OPOLOGY

THE BASIC₁ore

will be

Withdrawn

'A good read, with instructive boxes and useful summaries, and it will doubtless whet many's appetite for more.'
    Professor Thomas Hylland Eriksen, *University of Oslo, Norway*

Anthropology: The Basics is the ultimate guide for the student encountering anthropology for the first time. It explains and explores key anthropological concepts, addressing questions such as:

- what is anthropology?
- how can we distinguish cultural differences from physical ones?
- what is culture, anyway?
- how do anthropologists study culture?
- what are the key theories and approaches used today?
- how has the discipline changed over time?

Providing an overview of the fundamental principles of anthropology, this user-friendly text is an invaluable resource for anyone wanting to learn more about a fascinating subject.

Peter Metcalf is Professor of Anthropology at the University of Virginia, USA. His other publications include *They Lie, We Lie: Getting on with Anthropology* (Routledge 2001).

ALSO AVAILABLE FROM ROUTLEDGE

ARCHAEOLOGY: THE BASICS (SECOND EDITION)
CLIVE GAMBLE

ART HISTORY: THE BASICS
GRANT POOKE & DIANA NEWALL

PHILOSOPHY: THE BASICS (FOURTH EDITION)
NIGEL WARBURTON

RELIGION: THE BASICS (SECOND EDITION)
MALORY NYE

SEMIOTICS: THE BASICS (SECOND EDITION)
DANIEL CHANDLER

SOCIOLOGY: THE BASICS
MARTIN ALBROW

ARCHAEOLOGY: THE KEY CONCEPTS
COLIN RENFREW & PAUL BAHN

CULTURAL THEORY: THE KEY CONCEPTS (SECOND EDITION)
ANDREW EDGAR & PETER SEDGWICK

SOCIAL AND CULTURAL ANTHROPOLOGY: THE KEY CONCEPTS
NIGEL RAPPORT & JOANNA OVERING

ANTHROPOLOGY
THE BASICS

Peter Metcalf

Routledge
Taylor & Francis Group

LONDON AND NEW YORK

First published 2005
by Routledge
2 Park Square, Milton Park, Abingdon, Oxon OX14 4RN

Simultaneously published in the USA and Canada
by Routledge
270 Madison Ave, New York, NY 10016

Reprinted 2009 (twice)

Routledge is an imprint of the Taylor & Francis Group, an informa business

© 2005 Peter Metcalf

Typeset in Aldus Roman and Scala Sans by Taylor & Francis Books
Printed and bound in Great Britain by the MPG Books Group

British Library Cataloguing in Publication Data
A catalogue record for this book is available from the British Library

Library of Congress Cataloging in Publication Data
A catalog record for this book has been requested

ISBN 0-415-33119-6 (hbk)
ISBN 0-415-33120-X (pbk)
ISBN 978-0-415-33119-7 (hbk)
ISBN 978-0-415-33120-3 (pbk)

Taylor & Francis Group is the Academic Division of T&F Informa plc.

CONTENTS

List of Illustrations   vi

1   Encountering Cultural Difference   1
2   Misunderstanding Cultural Difference   21
3   Social Do's and Don'ts   38
4   African Political Systems   54
5   Anthropology, History and Imperialism   74
6   Culture and Language   89
7   Culture and Nature   115
8   The End of the Tribes   139
9   Culture and the Individual   163
10 Critical Anthropology   182

    Bibliography   207
    Index   213

ILLUSTRATIONS

Figures

2.1 One of the exotic forms of humans illustrated in the Liber
    Chronicorum of Hartmann Schedel   23

3.1 The island of Tikopia   42

4.1 A family tree as seen by a person in the Diel lineage   69

8.1 Map showing the Asian global economy   150

Boxes

1.1 Culture   2

1.2 Socialization   4

1.3 A cultural misunderstanding   15

1.4 The Third World   17

2.1 Darwinian selection   29

3.1 How "primitive"?   46

4.1 Cultural relativism   55

5.1 The British Empire   76

6.1 Montaigne and the "savages"   91

6.2 Language acquisition: learning the rules   95

6.3 Koko the talking gorilla   97

6.4   Part of an Ojibwa taxonomy of "living beings"   104

6.5   Restricted and generalized exchange   110

7.1   Symbolism   118

7.2   Orientation of the Atoni house   120

7.3   Shamanism   132

8.1   The Maori Wars   145

9.1   Psychology, psychiatry, and social psychology   167

ENCOUNTERING CULTURAL DIFFERENCE

Anthropology is an adventure. It offers you the opportunity to explore other worlds, where lives unfold according to different understandings of the natural order of things. Different, that is, from those that you take for granted. It allows you to escape the claustrophobia of your everyday life, but anthropology is not mere escapism. On the contrary, it will demand your best efforts at understanding.

FAR FROM HOME, CLOSE TO HOME

Anthropologists travel to every corner of the globe to conduct their research. The first generation of them in the late nineteenth century relied on the reports of travelers and explorers for their information. Consequently, anthropology can be seen as an outgrowth of the vast travel literature that accumulated in European languages following the great voyages of discovery of the fifteenth century. In the twentieth century, anthropologists decided that such reports were not enough, and that they needed to go and see for themselves. The modes of research that they initiated, designed to avoid as far as possible the pitfalls of prejudice, provide the basis of the modern discipline.

For most people in the contemporary world, however, it is not necessary to travel far from home to cross cultural boundaries. On the contrary, subtle cultural shifts go on all about us, and the more you know about anthropology, the more you will be able to detect them and assess their significance. Increasingly, anthropologists are convinced that there never was a time when humans lived in such isolation as to know nothing of others, and human history is above all a story of cultural collisions and accommodations. But there is so much mobility in the modern world that such interactions are for many people a part of daily life. Consequently, the issues of anthropology need not be abstract or remote; often we encounter them as soon as we cross our own doorsteps.

BOX 1.1 CULTURE

Culture is a key word in anthropology, but theorists emphasize different aspects. In general terms, we can define culture as all those things that are instilled in a child by elders and peers as he or she grows up, everything from table manners to religion. There are several important things to note about this definition. First, it excludes traits that are genetically transmitted, about which more in the next chapter. Second, it is very different to the common usage of the word to mean "high culture," such as elite art forms. Instead, it refers equally to mundane things such as how to make a farm or go shopping, as well as learning right from wrong, or how to behave towards others. Third, as these examples show, it covers an enormous range of things that people need to learn in each different culture, giving anthropologists an equally wide range of things to study.

AWARENESS OF CULTURAL DIFFERENCE

Meanwhile, the adventure has its hazards. In the 1970's the term "culture shock" came into circulation. As originally used by anthropologists, it described the disorientation that often overtakes a fieldworker when returning home from a prolonged period of immersion in another culture. All kinds of things that had once been totally familiar suddenly seem odd, as if one were seeing them for the first time. Consequently, everything becomes questionable: why have I always done this or assumed that? This questioning attitude is perhaps the most basic feature of anthropology. Most people most of the time simply get on with their lives. It could hardly be otherwise, given all that there is to do. It is only under special circumstances that we stop to reflect, and the experience of another culture is a common stimulus.

When journalists started using the term, however, they left out the reflexive angle. Culture shock came to mean simply the reaction to entering another culture, and that can be disorienting enough. Imagine yourself meeting for the first time a whole group of new people. Even if you are an outgoing person, you are likely to feel self-conscious, that is conscious of yourself. You start thinking about things that are normally automatic: how to walk, where to put your hands. The effort makes your movements stiff. For many people, it takes practice and an effort of will to behave "naturally" under these conditions. Being coached by a friend to relax only makes things worse. Culture shock is like this, except extended over a longer period. The momentary nervousness of walking into a room may be overcome in a few minutes of conversation, but culture shock may last for days or weeks at a time.

EMOTIONAL RESPONSES

Now add to this the complications of language. Even unfamiliar slang or a different dialect is enough to signal your status as an outsider. How much worse if you are only beginning to learn the language of those around you. When people are kind enough to talk to you, you are painfully aware of being a conversation liability, stumbling along and making clumsy errors. If your hosts talk slowly for your benefit, you know you are being talked down to, like a child. When you can't follow simple instructions you are liable to be taken by the hand and led. Such treatment can be hard to bear and you may feel a surge of resentment, even though you understand perfectly well that everyone is trying to be helpful. Such are the contradictory emotions of culture shock.

Emotions are not only confused, but also intense. Unable to follow everything that is going on, you do not know what expression to wear on your face. To avoid looking bored, you try to smile encouragingly at everyone. Soon the smile freezes into an insane grin, and before you know where you are you are close to tears. The problem of your own emotions is made worse by not being sure what the people around you are feeling. If they raise their voices, you wonder if they are angry, but if they are silent you ask yourself the same question. Moreover, cultural differences do not only express themselves in words. There is also what is commonly called "body language." If people stand closer than you are accustomed to you may feel overwhelmed, but if they stand further back you may feel isolated. Some people insist on making eye-contact to an unnerving degree. Others avert their gaze politely so as to avoid staring, making you feel even more that you do not know what is going on. At this stage, paranoia is not far away.

THE REALITY OF CULTURE

After an experience like this, you are never again likely to doubt the reality of culture. An alien culture seems to surround you, so that you can almost touch it. You seem to exist inside a tiny bubble that moves with you through a different medium. Moreover, having experienced it yourself, you can see it happening to others. Back in your own environment you can spot strangers moving around uncertainly inside their little bubbles.

Anthropologists are not immune to these reactions. The best that their training can do is to teach them what to expect. They understand that they have to allow themselves to be partly "re-socialized" (see Box 1.2). That is to say, they must unlearn all kinds of small

BOX 1.2 SOCIALIZATION

We defined culture in terms of "instilling" learning in the young person. The proper word for this process is socialization, and it covers both formal schooling – where such a thing exists – and also all those ways in which children are coaxed and prodded into behaving as their families think they should, and learning what the members of their communities think they need to know. Almost invariably, mothers play a central role in socializing young children, but as they grow more people become involved. Grandparents and elders often teach by telling stories. Brothers, sisters and friends are also important, since most young people are anxious to be popular with their peers. Young adults may also want to learn particular skills or join particular groups, and so may seek out specialized teachers.

things acquired in childhood, such as basic manners, conversational styles, and body postures, and relearn them in the new culture. That process accounts for the odd feeling of regressing to childhood, with all its vulnerabilities and frustrations. Anthropologists sometimes describe this as "full immersion" fieldwork, meaning that they jump right in to the new culture and stay put until they have managed to become reasonably comfortable there. They do it with trepidation, but they do it willingly, because they know what they want to achieve in the process.

WHAT IS TO BE GAINED?

The notion of "culture shock" emphasizes the unpleasant aspects of crossing cultural boundaries. But having done your best to over-come them, there follows all the excitement of discovery. Even if interaction is limited, any real attempt at communication soon yields results. Some detail catches your attention, and you need to know more. That curiosity is the wellspring of anthropology, and what it promotes is an intellectual drive. Putting that another way, travel on its own is not enough. International tourism is now one of the largest industries worldwide, but most tourists have only the most superficial interaction with local people. Where the "exotic" is thought to exist, most want it neatly packaged for easy consumption, in guided tours or "culture shows." For tourism, the exotic is something you can photograph. For anthropology, it is not.

Not only is travel not enough, it may be unnecessary. There are often other cultures to be explored within a single community, and they are certain to exist in major cities. Some anthropologists conduct research a mere bus journey away from home, and that can be just as demanding as fieldwork overseas. Culture shock must be negotiated anew on every visit, and it is a rare person who can move back and forth gracefully.

However it occurs, what follows is an expanded world in which to find interest and enjoyment. Nor need you give up anything in the process. You are no more at risk of losing your own cultural heritage than you would be if you learned another language. On the contrary, you can appreciate it in a deeper sense. Anthropologists are unstinting in their admiration of what we might call cultural fluency. Wherever it is found, it constitutes a unique expression of the human spirit. It is doubly admirable to have access to more than one.

ETHNOCENTRISM

Not surprisingly, throughout history many people have refused the adventure, finding in it only something disturbing and threatening. Their urge is to huddle down in the familiar, and turn their backs on other people. This reaction is called ethnocentrism, literally, being centered in one's own ethnicity or culture. In itself, ethnocentrism is neither unusual nor immoral. Most people most of the time need some clear sense of identity to lean on, and there is no reason why they should not value what their parents taught them. The danger is that ethnocentrism will harden into chauvinism, that is, the conviction that everything they do or think is right, and everything everyone else does or thinks is wrong, unreasonable, or even wicked. Anthropology cannot operate in the face of chauvinism, and normal ethnocentrisms must be set aside if there is to be any chance of entering, even partially, into the worlds of other people.

ANTHROPOLOGY'S PIONEERS

Travel writers are often drearily chauvinist, but there have always been a few whose curiosity overcomes their chauvinism. In the fifth century bc, Herodotus journeyed from Greece, through the Aegean and eastern Asia as far as Egypt. In his famous *Histories*, he gives lively accounts of the customs of the people he meets along the way. He does not, however, disguise his opinions. He finds it perverse, for instance, that Egyptians shave their heads as a sign of mourning. As a Greek, he knows that the proper thing to do is not cut the hair at all, but let it grow unkempt. If you find his reaction naïve, you might ask yourself what hair length, styling, and display signal in your own culture, and note how easy it is to have exactly Herodotus' reaction to the habits of others.

What the first generation of anthropologists did was to collect and compare all the travel literature they could lay their hands on, everything from Herodotus to the reports just then arriving from explorers in Africa. This included three centuries of writing on the peoples of the Americas, some fanciful, some observant. For example, in his seventeenth-century *Grands Voyages*, de Vrys gives a description of the Tupi Namba of the Brazilian coastline that remains invaluable because these tribes were so soon wiped out by disease and conquest. For scholars back in Europe, such accounts of what was literally the New World filled their imaginations. As far back as the late sixteenth century, the French essayist Michel de Montaigne insisted on the morality of exotic customs, even when they run counter to one's own moral code. His examples were taken from American Indian societies. In the late eighteenth century, voyagers in the South Seas caused yet more sensations. The expeditions of Captain Cook to Hawai'i and Tahiti were carefully documented by scholars who accompanied them. But such was the demand for information back in England that unofficial versions were rapidly put into circulation, based on the anecdotes of the ordinary seamen.

In the nineteenth century, theorizing on the basis of travel accounts jelled into a distinct field of study, and its exponents began to refer to themselves as anthropologists. Their material was increased by a wave of interest in the customs of European peasants, related to the rise of new nationalisms all over the continent. The trouble with all of this data was of course that it varied enormously in reliability. Moreover, at a time when amazing new discoveries were being made, it was hard to tell sober reportage even from pure fantasy. In 1875, for example, a French sailor claimed to have spent nine years in captivity in an undiscovered kingdom in the interior of New Guinea. His sensational account describes golden palaces and fantastic cities – all needless to say totally spurious. Even in less extreme cases, such was the thirst for information that uncorroborated sources were freely cited. The influential English anthropologist Edward Burnett Tylor used all kinds of sources in his global survey of "primitive" culture. One snippet was apparently obtained from a man he met on a train, who had traveled in Africa as a salesman of whisky.

FIRST EXPERIMENTS WITH FIELDWORK

At the same time, however, efforts were under way, particularly in the USA, to produce more consistent data on which to base anthropological theorizing. Lewis Henry Morgan, whose influence was equal to Tylor's, based his 1851 description of the *League of the Ho-de-no-sau-nee, or Iroquois* on information that he got directly from Iroquois informants in upstate New York. Frank Hamilton Cushing went further, moving into the pueblo, or mountain-top village, of the Zuni people of New Mexico, and learning their language. Interestingly, his colleagues from the Smithsonian Museum in Washington DC were initially shocked that he should do such a thing. It was only later that the director of the Museum saw the value of Cushing's work, and became his sponsor.

Men such as Cushing slowly moved the discipline beyond the "arm chair anthropology" of the nineteenth century and towards its modern form. The techniques of fieldwork are often associated, however, with the work of Bronislaw Malinowski in the Trobriand Islands, at the eastern tip of New Guinea. Malinowski liked to imply that his discoveries resulted from unique circumstances, so increasing his own originality. It was said for instance that he was interned in New Guinea during World War One because, as an Austrian citizen of Polish descent, he was classified as an enemy alien. In fact, the Australian administration placed no restraints on him, and the suggestion for more intense, long-term research had already come from his teachers W.H.R. Rivers and Alfred Cort Haddon. These two had earlier participated in a scientific "expedition" to the Torres Straits, an island-dotted channel lying between New Guinea and the northern tip of Australia. What that in practice meant was that a team of researchers had traveled through the region, stopping here and there to collect artifacts and administer various psychological tests on local people. From that experience, Haddon and Rivers concluded that progress in the discipline required better fieldwork.

THE TECHNIQUES OF FIELDWORK

There is no great mystery about the techniques of fieldwork. One way of thinking of them is as a controlled experience of culture shock. That is to say, the predictable feelings of disorientation are harnessed to focus attention on what exactly is different. For example, whenever a sensation of clumsiness occurs, it reminds you to pay close attention to how your hosts stand, move, and position themselves while talking. That in itself is a worthwhile study, and one that will rapidly allow you to fit in better.

In short, the three basic elements of fieldwork are:

(1) *Long-term residence.* Malinowski famously pitched his tent in the middle of the village of Kiriwina in the Trobriand Islands. But residential arrangements vary so much around the world that there can be no one way of doing things. In many places it would be impossible, or at least highly eccentric, to live in a tent. Sometimes there are clear rules of hospitality, which make things easier. There can be disadvantages even to such a convenient arrangement, however. If, for instance, custom requires that you stay with a community leader, you may be seen as his ally or client, so impeding communication with other factions. Alternatively, people may live in dispersed homesteads and you need to find a host family. This can be difficult. After all, it is no small thing to ask of people that they take in a total stranger for months at a time. In some places, it is improper for anyone not a close relative to enter the house at all, and the anthropologist must find an empty house to live in and interact as much as possible with people outside their homes. When the famous British anthropologist Edward Evans-Pritchard carried out fieldwork in the Sudan in the 1920's and 1930's his reception varied greatly from one people to another. "Among Azande," he reports, "I was compelled to live outside the community; among Nuer I was compelled to be a member of it. Azande treated me as a superior; Nuer as an equal" (1940: 15).

There are in fact innumerable complications and compromises. But the goal at least is clear: to make it possible to interact with people on a daily basis and in the most direct manner possible.

(2) *Language competence.* The same proposition applies to linguistic interactions. Effective fieldwork cannot be accomplished through an interpreter. The reasons for this are fairly obvious. It is only too easy for meanings to become garbled in translation. Moreover, there may well

be ideas that cannot be translated at all. Worst of all, it destroys all possibility of the kinds of casual open-ended conversations that are the key to rewarding fieldwork.

Consequently, fieldwork usually requires learning a language, and learning it in depth. Travelers may acquire a few phrases, enough to ask directions, book a hotel room, and such like. But anthropologists need to be fluent enough to take part in everyday social activities, and that takes months of continuous work. This requirement by itself makes clear why fieldwork needs to be extended over a long period. As a rule of thumb, a year is about the minimum, where it is possible to learn a locally relevant language in advance. That in effect means one of a couple of dozen of the most widely-spoken languages in the world, ones that are likely to be taught at universities. Even with the advantage of such training, it will take some time to become comfortable operating entirely in the new medium. But there are thousands of other languages in the world, and they may lack even the most basic learning materials, such as dictionaries and grammars. Consequently, anthropologists have often found themselves confronting an unwritten language to which they have no previous exposure at all. They then have no alternative but to construct for themselves the linguistic materials they need, beginning with an orthography, that is the letters and symbols necessary for writing down the sounds of the language. Where this is necessary, the minimum time for successful fieldwork may be two years or even longer.

The familiarity that anthropologists have with language diversity makes it plain why the discipline has always had a close connection with linguistics, and there will be more to say about that in subsequent chapters. We need to note, however, that there is no rule that says anthropologists have to work in languages foreign to themselves. It is entirely possible to cross cultural boundaries without switching languages, although there may be variations of accent or vocabulary. Think, for instance, of class boundaries, or immigrant communities in a major city.

Moreover, anthropologists may choose to return to their own countries for fieldwork, after training in anthropology elsewhere. An example would be an Indian anthropologist trained in the USA or UK, who then returned to India to conduct research. Crossing and recrossing a whole series of cultural boundaries would complicate his or her experience of culture shock.

(3) *Participant observation.* This feature of fieldwork is the trickiest to define.

Basically, it means that the anthropologist participates in the lives of local people, living as they live, doing what they do. In practice, however, this is a goal that can only partially be met. Most likely, the anthropologist is simply incompetent to do what local people do.

Malinowski made a point of going fishing with his Trobriand hosts, but he does not tell us how many fish he caught. Moreover, the anthropologist cannot spend the kind of time necessary to make a farm, for instance. He or she has to get on with research. Finally, it is likely that there will be activities from which the anthropologist will be excluded by reason of gender or status. There may be women's rites, or simply conversations, that will never happen if a male is present, anthropologist or otherwise. On the other hand, a woman anthropologist may be restricted in her movements, or have difficulty getting information on political things. In addition, there may be circles that are closed to everyone except the specially initiated.

What this adds up to is the near impossibility of living just as local people do. Nevertheless, the *attempt* to do so is important. When Malinowski went fishing he was not really trying to catch fish. Instead, he was learning first hand about fishing; its techniques, specialized language, and lore. In fact, this willingness to take part as best one can in everything that is going on can be seen as encompassing the other requirements, for long-term residence and language competence. Consequently, the techniques of fieldwork are often summarized by the phrase "participant observation."

UNSTRUCTURED RESEARCH

Another aspect of participant observation is that the learning experiences of the anthropologist are not programmed in advance. Malinowski did not tell people when to go fishing, but simply tagged along when they did. Specialists in neighboring disciplines such as sociology and social psychology often find such "unstructured" research sloppy or unscientific. Their preference is for surveys that yield quantifiable data amenable to statistical analysis. For them, participant observation implies a reliance on "anecdotal" material, lacking proper sampling techniques. Most anthropologists have exactly the opposite view of things. The trouble with "structured" research is that you have to know what you are looking for in advance. This works well if you need to know, for example, what percentage of a given population owns a car, or watches a particular TV show. It is very little use for studying different worldviews. Any questionnaire made up in advance is bound to incorporate exactly those prejudices the anthropologist is struggling to escape. For instance, in many places you will be wide of the mark if you begin a study of indigenous religion by asking people their name for God, or how often they go to church.

Instead, the topic must be approached repeatedly, first from one angle, then from another. As with the proverbial blind man describing an elephant, it will be necessary to feel your way around what cannot yet be made out in its entirety. In general, naturalistic contexts are better than contrived ones. That is, it is more rewarding to allow religious issues – or what may turn out to be religious issues – to come up in everyday activities. The process of unstructured research resembles detective work more than laboratory science. Controlled experiments are impossible. Instead, clues must be exploited as they appear, even though it may take months before their meaning is clear. Moreover, the anthropologist is, as it were, working on several cases at the same time. One case may be stalled for a while, only to be re-opened when fresh information appears, probably from an unexpected direction. An ever-growing but diverse corpus of information must be constantly re-examined, in search of new leads. By comparison survey research is easy, but its results superficial.

Unstructured research does not, however, prohibit asking questions. On the contrary, anthropologists question everything. What marked out Malinowski from Trobriand fishermen was no doubt his incessant questions: what is this called? why do you do that? It is this feature, more even than strange appearance or odd habits, that makes the anthropologist conspicuous. He or she is constantly asking questions. In fact, it is a mark of good fieldwork to find new questions to ask. For most of us, curiosity is soon blunted. After a series of questions you feel as much in the dark as ever, but cannot think of anything else to ask. What resourceful anthropologists manage to do is turn things over in their minds until they have framed a new question – which may or may not help. This is a skill that takes practice.

THE ROLE OF INFORMANTS

Inevitably, some questions are more difficult than others. Any native speaker can probably tell you the names of different fish hooks, but only a few are willing to respond thoughtfully to abstract questions about the nature of the world. Such people are rare in any society, and anthropologists count themselves lucky to discover them. If they become regular "informants," as the expression is, they may play a major role in research. What they offer is reflection on cultural meanings from the privileged viewpoint of the insider.

Informants provide a bridge between cultures because they tolerate questions that no local person would ever ask. Often these have a naïve quality, like a child asking why grass is green, or the sky blue. Such questions do have answers, but few adults bother to think about what seems too obvious not to be taken for granted. Once again the fieldworker is caught behaving like a child asking why grass is green. This tendency to ask questions that seem naïve is the origin of the old joke that an anthropologist is someone who asks smart people dumb questions.

Even a very good informant, however, does not simply hand over on a plate, as it were, all the information that the anthropologist needs. The interaction is invariably more complicated than that. A common experience in fieldwork is to ask what seems like a perfectly straightforward question and receive back an answer that seems completely irrelevant. You repeat the question, in case you misheard, and get the same reply. Then both of you stare at each other in blank incomprehension. Such moments may be a crisis in fieldwork, undermining everything that you thought you had learned. But they can also be valuable, signaling that you have stumbled onto something deep and interesting. Clearly, your informant is working with other premises than you, that is, one of those differences of worldview that it is your goal to discover. You must now find a way around the conundrum by trial and error, until insight comes. There are no guidelines other than persistence.

CHECKS AGAINST MISINFORMATION

In addition, of course, there is also the possibility that you are being misled. Lying is a very human activity. The complex layers of exaggeration, deception, and evasion of which we are capable are a measure of the subtlety of language. Moreover, it is not hard to imagine circumstances when even the most cooperative informant might want to hide things, or misrepresent them. This is because the relationship between informant and anthropologist does not exist in some ideal realm outside regional politics. On the contrary, the outsider must not only be somehow accommodated within a local community, with all its subterranean struggles for status, but may also be seen as a resource in dealing with government agencies and other "outside" forces. In either case, he or she is open to manipulation.

What defense do anthropologists have against deception? First, flat out lies are hard to maintain for months at a time in an intimate community. Sooner or later, someone will spill the beans; either by a genuine slip or through a covert wish to unmask the liar. The anthropologist has to keep cross checking, and wait. Meanwhile, he or she gradually gains a better grasp of what is going on in conversation. Routine boasting becomes easy to spot, as does teasing. Many an anthropologist has had the experience of being told ever more outrageous lies to see how long it is before he or she catches on. Attitudes to strict truthfulness vary widely around the world, and it takes time for the fieldworker to be able to spot contexts in which telling whoppers is a form of verbal play.

There is a further check against lying, and it is an important one. Anthropologists do not only listen to what people say they do, they also watch what they do in fact do. For instance, if a local leader boasts about his exalted standing, you can observe whether he is actually treated with deference. This in turn requires that you have participated in situations where senior people meet, and have observed the range of greetings from the casual to the respectful. Indeed, you will have already needed to learn these practices in order to interact with such people yourself. Again, you can check an informant's account of a ritual against what happens at an actual performance, and whatever differences there are will set you asking new questions. The technique of participation is exactly this feedback between watching and asking. As you learn more, you understand more of what you see, and in turn ask better questions.

ANTHROPOLOGICAL KNOWLEDGE

In the end, however, there is no foolproof defense against misunderstanding, whatever its origin. Most anthropologists are only too aware of this. They have had to revise their ideas enough times to doubt that any conclusion is final. Fieldwork is a humbling experience, and the effect persists. Recent debates about what kinds of knowledge are possible within the so-called "social sciences" have made anthropologists even more wary about what they claim to know.

It is not a problem of having no facts to report. On the contrary, an anthropologist just back from the field is a fountain of information on all kinds of things from what people eat to how they tell a joke. There is nothing inferior about this kind of data. It is often

BOX 1.3 A CULTURAL MISUNDERSTANDING

While doing fieldwork in Borneo, I had a friend visit me from the USA. Local people were surprised to find that he spoke no Malay. "Why doesn't he speak Malay?" they asked. Throughout a region of great linguistic diversity, Malay is the lingua franca spoken by everyone as a second language, allowing communication with traders in the markets and other strangers. "He's only just arrived," I replied. "Yes, we know that," they said, "but why doesn't he speak Malay?" After trying the question several times with increasing frustration, one man found a way to rephrase it: "When he is in the USA, how does he buy things?" What my audience did not know, and what I had considered too obvious to tell them, was that in the USA everyone speaks English, even shopkeepers.

intriguing, and invaluable for all manner of comparative purposes. The goal of many anthropologists is, however, to see the world as others do, and that is more delicate. There is no way to step inside someone else's head, and anyone who claims to do so is an imposter. Fieldwork soon teaches you that. Consequently, what an anthropologist must do is lay out his or her information, collected in all kinds of different contexts over months or years, and then offer an interpretation. That interpretation is not fact in the same way as reporting on your hosts' diet.

There is another aspect of anthropological knowledge that needs to be noted: it sometimes has the potential to hurt those who gave it. For instance, an anthropologist who learned family secrets of some kind would do well to make sure that they were not broadcast around the community. That would be a poor reward for the informant's trust. So fieldnotes will have to be kept out of the way and/or written in code. Later, it may be impossible to publish them, in case attempts to disguise the family's identity are penetrated. On a more serious level, information about illegal activities or subversive political involvements may imperil the hosts' livelihood or even lives. In extreme cases, an anthropologist may be placed in difficult moral dilemmas about what can and cannot be revealed.

FIELDWORK BECOMES STANDARD

By the 1930's the standards of fieldwork set by Malinowski had become generally accepted. Meanwhile, there were plenty of opportunities to apply them in the colonial possessions of Britain and France. That is to say, there were many ethnic groups about which very little was known, while imperial control provided conditions under which research could go forward. What exactly this meant for anthropology, now and then, has been a matter of considerable debate, of which more later. For the moment we only note the connection.

In the 1930's, there were only a handful of practitioners scattered around the world. Their findings soon attracted attention, however, and young people were drawn to the re-invigorated discipline. After World War Two, there was a rapid expansion as universities began to offer degrees in anthropology. The number of research projects mushroomed, and our knowledge of the peoples of Africa, Oceania, and Southeast Asia increased by leaps and bounds. The 1950's and

1960's were in many ways a golden age for anthropology, and a new genre was developed for writing about other peoples' cultures. This literature is called *ethnography* (literally, writing ethnicity) and the person who does it is an *ethnographer*. Since then, anthropologists have had two jobs: first, to conduct research and write ethnographies, and second, to speculate about the meaning of their findings and those of other fieldworkers. In subsequent chapters we will observe the varying interaction of fieldwork and theorizing.

BEYOND COMMUNITY STUDIES

Since the 1960's, the range of locations in which anthropologists work has steadily expanded. Already in the 1950's, anthropologists had confronted the fact that a large number of Africans no longer lived in villages but in towns and mining camps. However, the fieldwork techniques of Malinowski were clearly designed for smaller communities, ones where it was possible for the anthropologist to get to know a fair proportion of the inhabitants, and keep track of the important goings-on. Methods had to be adapted to work in cities. Some long-established cities in many parts of the world were found to contain tight-knit neighborhoods, cross cut by alleys that could be treated as villages within the urban environment. It was more common, however, to find shanty-towns in which all kinds of newcomers

BOX 1.4 THE THIRD WORLD

In the 1950's it became common to divide the world into three parts. The First World consisted of the Western democracies, the Second was the communist bloc, and the Third was the poor or "developing" countries of Africa, Southeast Asia, South and Middle America. After the collapse of the Soviet Union, the phrase Second World lost much of its meaning, and some scholars objected to the pejorative implications of numbering worlds as if in declining order of importance. So an alternative came into fashion, contrasting an industrialized North with the postcolonial South. Some anthropolgists have maintained the old usage, however, in part because they concern themselves with a Fourth World, that is, small ethnic groups that are virtually powerless in modern nation-states, whether of the North or the South.

were crowded together; anthropologists then needed to be inventive in finding ways of participating in local life. One technique involved exploring social networks extending beyond local communities.

By the end of the twentieth century, the great majority of research projects in anthropology were done in circumstances more complicated than Malinowski's in the Trobriand Islands. That was because of the accelerating rates of change worldwide. The global economy reached into every corner of the world, changing local lifestyles for better or worse. People migrated regionally or internationally, fleeing crises or looking for work, and television gave people in all but the most remote places a view of the outside world. In the same way, the line between the First and the Third World became hazy, as each penetrated the other, and anthropologists increasingly worked in both.

Under these circumstances, the techniques of participant observation had to be adapted to suit a thousand different circumstances. The goal, however, remained the same: to find ways to enter into other peoples' worlds, to learn their language, follow their lifestyle as far as possible and for an extended period, and to allow social interaction to unfold in a natural way.

OTHER MODES OF RESEARCH

A final caveat is necessary before ending this chapter. I have characterized the interests of the discipline by talking about the research techniques typical of what is called social or cultural anthropology, or sometimes, rather clumsily, socio-cultural anthropology. It must be pointed out, however, that there are anthropologists who do not use these techniques at all, because they are not suitable for their research problems.

This leads us to the considerable differences in the way anthropology has taken shape in different countries. In particular, anthropology spreads a much larger tent in the USA than it does in the UK. That is to say, there are branches of anthropology that have always been important in the USA, but are not well developed in the UK. Examples are linguistic and physical anthropology. Archeology, meanwhile, has been treated as a separate discipline in the UK, whereas in the USA it is most often seen as a branch of anthropology. Just why this is so, and what is covered in the various sub-disciplines, will become clear in subsequent chapters.

Summary

As we go about our daily lives, we are not aware of all the things we learned as children, the taken-for-granted ways of behaving, the general understandings of the way things are. In this sense, "culture" is invisible. If we suddenly become self-conscious about it, it is usually because we have crossed some kind of cultural boundary. Such crossings are by no means restricted to anthropologists. Instead they are a common human experience, almost inescapable in the modern world. All that anthropologists can claim is that they knowingly seek out such cultural boundaries. Their techniques of fieldwork are not esoteric, involving little more than an attempt to meet other people on their own terms. That attempt can be arduous, however. It involves at a minimum acquiring the necessary language skills, and being prepared to commit a great deal of time and effort. Fieldwork situations vary so widely that adaptability and resourcefulness are required. Moreover, anthropologists are not immune to the disorientation of cultural displacement. They are as likely as anyone else to feel lonely and vulnerable. Nor are they immune to manipulation. People everywhere communicate their emotions and intentions in the most subtle ways, ways that the newly-arrived stranger is not likely to follow. Consequently he or she is easily misled, whether maliciously or merely in fun. The only defense against gullibility is a slowly increasing sophistication, and constant cross checking. This can be effective, given the right opportunities, but even so a proper humility is in order. Most fieldworkers are only too aware of the limits of what they know. Facts there are aplenty, about such readily observable things as mode of residence or farming techniques. But those things that interest us most, the cultural webs in which we all hang suspended, are more elusive.

FURTHER READING

One of the earliest pieces of travel literature to make a major impression in Europe was Marco Polo's *The Travels*. It circulated in over 119 manuscripts in the late thirteenth and fourteenth centuries, and brought the first detailed report of the fabulously wealthy and exotic civilizations of South and East Asia. Appropriately, scholars are still debating which parts are genuine, and which fabricated (Polo 1997). From the sixteenth century onwards, the trickle of travel literature rapidly expands to a flood. To pick just one charming example, Lady Mary Wortley Montagu spent several years in Turkey, as the wife of the English ambassador. She took the trouble to learn Turkish, and translated Turkish poetry. She gained entrée into the Sultan's palace, and even his famous seraglio, and recorded her adventures in her *Turkish Embassy Letters* (1994, original 1763). There are now many books by anthropologists describing their fieldwork experiences, as opposed to their findings. It fact, it has now emerged as a genre of its own, sometimes disparaged as "navel-gazing" ethnography. A treatment that does not deserve disparagement is Jean-Paul Dumont's *The Headman and I: Ambiguity and Ambivalence in the Fieldworking Experience* (1978). Nigel Barley wrote several humorous accounts of his fieldwork encounters, drawing a large audience into anthropology. An example is *A Plague of Caterpillars* (1987). Barley's style drew criticism, however, as being condescending. Nevertheless, Barley promoted a trend towards less dry modes of ethnographic reportage. Regarding the delicate balance of truth and error in fieldwork, see Metcalf's *They Lie, We Lie: Getting On With Anthropology* (2002). To get a taste for Malinowski's fieldwork, you can do no better than looking at what is arguably the first modern ethnography, his *Argonauts of the Western Pacific* (1961, original 1922), original. It is an account of the sea voyages made as part of an extensive system of trade, particularly the circulation of high-prestige objects. It is a forbiddingly massive tome, but not difficult reading, and delving into it even briefly demonstrates the amazingly rich detail that ethnography can produce about things that were previously totally unknown to Europeans.

2

MISUNDERSTANDING CULTURAL DIFFERENCE

"Anthropology," translated literally from the Greek, means "people study."

The formula has a satisfying brevity, and it is certainly what anthropologists do. But it will hardly serve as a definition, since all other social scientists, such as sociologists and psychologists, do the same thing, not to mention historians and economists. Moreover, studying literature, we are told, gives insight into the human condition. In fact, there is hardly anything in the arts and humanities that is not concerned with people.

What then is special about the way anthropologists study people? My answer is that we are concerned with how people differ among themselves, from one place and time to another, and what those differences signify. In this sense, anthropology is not something invented in the nineteenth century, but something that has always been with us. Throughout history, and before it in prehistoric times, people certainly encountered others different to themselves. They must then have discussed what the differences were, and what sense to make of them. This is simply the inverse of the phenomenon of ethnocentrism described in the previous chapter. Moreover, anthropologists frequently run across such indigenous theorizing, if only because they themselves are usually "different" from their hosts.

THE LUGBARA WORLDVIEW IN THE 1940'S

John Middleton, who worked with the Lugbara people of Kenya in the 1940's, provides a nice example. The Lugbara homeland is a high plateau, flat and treeless. The rainfall and soils are good, so that they have a productive agriculture and no need to travel far from home. Middleton describes a very literal worldview: from atop his house a Lugbara man looks out on his social world laid out before him. Under him, his own house, circular as it happens. Close by are his close kin, people he has been familiar with all his life. A little further off he sees the villages into which his people marry. That is, his wife and the wives of his male kinsmen come from those villages, and their sisters and daughters go off to live there when they marry. Consequently, he has visited all these villages many times, to participate in weddings and visit in-laws. These people he regards as just like his own people, except that one cannot quite be sure that there are not witches among them. Witchcraft is known to exist, but no man suspects his close kin. If harm befalls therefore, a man looks to his in-laws, and that suspicion is enough to maintain a definite social distance. Beyond the circle of his kinsmen's affines there are people who are known to be Lugbara, but with whom our observer has had only brief encounters. More remote again are Africans who do not even speak Lugbara. The witchcraft tendencies of these strangers are unknown, but deeply suspect.

Finally, across the very rim of the world exist the white men, who had appeared in Lugbara country only a few decades earlier. Though rarely seen in the villages, they had transformed the Lugbara way of life by imposing a colonial order and introducing new commodities. So thoroughly had the whites turned their world upside down that the Lugbara took them to be literally inverted people, so that they ran around on their hands, their feet waving in the air. When Middleton pointed out that he and the colonial officers they had seen all walked around on their feet, the Lugbara gave him a knowing look. That was what happened when Lugbara people were watching, they said, but at other times ... well ... .

After the 1950's the Lugbara were rapidly drawn into a wider environment, and the neat concentric circles of their worldview became more complicated. If, meanwhile, you find it naïve, you might ask yourself who lies close to the center of *your* worldview, and who or what is at its edges, inverted in some way or another.

HOMO MONSTROSUS

Moreover, we need not go very far back in European history to find similarly innocent ideas. When in the eighteenth century the Swedish botanist Linnaeus began the scientific classification of all the animals and plants in the world, he gave our species the name it still bears: *Homo sapiens,* "clever humans." At the same time, however, he made room for another species of the same genus that he called *Homo monstrosus,* "monstrous humans," and into that category he put all the strange half-human creatures that had inhabited European folklore since the middle ages. Some of these had origins dating back to classical Greece. Herodotus, for example, not only reports the odd customs of the Egyptians, but also repeats stories that he collected in Egypt of people yet further to the south. In those distant regions, it was said, there was a tribe of people that had no heads; instead their eyes and mouths were in the middle of their chests. In this way, Herodotus' worldview matches that of the Lugbara, extending from the familiar to the strange to the monstrous.

Figure 2.1   Medieval image of a uniped (*Scientific American.* October 1968. Page 113. "Homo Monstrosus" published by kind permission of the Science, Industry & Business Library, The New York Public Library, Astor, Lenox and Tilden Foundations.)

During the middle ages, woodcut prints of monsters were often sold at country fairs. They were copied from illustrations in books such as the thirteenth-century encyclopedia *On the Properties of Things* by Bartholomeus Anglicus, which remained popular for centuries, and was translated into six European languages. After the invention of printing, it reached forty-six editions. A late-thirteenth-century map in Hereford cathedral in England shows various tribes supposedly living in India, including one-legged creatures who could move only by hopping. Their huge single feet did, however, prove useful as umbrellas.

NEAR-HUMANS

Aside from such fantasies, there are of course real near-human creatures to be found. They are the chimpanzees, gorillas, and orangutans, our closest living relatives in the animal kingdom, fellow members of the category that Linnaeus called *Hominoidea*. Their existence on the edges of the known world confused medieval observers, who thought that they were another kind of monstrosity, a variety of hairy men. Their mistake was not unusual: the very name *orangutan* is taken from Malay and means literally "people of the jungle." In parts of Borneo where headhunting was once practiced, orangutan heads could substitute for human ones.

Obviously the great apes, as they are called, are fascinating to anthropologists because they provide an opportunity to see what is uniquely human in comparison with them. For instance, there has been a great deal of research in the last few decades on whether it is possible to teach chimpanzees to "talk," that is, to use a complex system of signs that approximates human language. What was learned is described in Chapter Four, but in the meantime we should note that this research further undermines the definition of anthropology as "people study." Not only do other disciplines study people, but some anthropologists also study other animals.

LIMITS OF THE SPECIES

Meanwhile, there is no longer any possible confusion concerning the boundaries of our species. That is because there is a simple test, and its results are unambiguous. If two populations can interbreed and produce fertile offspring, then they belong to the same species. As everyone knows, you cannot breed a sheep with a goat, or a dog with a cat. Sometimes, when animals are very close in the Linnean classification, you can cross them, but the offspring are sterile. The best-known examples are mules, which are produced by mating a horse with a donkey. But mules cannot be bred among themselves; you have always to go back to the different parents. Consequently, horses and donkeys are different species, and there is no species of mules.

If all this sounds complicated, the situation with regard to humans is much simpler. All human populations are readily cross-fertile and produce offspring as fertile as any other. We know this because, in all the turmoil of the last few centuries, wars and migrations and trafficking in slaves have moved large populations from one continent to another. Consequently, there have been opportunities to try just about every possible combination of peoples, and the result is always the same. We are unmistakably one species.

THE HOMINID LINE

Moreover, we now know a considerable amount about the origins of our species, vastly more than was known in the eighteenth or nineteenth centuries. This is because of a series of amazing discoveries in the second half of the twentieth century, mainly in Africa. The discoveries comprised fossil remains of creatures that in some ways resembled apes and in other ways looked like humans. Some were perhaps hominids, that is, ancestral to ourselves. But others were precursors of the living species of apes and monkeys, or represented lines that later became extinct. As the data accumulated, each sensational discovery triggered intense debate among specialists about what it meant. There was room for controversy because, of course, you cannot crossbreed old bones. Consequently, just how many species were involved, and how they were related to each other, remains open to interpretation.

Nevertheless, by the beginning of this century we had a reasonable picture of human origins. Inevitably, there will be revisions as new data appears, but we can say with some confidence that fully bipedal, tool-using hominids appeared in East Africa about 2 or 2.5 million years ago. Tool use is what defines the genus *Homo*, and that is odd since all the other categories by which animals are classi-fied are based on physical features. This eccentricity dates back to Linnaeus, who saw tools as the essential feature of humanity. It adds further complications to the search for our ancestors, however. Not only do the specialists have to find bones, but also establish that there were stone tools – however simple – associated with them. At the same time, there were other species of *Hominoidea* in existence, whose skeletons reveal that they were not fully bipedal, and whose remains cannot be associated with tools.

The next burning question is how many species there have ever been within the genus *Homo*. The current consensus of expert opinion is that there have been just two. The first was *Homo erectus* ("upright human"), who managed to spread from Africa to all the continents of the Old World. Not surprisingly, there are physical differences between *H. erectus* skeletons from different time periods and places, but they are so slight that specialists conclude that they comprised one species. Then, about 100,000 years ago, a new type of human appears with tiny adjustment to the skull and pelvis characteristic of modern humans. These "anatomi-cally modern humans" evolved from some population of *H. erectus* probably in East Africa, and then spread even further around the world than their forebears, gradually displacing them as they went.

VARIATION WITHIN THE SPECIES

What this means is that all living human populations are much more closely related than anyone understood in the nineteenth century. At that time, popular opinion had it that the different races of mankind were profoundly different, or even that they had diverged before the appearance of genus *Homo*. It was doubted for instance that children of white settlers and Australian Aborigines would be fertile, as if the two populations could only breed like horses and donkeys. "Half-breed" American Indians or mixed-race Asians were described as decadent, as if the very fact of their mixed ancestry made them less viable.

These fantasies came from the same medieval sources as *H. monstrosus*. By 1757, Linnaeus had divided *H. sapiens* into five categories, described as follows:

(a) Wild man. Four-footed, mute, hairy.
(b) American. Copper-colored, choleric, erect. Hair black, straight, thick; nostrils wide; face harsh; beard scanty; obstinate, content, free. Paints himself with fine red lines. Regulated by custom.
(c) European. Fair, sanguine, brawny; hair yellow, brown, flowing; eyes blue; gentle, acute, inventive. Covered with close vestments. Governed by laws.
(d) Asiatic. Sooty, melancholy, rigid. Hair black; eyes dark; severe, haughty, covetous. Covered with loose garments. Governed by opinions.
(e) African. Black, phlegmatic, relaxed. Hair black, frizzled; skin silky; nose flat, lips tumid; crafty, indolent, negligent. Anoints himself with grease. Governed by caprice.

The items on the lists are worth attention. Category a. is presumably the great apes, with whom Linnaeus evidently thinks humans are cross fertile. The others constitute four of the familiar European folk categories of race: black, white, red, and yellow, to which is often added a fifth, brown. The terms choleric, sanguine, melancholy, and phlegmatic relate to medieval theories of medicine based on the Greek notion that each person constitutes a balance of various "humors." Somewhat ethnocentrically, the Swede Linnaeus seems to think that all Europeans have blue eyes.

Most significant of all, however, his lists naïvely mix physical characteristics like hair type with cultural ones like dress and political organization. That is the key flaw, one that echoes on into subsequent centuries, and is the root of all racism.

THE PARADOX OF RACE

The great paradox of race is that, despite all the evidence of our senses, it is not there. At first sight, this claim looks like one of those contrived jokes that academics like to play just for the fun of turning common sense on its head. Surely we can all see that some people are black, others white, some have straight hair, others wavy, and so on. Doesn't that show there are races? Isn't that what race is?

The answer is no, these manifest physical differences are not enough to show that races exist in humans. The extra feature that is needed is that physical traits cluster together so that everyone can be sorted into a limited number of distinctly identifiable types of people. But this is not what we find when we go beyond "common sense" and take a careful look at human populations around the globe. Instead we find such constant variation that we can find populations with just about any combination of traits you can imagine. If Black or African people are supposed to be tall, what to make of the pygmies of the Ituri forest? If "Asiatic" people are supposed to be "yellow," how will you classify the Tamil peoples of southern India, who are as dark-skinned as many Africans? If you hypothesize that their ancestors came from Africa, how will you account for the fact that their faces look more European than African? Did they get their skin from one continent and their faces from another? Does genetic inheritance work that way? Why wasn't it the other way around?

COLOR

Since we are dealing here not only with a paradox, but one that has been fateful for recent human history, it is worth rephrasing the proposition in a couple of ways so as to make clear what it means. First, let's deal just with the simplest item: "color." In biological terms, human beings vary in the amount of melanin in their skin. Why that is so is well understood. It is an adaptation to different degrees of solar radiation in different parts of the world. In the Sahara desert or the Australian outback a high density of melanin helps protect against ultra-violet rays that can damage the skin, as anyone knows who has had sunburn, not to mention skin cancers. In a cloudy northern environment, however, the same rays taken in small doses promote the production of vitamins in the skin. This means that Darwinian selection is working in different directions in different places, over many generations pushing some populations towards ever more melanin and others towards ever less. Not surprisingly, then, a map showing at the same time the amount of sunshine and density of melanin reveals a broad correlation.

The exceptions to this correlation are also not hard to understand. From Alaska, through tropical Middle and South America, and on to Tierra del Fuego, American Indians show far less variation in skin color than do populations spread across the same

BOX 2.1 DARWINIAN SELECTION

Charles Darwin's famous book *On the Origin of Species by Means of Natural Selection* (1859) set out the theory of biological evolution. By selection, Darwin meant that the characteristics of those individuals best adapted to survive and reproduce in particular environments would, generation by generation, gradually become more common in a population. As a species occupied more terrain, so its component populations became differentiated. If the process continued for long enough, they might then become different species. Climatic change hastened the process, so that biological evolution was the story of the rise of species, some of which survived over whole geological epochs while others became extinct.

latitudes in the Old World. That is because their ancestors arrived only recently in the Americas, that is, in terms of evolutionary time spans. Moreover, they already had the necessary technologies to make clothes for themselves to deal with different climates. That is to say, cultural adaptations had already begun to affect the ways in which biological adaptation worked.

With the nature of skin color variation clear, we can take the next step and ask what it means for race. In short, what we find simply is that there are populations with every degree of melanin density along a scale from most to least:

Black .... White

Now, how many races does this indicate? Should we divide the spectrum down the middle, and conclude that there are two races, black and white? Or would three be better, black, brown, white? Or five: black, brown, red, yellow, white? Or ten, or twenty, or a hundred? The answer is that there is nothing in the data itself to make one number more "correct" than another. There are as many "colors" as one wishes to distinguish, *ad infinitum*. (I leave aside the obvious comment that "white" people are not really white, nor "black" people black, not to mention the supposedly "yellow" and "red" people.)

What this demonstration shows is that any particular classification of people into different color categories is not "natural." That is, it is not a feature of the world, such that any two scientists looking at the same data would come to the same conclusions about it. Just the contrary is true, and that is what physical anthropologists mean by telling us that the supposed races are not really there. These same specialists remain interested in the ways human populations vary, and there is nothing wicked or prejudiced in pointing out that people vary in skin color, just as they do in innumerable other features. So they contrast particular populations, according to what variables interest them in any given research project. But they no longer bother with any kind of master classification of all *H. sapiens*. Such grandiose taxonomies are obsolete.

Consequently the paradox of race can be restated in this way: contrary to what we always imagined, "race" is not a phenomenon of nature at all, but rather a cultural construct. That changes everything about it. Instead of asking what is genetically peculiar about other people, we need to find out what it was in our historical experiences that led us to divide people up in the ways we do. It helps to shift perspectives. To a European or an American, for instance, it seems bizarre that Koreans and Japanese, or Singhalese and Tamils, should see themselves as racially opposed, when the briefest glance at their entangled histories reveals the cultural nature of the clashes between them.

BLOOD TYPE

To drive that lesson home, let's look quickly at another physical feature, this time one that could not possibly have appeared in Linnaeus' classification or medieval folklore. It was only in the nineteenth century that it was discovered that human blood was not the same in everybody, but differed chemically in many different ways. The first and best-known classification was into blood types A, B, and O. Unlike skin color, which can vary infinitely along a scale, everyone has blood of one type or another. Consequently, it looks like blood type might provide a solid basis for a three-part classification of races. The problem with this is that people with each blood type are distributed all over the world, mixed up with people who externally look similar, but belong to other blood groups. These spotty distributions of people here and there are not what are usually thought of as races. To compare whole populations it is necessary to count the frequency of different blood types. The result can be shown on a map, high frequencies here, lower frequencies there. As far as possible, blood samples are taken only from indigenous populations so as to avoid the effects of mass migrations over the last couple of centuries. In the Americas, for instance, it is the figures for Indian populations that are mapped, not those of European descent.

A nineteenth-century view of race would lead us to suspect that any one "race" would share similar percentages of blood types, in contrast to other races. By now it will come as no surprise to learn that this is not what we see. Instead the lines showing different percentages of different blood types weave across the continents, chopping them up into blobs and slices that bear no resemblance whatsoever to our ideas of where the different "races" come from. In addition the lines for different blood types cross each other, so that it is hard to make any sense of the maps at all. For example, a broad band of Aborigine populations running East–West across the center of Australia have about 50% of people with blood type A, while their neighbors to the north and south average about 20%. But no one has ever hypothesized two races of Aborigines. Again, blood type A is very common in large parts of South America and also across what is now Canada, but rarer in the rest of North America. The Swedes have more of blood type A than Norwegians, and so on.

Once again, the reason for these seemingly random distributions of blood types is not hard to identify. As far as we know, there is no particular adaptive advantage in one blood type rather than another. None aids or hinders adaptation to particular climates or habitats. Consequently, the variation in populations is a result of what is called "drift," that is populations diverge over the generations according to chance patterns in mating. The key issue, however, is that if there really had ever been "races" separated for long epochs from each other, then the data would reflect those boundaries. It does not, and nor do other variables.

INTELLIGENCE QUOTIENT

Since there has been endless debate about race and IQ, the topic calls for a little attention. The first thing to note is that measuring the IQ of individuals is hardly as straightforward as figuring out to which of the three major blood groups they belong.

An IQ test is anything but simple, as anyone who has taken one knows. They consist of batteries of tests, whose scores have to be computed and compared to those of whole populations. But what exactly is each of these tests measuring? Verbal tests in English obviously favor people who speak standard English rather than any dialect. Diagrammatic tests have other built-in ethnocentric features. For example, Australian Aborigine children achieved genius scores on tests where they had to decide from a drawing whether two pieces of entwined rope were knotted together or whether they would simply pull apart. Those administering the tests were astonished, until they discovered that the children spent hours playing string games, that is, making patterns by pulling a loop of string around their fingers, and then transforming the pattern with a flick of the wrist. That particular test was then of course dropped, since it was obviously "biasing" the results.

Second, we should note that populations can only be compared by taking an average. Individuals do indeed vary on whatever it is that is being measured in IQ tests. That comes as no surprise; it is our general experience that some people are smarter than others. But if you bunch people together at random in groups of a dozen, the effect becomes less noticeable because unusually high or low scores are outweighed by the others. That means the differences between average scores of groups are less than that between individuals. The effect intensifies as one compares populations of a hundred, and then a thousand, and so on. Very rapidly, the differences *between* populations become tiny compared to the differences *within* populations. Once we get to populations the size of whole segments of the world's population, such as the traditional five "races," whatever differences there might conceivably be would be so vanishingly small as to be undetectable by our crude measuring devices, and completely irrelevant to everyday life.

To sum up: if all you know about a person is the concentration of melanin in his or her skin, then that is all you know about that person. You know nothing about his or her height, blood type, IQ, aptitudes, industry, or inherent tendency towards a phlegmatic or choleric personality. And that is all there is to say about that.

RETHINKING "RACIAL" CHARACTERISTICS

So clear is this result to anthropologists in the twenty-first century that we take it for granted that just about all supposedly "racial" characteristics are really cultural characteristics. What that means is that we have to rethink all of the former in terms of the latter. There are innumerable possible examples, but just two will suffice to make the point:

African musicality. In America many people both black and white take it for granted that black people are inherently gifted musically. For Afro-Americans this constitutes a proud claim to hipness, and for Euro-Americans a generous concession on a nonpolitical issue, but it remains a racial stereotype for all that. What an anthropologist would want to study is African traditions of rhythm, dance, and music, and how they were maintained and transformed when transported to the New World. That is a long and fascinating story, with much research actively in progress. Briefly, we can report that interest in music and dance is not uniformly distributed across the whole of sub-Saharan Africa. It so happens that some of the West African peoples most heavily victimized during the slave trade did have complex styles that were practiced in the villages and patronized by kings. On the plantations of Brazil, the Caribbean, and North America, cultural outlets for slaves were extremely restricted. Music and story-telling were the most available, and the former had the advantage that it needed no translation between peoples thrown together regardless of ethnicity. Consequently, their music thrived, largely out of sight of their masters. To this day, researchers have found, the play of African-American children in the street and in school playgrounds is dominated by games of verbal and physical dexterity, a perfect training for music.

By the 1950's, even before de-segregation, black music was beginning to find its way into mainstream American culture. Needless to say, white musicians who were attracted to it rapidly learned its complex rhythms and styles, and melded them with their own. In fact, music in the modern world is surely the most mobile of mediums. New styles spring up constantly, mixing elements from around the globe in an endless riot of creativity. Meanwhile, African-American music is so familiar around the world that, viewed from outside the continent, American culture to a large extent *is* African-American culture.

Jewish bookishness. In much the same way, it is stereotype, racist even if taken as complimentary, that Jews make good lawyers. The relevant quality is concern with books and with written codes, and it does not take much research to become aware of their crucial significance in Jewish history. In European and Middle-Eastern theology, there are three "peoples of the book": Jews, Christians, and Muslims. That is to say, for adherents of all these faiths it is important to study the sacred texts, and people with a deep knowledge of them are greatly respected. For Jews after the diaspora, during epochs of poverty and oppression, their texts became the only thing holding dispersed Jewish communities together. Consequently, Jewish children have for centuries been raised to aspire to literacy and to scholarship, even more so than Christian and Muslim children. It is not surprising that they have made such major contributions to the culture of the West.

Meanwhile, better access to education in many parts of the world has increased literacy and the demand for books. Contrary to what nineteenth-century observers might have expected, everywhere that this occurs, it is not long before writers, scholars, and teachers emerge in response to the new opportunities. Bookishness is not the preserve of any "race," but the result of historical experiences and cultural responses to them.

MITOCHONDRIAL EVE

By way of closure, there is a recent finding of physical anthropology that neatly confirms this view of human difference. It has been discovered that there is a type of genetic material found in the outer layer of cells, the mitochondria, that is transmitted directly from female animals to their offspring. Consequently, it is not changed in the processes of sexual reproduction, nor by drift. It changes only by mutations, which occur rarely and remain in all subsequent generations descended from that female. Slight differences in mitochondrial genetic material can consequently be used to compare the degree of closeness of populations all over the world. Out of this research came an amazing result: all currently existing human populations are descended from one small population that existed about 50,000 years ago. It is not literally the case that we all share one ancestress, but the reality is close enough to that for us to speak of a "mitochondrial Eve."

What this result shows is that human beings are even more closely related to each other than we had imagined before. In evolutionary terms, 50,000 years is the mere blinking of an eye, and the physical variety of our species is superficial. All of us have the inherent capacities to acquire any cultural repertoire at all, and that confirms what we see about us. Children from any part of the world can be raised in any other, and, if they are allowed to, they will become as culturally competent as any other.

AFTERWORD: THE FIELD OF PHYSICAL ANTHROPOLOGY

This chapter makes clear the importance of the findings of physical anthropology for the entire study of humanity. Before we move on, however, it is worth pointing out that the field is not exclusively concerned with "race." In fact, there are many types of specialists within the field, and they each have their own skills and techniques of research. Experts on hominid evolution, for instance, need to know enough geology to spot potential rewarding areas to search for fossils, and then use careful techniques of excavation so as to preserve their data. This is in addition of course to knowing a great deal about comparative human and primate anatomy, so that a range of both "field" and laboratory skills are required. The same is true of physical anthropologists who study the prevalence of diseases in different populations. As we saw above, deconstructing "race" does not mean denying genetic differences between human populations. On the contrary, it is possible to target populations for particular research purposes, so as to study such things as the genetic components of different medical conditions, or dietary needs. The practical value of such work augments the theoretical impact of the field.

Summary
It is only during the last century that the nature of human physical variation has become plain. It involves a paradox. Everyone can see with their own eyes that human populations vary in skin color, body dimensions, blood type and any number of other variables. But this does not mean they have races in the biological sense of the term. That is to say human

populations cannot be sorted into a small number of boxes, each containing populations resembling each other in a range of variables. The reverse is true: the more variables one measures, the more boxes are needed to contain their diversity, *ad infinitum*. Consequently, there are as many races as one cares to see. Since physical anthropologists have looked the closest, they have simply abandoned any notion of a master taxonomy. Two important things follow: first, racial stereotypes are bound to be misleading. There is no possibility that large segments of humanity that cannot even be differentiated by obvious physical features will differ as a whole in such subtle and elusive matters as IQ. From this follows a second conclusion: when people discuss "race" issues, they are really talking about a cultural phenomenon. What the anthropologist wants to ask is what historical circumstances made this "racial" distinction important at this place and time. How are the categories mobilized in social and political situations?

It is important that the objective findings of physical anthropology be widely understood, but it must be conceded that they are not. Everyone assumes that anthropologists are saying that racism is wicked, when in fact we are saying it is meaningless. Against such resistance, it is the duty of anthropologists to expose the illusion of race at every possible opportunity. If you are convinced by the arguments in this chapter, it is now your duty as well.

FURTHER READING

Regarding the Lugbara of Kenya, my source is John Middleton, who wrote many articles and books about them. The best known is *Lugbara Religion* (1960). The material about medieval European notions of "Homo monstrosus" comes from a fascinating article with that title, written by Anne de Waal Malefijt (1968). One of the earliest and most influential attacks on the notion of "race" was Ashley Montagu's *Man's Most Dangerous Myth* (1945), in which he sets out the intellectual position that is now taken by virtually all anthropologists. There are many textbooks on physical anthropology, describing both what is known about the evolutionary origins of our species, and the nature of the current physical variations within the species. One that I have frequently consulted is

Bernard Campbell's *Humankind Emerging* (2001). Since new fossil discoveries are constantly causing revisions in the details of the hominid story, most of these texts appear in regularly updated editions. Finally, the pitfalls of IQ testing across different cultures are discussed in Stephen Gould's *The Mismeasure of Man* (1981).

3

SOCIAL DO'S AND DON'TS

For all but the most blinkered chauvinist, it comes as a relief to see that the things that most divide people are not immutable genetic traits, but changeable cultural ones. Not only *can* they change, by all kinds of accommodations and borrowings, they *will* change, as everything in our modern world shows clearly.

That does not mean, however, that cultures are superficial. On the contrary, the process of socialization shapes individuals in a fundamental way, and often provides their most intimate understanding of who they are. Consequently, cultural identities cannot be changed at will. Nor can they be eliminated by government regulation, and efforts to do so invariably provoke resistance. What follows has only too frequently been oppression, violence and war.

Evidently, cultures have a strange quality: always and everywhere changing, but not at the will of those who supposedly possess them. It seems almost as if cultures have a will of their own, but that thought brings us close to the logical fallacy of teleology. That is to say, "cultures" become mystical beings, like the ancient Greek gods on Mount Olympus, manipulating the lives of the uncomprehending humans below. If there is some grand plan or meaning to history or society that we humans are not aware of, then whose plan is it? No answer to that question gets us very far in understanding the phenomenon. Instead we need to resolve the apparent contradiction that cultures seem to be inside us and outside us at the same time.

INSIDE YOUR HEAD

To help think this through, let us take a simple example. Suppose you sit down at a table in a coffee shop, and then notice that there is a pair of sunglasses left there. You get your coffee and drink it, but no one shows up to claim them. So what runs through your mind? Perhaps your first thought is: what luck! I could do with a spare pair of sunglasses. This is followed almost immediately by: I suppose I really should give them to the person behind the counter (to keep for whoever left them behind). Then, typically, there follows a brisk internal debate – ah, no one's going to come back for them. I'll just pick them up casually and walk out. No one will notice – Hah! Look at the great criminal mastermind! Don't be so petty. You need sunglasses, go buy some – well, finders keepers, you know – so now we're back in primary school are we? (Internal voices can be very sarcastic.)

If we now ask why this dialogue occurs, the answer is obvious. There is a rule: do not steal. Without the rule there would be no debate about whether this constituted an infraction, and whether to do it anyway. Moreover, if you are the kind of person who would not dream of walking out with the glasses, I can easily find some other example. For instance, are there no occasions when you might be tempted, out of sheer tact, to tell a "white lie"? Or on the other hand, if you are entirely comfortable with acquiring objects from here and there that no one seems to be needing at the present moment, how would you feel about walking off with something belonging to a good friend? Such qualms are the thin end of a large wedge. What the wedge divides, through the process of socialization, is your social self from your psychic self.

PSYCHOLOGY AND ANTHROPOLOGY

This is important, because otherwise anthropology would be a branch of psychology. If teleology is to be avoided, if cultures are not to be made into entities that exist somehow on their own, we have to concede that they exist inside peoples' heads. It is true of course that rules may be written down, like the Ten Commandments. There may even be watchdog organizations that try to maintain cultural purity, like the Académie Française (the "French Academy," an elite organization of senior scholars). But the Ten Commandments would have no cultural impact if they were *only* words on paper, and the Académie is singularly unsuccessful at stopping French people from borrowing words from English. More importantly, people who lack writing, or any kind of authoritarian institutions, still manage to have cultures.

Meanwhile, we all know that individuals vary in all manner of idiosyncratic ways. Some people are sociable, others less so. Some are dreamers, others have a practical bent. Everywhere in the world people differ in temperament and aptitudes, even from the members of their own families. No one could deny the fascination of such differences – we gossip about them endlessly. But they are not what concerns anthropology. Instead, we must distinguish a level of cultural reality, neither biological nor psychological, neither common to the species nor peculiar to the individual. Moreover, it requires its own level of explanation. To reduce cultural phenomena to the other levels is to engage in either "biological reductionism" or "psychological reductionism," both of which have repeatedly bedeviled the discipline.

OUTSIDE YOUR HEAD

This argument does not of course deny the validity of psychology as a field of study. The shoe is on the other foot: in the late nineteenth century anthropology needed to define its own concerns, as distinct from psychology. The man who accomplished this was Emile Durkheim, who taught first at the University of Bordeaux and then in Paris. He argued that our everyday actions were influenced by what he called "collective representations." This cumbersome term was designed to emphasize that these influences applied to many people simultaneously, that is a collectivity, and at the same time that they expressed, or represented, the existence of this collectivity. In later years, British anthropologists substituted the simpler terms "norm" or "social institution." Below I use all three terms interchangeably. For present purposes, collective representations can be described simply as all the social rules upheld in a particular population, all the do's and don'ts instilled in children in the process of growing up, or acquired by identification with a particular moral system.

I must emphasize that Durkheim argued that collective representations *influence* individuals; they do not *control* them. If they did, there would be none of those debates going on inside our heads that Durkheim pointed to. Nevertheless, some critics have accused him of reducing people to mere puppets, their strings pulled by some mysterious collective entity. For some, Durkheim's views even smacked of socialism, but this claim is absurd. Could you even exist as a social person without sharing ideas of right and wrong? Does individualism require living in a cave? What would be the result of letting such "individuals" drive on our roads?

On the contrary, collective representations constitute an important part of the person, precisely because they are *internalized*. Imagine, in my example, if there were no other customers in the coffee shop, and the person behind the counter had ducked out for a moment. The internal debate would be the same. If, on the other hand, you sat down at the table with one or two friends, the debate might occur out loud. Or perhaps in gestures: one of you pockets the glasses with a certain swagger, to imply a worldly cynicism, while the others exchange a glance, and raise their eyebrows in disapproval. This demonstrates the social nature of the rule. Everyone at the table shares it; it is both internal and external.

THE RAISED EYEBROW

This example also shows the usual sanction that "enforces" social rules. If you are caught robbing a bank, then what follows is a matter of written codes: arrest, trial, sentencing, prison. Nation-states maintain elaborate codes of law, defining exactly what constitutes a crime and what punishment is proportionate, for everything from a parking violation to murder. The great majority of infractions of collective representations, however, are not crimes or felonies, nor can you sue someone for committing them. Instead, there are rules about proper behavior in a thousand different contexts, and what urges compliance is nothing more than social approval. A child looks up into his or her mother's face, and is rewarded with a smile, or corrected with a frown.

AVOIDING THE ANCESTORS' MATS

An anthropologist beginning fieldwork must learn a host of social rules appropriate to the new environment. But this is not a preparation for fieldwork, this *is* fieldwork. Social rules are among the most accessible things to study because they can be observed in action. There is nothing hidden about them; sometimes they are even stated explicitly.

When the New Zealand anthropologist Raymond Firth began work in the remote Polynesian island of Tikopia in 1928, he had to

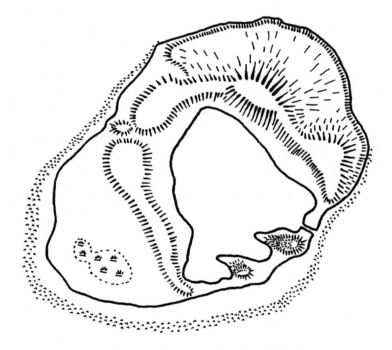

Figure 3.1 The island of Tikopia is about two miles wide, and three long. Moreover, as the map shows, a lake takes a large part of its area, and the north end is not suitable for gardens. Consequently, the island supports only a small population, about 1200 in 1928. It is also remote: over a hundred miles to the nearest inhabited island, and over two hundred from the nearest of any size, in the New Hebrides chain. Moreover, these islands are not inhabited by Polynesians. The major islands of Polynesia, such as Samoa and Tahiti, are far away to the east. Consequently, Tikopia is referred to as a Polynesian outlier.

acquire some new habits in moving about the houses of his hosts. It was the Tikopian custom to bury their dead within the house, or under the eaves just outside. This sounds shocking to us, but Firth insists that corpses were buried deep enough in the porous, sandy soil that there were no odors. For the Tikopians, the practice was simply a mark of attachment. Deceased family members should continue to be shielded under the roof that covered them in life, and even after conversion to Christianity there were almost no church-yard burials. The side of the house where burials occurred was called *mata paito*, the "eye" or "face" of the house, and it was used only on ceremonial occasions. The graves of distinguished ancestors were covered with special mats, but the residents slept on other mats with their heads facing the ancestors.

Firth describes his learning experience as follows:

It is surprising how soon the anthropologist himself becomes accus-tomed to treating the *mata paito* in native fashion. When I was introduced to Taurangi, my home in Ravenga, the two grave mats of the father and grandfather of the present owners were shown to me and I was requested not to walk on them or use that portion of the floor – which of course I readily promised not to do. And though the graves were only a couple of feet from my table I observed the promise, skirting the mats punctiliously as I moved about the little dwelling. After a few weeks the habit of avoiding this portion of the floor was so far ingrained that it was not a conscious practice, and I remember that on one occasion it came as a slight shock to find how completely I had been ignoring the prohibited space and the company of the relics of the dead.

(1983 [1936]: 79)

Note how many Tikopian things were articulated with this one institution. As he came to understand it, Firth learned not only about indigenous concepts of social space, but also of kinship, poli-tics, and religion.

SELF-EXPRESSION

In contrast to so serious a matter as respect for the ancestors in a traditional society like Tikopia, the mere choice of commodities in

European or American shops might seem to be a matter of individual whim. That, however, would discount the force of fashion. The test of Durkheim's collective representations is that individuals feel them to be somehow external to themselves. Specifically, they know that they did not make up the norms themselves, and that everyone around them is aware of the same norms. Such rules could apply even to such individual things as taste. In England, for instance, there is a saying that "red and green should never be seen." If you should be so incautious as to wear, say, a red sweater with green slacks, your punishment will be to have people constantly and irritatingly repeating the maxim to you all day long. In America, people will ask you if it is Christmas yet.

Most clothing styles, however, come and go too rapidly to become the subject of folklore. You may claim to have no interest in them, and to despise people controlled by the "fashion police." But it is not so easy to ignore fashion. To start with, you probably do not make your own clothes. That means you will have to choose from what is available in clothing stores, whose managers are trying to guess what will sell. Having acquired a wardrobe over the years, you will have to make a selection from it at least once a day. Selecting at random is almost impossible. Whether you like it or not, you have internalized literally hundreds of rules about what goes together, and what is suitable for this or that activity or occasion. Consequently, you cannot avoid making some kind of "fashion statement." Even if you doggedly wear the same T-shirt and jeans day after day, *that* will constitute a fashion statement, and a strong one at that.

If this proposition sounds grim, try standing it on its head. The fact that there are norms about clothing, especially changeable ones, provides a means of self-expression. Your knowledge is a resource. You can choose to dress "down" or "up," modestly, or to attract attention. You can show who you are, or who you want to be, or experiment with being a goth, or a hippie, and perhaps "discover yourself." For the most part, you cannot get away with walking around nude, or in a grass skirt. Beyond that, you have liberty of choice. Would it have been better to have lived before the Industrial Revolution, when clothes were too expensive for any but a tiny elite to have more than one suit of clothing, or at most two? Or would you prefer Mao's China, where everyone went around in the same regulation garb?

STATUS AND ROLE, RIGHTS AND RESPONSIBILITIES

Moreover, the force of norms varies according to context. You would probably not want to spoil the sense of occasion by turning up at a friend's wedding in a tracksuit. Norms also vary according to who you are. Though this may change in a generation or so, most of us would not be reassured to find our bank manager dressed as a Hell's Angel.

In the 1940's British anthropologists elaborated a technical jargon for discussing the variability of norms from one person to another. The basic proposition is that you have a social existence insofar as you have relationships with other people. That seems obvious enough, but there is a twist: a relationship is not just a matter of liking someone, it is also a matter of assuming *rights* and *responsibilities* towards each other. Suppose you make friends with someone, but then he or she purposely makes you look foolish in front of other people in your circle. You might reasonably respond: I thought you were my friend. What that implies is that there are certain things you can expect of a friend. Your sense of betrayal comes from the assumption that both of you know what rights and responsibilities go with friendship, not just your friendship, but any friendship. In the British jargon, that person had assumed the *status* of a friend, but failed to perform the *role* of a friend.

You will notice once again the distinction that Durkheim made between people as individuals, whose personalities do or do not allow them to take pleasure in each other's company, and the culturally specific collective representations that define the role of friend. These rules can be explicitly mobilized. You can try to coerce someone into doing something by saying: "come on, you're my friend. Do it for *me*." If they fail to comply, you can legitimately punish them with a pout.

KINSHIP ROLES: FATHERS AND SONS

The next point to note is that the status relationships are not always symmetrical, like that between friends. The role of a father towards his son can hardly be the same as the role of the son to his father. Moreover, exactly what these roles are varies enormously from one society to another. For an example let us return to Tikopia.

BOX 3.1 HOW "PRIMITIVE"?

One of the questions that anthropologists who work in remote places are often are asked is "just how primitive is it there?" The usual response is for the anthropologist to look sideways at the questioner and ask warily "what exactly do you mean by primitive?" Is it a question about plumbing? Or is there some sensational fantasy of wild savages whose existence is barely above that of animals? Firth makes it plain that the technology of the Tikopians was simple even by the standards of 1928: no radios, no outboard motors. They had no knowledge of the use of money. But at the same time, the Tikopians were healthy and vigorous, courteous to one another, and enjoyed a rich communal life. Who is to describe that as "primitive"? On the contrary, one is struck by how civilized the Tikopians were.

At the same time, people often ask themselves whether the anthropologists sensationalize their accounts, making their hosts out to be more naïve than they really are. This is a very proper skepticism, since this kind of romanticism is a constant vice of travel literature. Firth addresses the issue squarely at the outset. Even though Tikopia was so remote, it had already been influenced deeply by outside contacts. To start with, half the population was Christian, at least nominally. The miracle was that any Tikopian continued in their traditional rituals. Across the rest of Polynesia, indigenous religions had long since disappeared. All iron tools came from traders, who visited the island perhaps once a year, and knives were always in heavy demand. At one time the island was overrun with rats who stole large amounts of food, until an overseas expedition brought back a pair of cats. Plants such as bananas and sugar cane were also imported, but also unfortunately diseases such as ringworm. All of this Firth notes carefully.

The cartoonist Gary Larson likes to poke fun at anthropologists. One of his cartoons shows people with bones in their noses pushing television sets and VCRs under the bed, while through the window of their grass hut two men in solar topees can be seen paddling up to the beach. The caption reads "Anthropologists! Anthropologists!" Is it possible that Firth overlooked something that arrived after contact with Europeans? Certainly it is, but it is not too likely that he missed TVs or VCRs.

Firth provides a lengthy account of child rearing in Tikopia. Not surprisingly, all parents are not equally conscientious, but there is broad agreement on what is expected from them. Of a child who is a nuisance at a public gathering, or lacks elementary notions of decorum, people say: "Why do not its parents instruct it? Why is it not told by its parents not to act thus?" (1983: 139). This is despite the fact that most children are subjected to a chorus of exhortation to behave properly. The most blood-curdling threats, Firth tells us, may be hurled at a gang of boys bent on mischief: "I shall come out to you, take a stick and split open your heads," or, "May your fathers eat filth! I come out, you will die on the spot!" (1983: 143). Yet the children stand their ground, grinning, confident that nothing will happen. In fact, Firth says, "conformity to the will of a senior is regarded as a concession to be granted, not a right to be expected; an adult behaves to a child as one free spirit to another" (1983:145).

Evidently, this is not an authoritarian society. Yet the respect of children for their parents, and especially a son for his father, is very marked. A son who shouts in the house, or waves a stick about, or stands up in front of elders, is constantly reproved: *A mata tou mana! A mata tou puna!*, literally, "Face of your father! Face of your grandfather!" By ten years of age, he has thoroughly internalized a set of appropriate body postures, and a style of controlled language, appropriate to male elders.

MULTIPLE FATHERS

It is not uncommon around the world for children to be taught to respect their fathers, and you may well recognize parts of the above description in your own upbringing. There is more to follow, however. A child in Tikopia refers not just to one man as father, but many. When anthropologists discovered examples of this in several parts of Polynesia, their heads were filled with sensational fantasies. Perhaps it was the custom some time in the past for whole groups of men to capture women from other tribes, and mate with them promiscuously, so that a child did not know which of them was his or her father. Such ideas may have sent a shiver of excitement down the spines of repressed Victorians, but the truth is simpler and less melodramatic.

The crucial feature is that a Tikopian child is not only born into a family of mother, father, brothers, and sisters, but also into one of much wider extent. A child, girl or boy, is born into a "house," but the Tikopian word *paito* means more than a physical structure of palm-leaf roof supported on posts. It denotes a social group that survives the passage of generations, and is housed in innumerable structures rebuilt on the same site. But a "house" may own several house sites in different parts of the island, since brothers may build separate houses while choosing to remain in the same *paito* for social and ritual purposes. Each "house" is also linked to other groups of people of the same kind. A pair of brothers, for instance, might be acknowledged as founders of two separate *paito*, and in each generation the eldest son of the senior living generation become its titular head. All these related houses in turn constitute a *kainanga*, a term that Firth glosses as "clan," and each clan has a chief, or *ariki*, who is first-born son of first-born sons, back to a semi-mythical founding ancestor. There are just four *ariki* in Tikopia, and their lineage continues back to the gods themselves.

A person's primary allegiance is to his or her *paito*, and consequently it need come as no surprise that all men in the preceding generation are addressed as "father" (*tamana*) since their relationship to the child is as a father. Indeed, all such men in the entire clan are addressed in the same way, and all must be respected in word and gesture. At the same time, the child is not at all confused about the different degrees of relatedness of the various fathers, nor which father fathered him or her.

SOCIETY

By this stage, you may be convinced that there is more social complexity in the tiny island of Tikopia than you had bargained for. But this is just the beginning. The links that a child has with his or her mother's house are also very important. A boy who feels that he is being treated too severely by his father or fathers seeks comfort and support in the house of his mother's brother. In fact, of all the people he comes in contact with, a boy is most relaxed with his brothers and with his mother's brothers. But what if the boy's mother has no brothers? Simple – just as there are many fathers, so there are many mother's brothers (*tuatina*; note that there is no word in English to translate this term since "uncles" include father's brothers as well as mother's brothers). That is because the boy's mother addresses all the men of her generation in her house and her clan as "brother," just as the boy addresses all the other boys in his clan as "brother" (*taina*). All these terms, *tamana*, *tuatini*, *taina*, are examples of what are called *classificatory kinship terms*, meaning that they apply not to one person but to whole categories of people.

Then again, when a young man is ready to marry, he enters into a whole series of new relationships, covered by other kinship terms, each conferring its own rights and responsibilities. His bride may come from another clan, but if not, some "brothers" will have to be re-classified as "brothers-in-law." Moreover, all of these many relationships will have to be reconfigured from a woman's point of view, which is different in many important respects. Her experience of growing up is different to a boy's, and so are all the relationships with her kin. Importantly, she is born into one house, but her own children are born into another. Then there are all the issues of land tenure and inheritance to discuss, not to mention the ritual roles of different kinds of kin, both male and female.

To describe all these relationships in sufficient detail to give a firm grasp of Tikopian society takes Firth over 450 pages. But for our purposes, we need go no further. The point of this sketch is to make it plain what we mean when we speak of Tikopian "society." It consists of all the links that stitch the Tikopian people together, not in terms of idiosyncratic emotional responses, but rather culturally-defined roles, each involving specific rights and responsibilities.

THE SOCIAL PERSON

In this network, one individual is connected to many others, and each connection implies a status and role relationship. A woman has the status of daughter, as regards both her mother and father, but there are also many classificatory mothers and fathers. We may say she is the daughter of an entire house (*paito*). In the same way, she has multiple sisters and brothers, including ones that we would call cousins. She may have children, and if she does, then she also has in-laws of several kinds. Tikopia is small enough, Firth tells us, that everyone on the island can in the end find some kind of kinship link to everyone else. Her allegiance to particular chiefs' elders is also governed by her kinship connections. In the terminology of social anthropology, all the statuses she holds by virtue of all these one-to-one relations constitute what she is as a *social person*.

The social person of a Tikopian, male or female, is largely defined by kinship statuses, but this is not true elsewhere. In Europe or America, being a citizen of one country or another is an important status, with crucial legal rights and obligations. One's work involves other statuses, with employers, employees, managers, and colleagues. There are innumerable organizations that one may be involved in, everything from insurance plans to sports teams, and each confers a status, whether significant or not. The number of different statuses that an individual may potentially hold becomes large – but not infinite. Moreover, for everyone there are a relatively small number of statuses, kinship and otherwise, that largely define the social person, so that it is a manageable task to describe it.

It is important to be clear that your identity as a social person does not include everything that you are as an individual. If someone asks "who is that?" the answer tends to be in terms of the social person: she is so-and-so's daughter, or, he is the plumber, or, she is an exchange student from such-and-such a country. But none of these descriptions penetrates very far into the individual, his or her genius or neuroses. The social person makes no room for hopes and dreams, or secret fears. The value of this approach is precisely that it leaves out of consideration a great deal about what makes us individuals, loved, hated, or ignored by other individuals. It allows precision by focusing on just one clearly defined element of what makes us who we are.

SOCIAL STRUCTURE

The anthropologists who pioneered this approach referred to themselves as structuralists, and they had a clear idea of what they meant by that. Subsequently, things have become more confused, as we shall see below, and the casual use of the word often baffles beginner students. There need be no great mystery, however, provided we go a step at a time. So let me offer a straightforward definition:

To describe the structure of a particular society means making an inventory of its most important statuses and roles, together with their associated rights and responsibilities, which are conferred by membership in social groups and categories.

All the terms in this definition are now familiar, except for the last two. A social category is a way of dividing people up in a manner that is socially significant. So, for instance, it matters whether or not I belong to the category of people who are covered by health insurance. A group, or more forcefully a corporate group, is a category of people who in addition share some of the following features: (a) they own property in common; (b) they assemble regularly, that is at predictable times; (c) they have a proper name, that is one that we might put in capital letter and (d) they have someone who can represent them collectively, sometimes called the "corporate sole."

There is the possibility of movement between group and category. If, for example, some activists get together to found an organization to agitate for better health insurance coverage. They begin by giving it a name, Medicine For All. They elect a steering committee, and send out flyers inviting people to join. With the money they collect, they buy office supplies, and organize a national convention. Before long, the MFA has a president, a budget, a nationwide membership, and employs a team of lobbyists.

Returning to Tikopia, it is clear that *paito*, "houses," are corporate groups: they own land in common, they have an elaborate ritual life that brings them together for marriages and funerals, they are named for their oldest house sites, and they are represented at island councils by their senior living member. Meanwhile, "children" are obviously a category, free spirits, running here and there as they please. The category *tuatina*, "brothers-in-law," requires a little more care. When a house needs to provide food for a ceremonial occasion, it is the duty of the men married to women of the house to perform all the hot and tedious chores of cooking. As a group, they are referred to bluntly as "the firewood," or "the oven stones," since the cooking is done in a pit oven lined with stones. For the occasion, camaraderie springs up between the men from other houses who are doing the cooking, but afterwards they disperse to their own houses. Moreover, any married man will be a

Summary

A crucial feature of the anthropology of society, or social anthropology, is not only what is included, but also what is left *out* of consideration. In everyday speech, the words "person" and "individual" mean more or less the same thing. But Durkheim's approach makes a sharp distinction between them. Social persons are defined by the statuses they occupy with regard to other persons, such as "friend" or "father." The roles that these statuses imply – the appropriate social do's and don'ts – are never unique. Instead everyone participating in that society understands them in roughly the same way. They are defined in norms (institutions, collective representations) covering everything from the obligatory to matters of taste, from deference to one's superiors, to fashions in clothing. In all these things, the individual is aware that others may judge him or her, even if the sanction is only a raised eyebrow.

We all know, however, that there is more to us as individuals than that – all our private dreams and ambitions, frustrations and fears, however unrealistic or irrational. It is important to note that even in this internal domain, revealed only to close friends and confidants, culture plays a major part. After all, our upbringing largely frames the kinds of fears and ambitions that we may have. No Tikopian child grows up longing to be an artist, living a bohemian life in a garret. But few British or American children can experience the sense of belonging that comes from being born into an ancient "house" providing dozens of "fathers," "brothers" and "sisters." Nevertheless, beyond such cultural understandings, there does indeed lay a mental realm that is genuinely idiosyncratic, penetrable only in terms of individual experience. This is the realm of psychology.

Social anthropology gains its incisiveness precisely by restricting itself to the study of social persons. When Durkheim framed the principle that we should "treat social facts as things" he was much criticized for making material what was clearly mental. But what he meant by the maxim is simply that there is reality to collective representations. Anyone who has experienced culture shock, as described in Chapter One, knows the feeling of having run into something that is really "out there," almost like walking into an invisible wall. What that wall consists of, says Durkheim, is all those little internalized rules about ways of doing things, even such simple things as body posture and conducting a conversation. Moreover, even these norms often vary for men and women, not to mention the status of whoever is being communicated with.

In beginning fieldwork, these norms are the first thing that an anthropologist encounters, and the first thing that he or she must grasp. That is to say, fieldwork almost invariably begins by understanding social arrangements. That is necessary even to understand who the people are that he or she is interacting with. This is the enduring value of Durkheim's ideas and the terminology elaborated by his British followers.

brother-in-law on some occasions and a wife's brother on others. However hard the work, there can never be a cooks' union in Tikopia.

FURTHER READING

The basic concepts of Durkheim's sociology are laid out in his *The Rules of the Sociological Method* (1982, original 1893). The British version is set out in A.R. Radcliffe-Brown's *Structure and Function in Primitive Society* (1952). Neither book, it must be conceded, makes lively reading. Not surprisingly, Durkheim often gets caught up in issues that now seem dated and irrelevant. It takes a deal of sifting to find those pieces of his program that are still useful. Durkheim is a founding ancestor of both sociology and anthropology. Sociologists mostly read his early work, but in mid-career Durkheim became fascinated by the societies of the Australian Aborigines, as described by early European travelers. His most important work for anthropologists is his massive account of Aborigine religion, *The Elementary Forms of the Religious Life* (1965, original 1912), to which we will return in Chapter Nine. The details of Tikopian life given here come from Raymond Firth's first ethnography *We, the Tikopia* (1983, original 1936). Several more were to follow, including the invaluable *The Work of the Gods in Tikopia* (1967), the only ethnographic study of a still-functioning indigenous Polynesian religion. In the rest of Polynesia, conversion to Christianity had occurred long before anthropologists arrived on the scene.

4

AFRICAN POLITICAL SYSTEMS

In the 1940's and 1950's, anthropologists took this notion of society to all parts of the world, applying the theoretical tools of status and role, rights and responsibilities, groups and categories. They set out to discover how other societies worked by dismantling them down to particular institutions. This project was a brilliant success. Within a few decades we had a new understanding of the diversity and originality of other societies. What anthropologists learned had a major impact on all the other social sciences, including sociology, political science, and psychology. At the same time, anthropology became solidly established in universities in Europe and America, and a new generation of students was attracted to it.

DEFINING "POLITICS"

One aspect of this program was a special kind of relativism (see Box 4.1) appropriate to social anthropology. It was taken as axiomatic that different kinds of social activity had to be defined in ways that could be universally applied. For example, when westerners talk of "politics," they are usually referring to the machinations of political parties, their success or failure in elections, and their policies once in power. But what if a society lacks all these things, parties, elections, and even governments? One option is to say that it simply has no

BOX 4.1 CULTURAL RELATIVISM

In philosophy, relativism is the proposition that there are no standards of truth or judgment whatever, outside individual preference. It is a tempting doctrine because it makes many classical philosophical issues irrelevant, but by the same token it brings all further discussion to a complete halt. For anthropologists, it is not necessary to take so extreme a position, and there are varieties of *cultural* relativism available that raise interesting new questions. The most general might be that anthropologists do not judge other peoples' ways of knowing the world (their "epistemologies," in philosophical jargon), but simply seek to understand them. It is not their business to make judgments of which ones are ultimately "true." Instead, their task is to grasp them for what they are, and that is certainly difficult enough. At the minimum, however, it invites exploration rather than paralyzing it.

The relativism of social anthropologists of the 1940's and 1950's begins by assuming that whatever aspects of Western societies may be identified, the same must be found in all others. The fact that we have difficulty in perceiving law without lawyers, or economics without money, or religion without gods, only goes to show what we have to learn from comparative studies. Note that there is no assumption that indigenous institutions will be divided between legal, economic and religious ones, or even that there will be any words for "law," "economics," or "religion." On the contrary, people live in a seamless reality, without the need for such categories. It is only the ethnographer that uses them, and only for specific comparative purposes.

politics, and that was the conclusion often reached by travelers and colonial administrators. But that immediately hobbles any chance of a comparative study of politics. You cannot learn anything new if you assume you know the answers before you begin. The anthropology of the mid-twentieth century launched itself directly against such smugness, and that was why it struck so many as new and refreshing.

Consequently, a definition of politics was framed in sufficiently basic terms that it would follow from the notion of society itself. As we saw in the last chapter, a society consists of persons linked together by statuses. These in turn are defined in norms of behavior that are socially sanctioned. Most infractions result in a frown, or perhaps the temporary shunning of the individual for his or her unruly or boorish behavior. But everywhere there are crimes that elicit a violent response, if only in self-defense. What anthropologists wanted to emphasize was that some types of violence were widely felt to be legitimate while others were not, and that distinction was the nub of politics, whatever widely divergent forms it took.

By the new definition, then, politics concerns the maintenance of social order by the legitimate threat or use of physical force. Viewed from outside, this means defense against invasion or enslavement. Viewed from inside, it means the punishment or restraint of deviants and sociopaths: murderers, bandits, thieves and the like. Consequently, the definition is often summed up in the phrase "law and war." As a by-product, we also have a definition of law, as one aspect of politics. The same generation of anthropologists came up with equally embracing definitions of economics and religion, but for the moment let us follow up the implications of the new approach to comparative politics.

A landmark in the development of social anthropology was the appearance in 1940 of an edited volume called *African Political Systems*. It contains accounts of eight different African polities. To show their variety, let us look briefly at three of them.

FIRST EXAMPLE: AN EXPANSIONARY KINGDOM

SHAKA CREATES A STANDING ARMY

At about the same time that Europeans were establishing a colony on the very southern tip of Africa, new states were emerging among the Nguni peoples to the north and east of them. The Nguni had been in the vanguard of the great Bantu expansion across sub-Saharan Africa. As they moved, they herded cattle and made temporary farms. Typically, they lived in dispersed homesteads not unlike the Tikopian "houses," with a group of male kinsmen and their in-marrying wives. They also had chiefs drawn from senior houses. There, however, the similarity ends, because the Nguni chiefs engaged in raiding and warfare, and some managed to establish small kingdoms. Royal houses claimed ancestry going back to prestigious and long-established kingdoms in the Congo region, and consequently mystical powers over the fertility of the land. Their role was largely ritual, but they could raise armies by summoning the sub-chiefs and their followers, just as a medieval king in Europe called his dukes for military service. The soldiers were, however, neither knights nor serfs, but independent farmers temporarily mobilized between busy seasons in the agricultural cycle.

In the late eighteenth century, Shaka Zulu changed this system for raising armies and built his small kingdom into a major force in the region. His innovation was to turn ritual age-sets into military regiments. Traditionally, young men were initiated in festivals held regionally every six or eight years. Together they formed a named *age-set*, and for the rest of their lives shared a bond of comradeship, especially in warfare. In times of peace, however, they lived in their own villages. Shaka's innovation was to not allow new age-sets to disperse. Instead, they were housed in barracks, where they tended the royal herds and farms, and were trained in military maneuvers. When a new generation of young men were ready for service, the retiring age-set would finally be allowed to return home and marry. In this way, Shaka changed the responsibilities associated with the status of age-set membership, organized initiates into new corporate groups called regiments, and in the process acquired a standing army such as no Nguni king had ever before commanded.

CHIEFS WERE "RAISED UP" BY THE KING

Shaka's heirs followed his expansionary policies, conquering neighboring peoples in annual military campaigns. Needing local representatives to administer their new territories, the kings "raised up" chiefs, that is to say they appointed them and defined their status. The result was a complex administrative structure that would need a lengthy account to describe in full. For example, some chiefs were recruited from among the royal families of kingdoms annexed by the Zulu. That might sound risky, since the chiefs might look for an unguarded moment to rebel and regain their former independence. But local chiefs could only raise armies by summoning the older age-sets from their farms. Meanwhile, the Zulu king carefully retained control of the most vigorous young men in his permanent regiments. Moreover, the regiments soon built a strong sense of national loyalty because teenage boys looked forward to joining them. There was the fun of living together in the barracks, where they were subjected to discipline, but also feasted from the meat of the royal herds. When they danced for the king, their coordinated mass agility and singing inevitably impressed everyone who saw them, including European visitors.

Another obvious source of chiefs in newly conquered areas was the Zulu royal clan itself, but there was a danger here. Close relatives of the king were also his major rivals. When a king became excessively tyrannical, it was to them that people looked for a replacement, and things were usually settled rapidly. Shaka himself was murdered by his brother, Dingane, who succeeded him. All Shaka's regiments could not defend him against a palace coup. Whether or not Dingane intended rebellion, he had no alternative but to move first when he came under Shaka's suspicion. Consequently, the politics of the royal clan were a complex matter all by themselves, and kings "raised up" only distant relatives who would become loyal clients. More often, they preferred to ennoble commoners whose fate rose and fell with their royal patron.

CHIEFS AND DISTRICT ADMINISTRATION

At its zenith of power, the Zulu nation was divided into dozens of districts, each administered by a chief. Within his district, a chief behaved like a king, though on a more modest scale. He too was surrounded at his official homestead by advisors, clients, priests and dancers. Consequently, he presided over a more localized version of the politics of the royal court, appointing sub-chiefs so as to avoid rivals and balancing different interests so that no one would go over his head and complain to the king. Even sub-chiefs maintained some state on a yet smaller scale, and runners traveled regularly back and forth carrying orders and news from center to periphery.

At the bottom of the administrative ladder, sub-chiefs dealt with village headmen, who maintained a strong sense of independence. No headman could be appointed who lacked the confidence of the villagers, and from their point of view his job was to keep the chiefs out of local affairs. Outsiders were unpredictable, and a skillful headman could often pressure local people into settling their differences merely by threatening to send them all to the chief. At the same time, chiefs did not involve themselves in the everyday affairs of villagers, such as farming. This disjuncture between the local and the national, typical of many African kingdoms, has led ethnographers to describe the state as superimposed on some pre-existing structure of clans. It is a tempting hypothesis, but it does not in fact explain much about Zulu villages. Whatever existed before has certainly been changed fundamentally by the existence of the state. Inevitably some disputes, often over land, could not be contained, and the apparatus of the state entered directly into village life. Some matters indeed could only be handled by the king's court. Like other African kings, Shaka reserved to himself the right to pronounce a death sentence.

VILLAGES AND FARMSTEADS, LINEAGES AND CLANS

A headman clearly had a difficult job. It was possible only because he could invoke the responsibilities of villagers not only as citizens, but also as kinsmen. A village comprised several farmsteads, each of which resembled a Tikopian "house" in that it contained a small group of men closely related as fathers and sons, or as brothers. This arrangement is in fact common in many parts of the world, and it is described in technical jargon as a *localized patrilineage*. A *lineage* is a number of people descended from a common ancestor, in these cases through men (the prefix patri- is derived from the Latin *pater*, meaning "father"). The lineages are "localized" in that their members live together in one place. Of course, local groups do not consist only of men. Invariably patrilineages include unmarried daughters and in-marrying wives, and there are often other people attached for a host of particular reasons. Typically, where patrilineages exist, they are connected through distant male ancestors to other patrilineages. The common ancestor may be several generations ago, and the links may be hazy. Nevertheless, all men who claim to be related in this way, plus their daughters, constitute a *clan*. In Zululand clans were neither localized nor corporate. Instead, villages contained lineages from several clans, often vying among themselves for local influence.

SIMPLICITY AND COMPLEXITY

For Zulu themselves, it was possible to see the state as simply an elaboration of familiar kinship structures. Everyone belonged to a clan after all, even the chiefs and the king. To address chiefs as "father" was only to extend a courtesy routinely accorded to clan elders, and the most common way to refer to the king was as "father of the nation."

When ethnographers set about describing the most important statuses, however, they found it not so easy to specify rights and responsibilities. What clan membership meant varied widely. Some clans were dispersed all over Zululand, others not. Even commoner clans had their senior lineages acknowledged by the state. Meanwhile, many members of the royal clan in effect lived like commoners, except for a few affectations. Less important royal lineages might even be outranked by chiefly lineages, but the latter were just as prone to internal rivalries and intrigues as their royal counterparts. A Zulu Shakespeare would have had no difficulty finding plots for his dramas. Then again, the king had to distance himself from his own clan. If he constantly favored his close kinsmen in legal disputes, he could not maintain his image as "father of the nation." In technical jargon, the king stood in *structural opposition* to the royal clan, meaning that he had to balance its power against those of chiefly and commoner clans. His allies in this were the senior members of his mother's clan. In fact, the Queen Mother was the second most important personage in the nation after the king, and in effect controlled a parallel political structure.

This outline hints at the sophistication of Zulu politics. In the mid-twentieth century dozens of African kingdoms were studied, and every one revealed its own subtleties. There were in them echoes of European history, but there were also features that were entirely original and unexpected. Meanwhile, many Africans lived outside state structures like that of the Zulu, so their political systems held more surprises. From Max Gluckman's account of the Zulu in *African Political Systems* we turn to Audrey Richards' description of the Bemba.

SECOND EXAMPLE: A MATRILINEAL REALM

MATRILINEALITY

Local Bemba groups were based on lineages, just as in Zululand, but they were *matrilineages* instead of *patrilineages*. That means that children belonged to the lineage of their mother, not their father (from Latin *mater*, "mother"). This way of doing things occurs worldwide, but it often confuses Westerners who are unfamiliar with it. As a system, however, matrilineality is no less logical or practical than patrilineality, and it only takes a little effort to grasp how it works. For a Bemba, it means that he or she is permanently identified with a group of relatives comprising the maternal grandmother and her brothers and sisters, the mother and her brothers and sisters, and his or her own brothers and sisters. These groups have no distinct names, but are simply referred to as the "house" (*inganda*) of this or that person. A matrilineal kinship system does not imply any radical difference in relations between the sexes; the chiefs of the Bemba are men just as they are among the Zulu. However, a Bemba man does not inherit the status of a chief from his father but from his mother's brother, that is, his closest male relative of the previous generation within his own matrilineage.

The Bemba rule of residence after marriage also emphasizes descent through women. In technical jargon it is *matrilocal*, which is to say a newly married couple take up residence at the village of the bride's mother. In this way mothers and daughters live together in a localized matrilineage, together with their in-marrying husbands and their children. Boys grow up in the place of their own matrilineage, but move away at marriage – a mirror image of the Zulu practice, where it is girls who move away from their own patrilineage on marriage. Among the Bemba there are matriclans, just as there are patriclans among the Zulu.

BEMBA VILLAGES

The neat symmetry of patrilineal and matrilineal systems breaks down, however, when politics enters the picture. Bemba villages are less stable than Zulu ones because men are torn between their responsibilities to their children in one place, and their matrilineage in another. If a man is eligible to inherit the role of headman from his mother's brother, he will need to move back to his natal village. His wife's relatives may object, but there is little they can do to stop him. It is only newly married men who can be forced to observe the rule of matrilocality. Consequently, village politics consists of trying to retain current residents and recruit new ones. Rather than wait to inherit a headmanship, an ambitious man may found a new village, bringing together his sisters' daughters, their husbands and children, and also where possible poaching his sons' families and his sisters' sons away from villages in decline. This strategy is possible because there is a great deal of spare land. The Bemba occupy a high plateau in north-eastern Zambia where soils are poor and population densities low. The overall result is that most villages are small, and last only a few generations before being abandoned. The only exceptions are those of chiefly "houses."

CHIEFS AND THE STATE

In the 1940's, a chief's village was much larger than a commoner's, and his standing was largely assessed by the size of it. It contained his noble relatives and commoner followers, and also clients of all kinds attracted by the sophistication and ceremony of his court. Every capital was a religious center, where the chief and his priests performed rituals that governed the fertility of the land and the coming of the rains.

To this extent, the Bemba political system resembled that of the Zulu, but there were fundamental differences. Compared to the subjects of the Zulu state, the Bemba were culturally uniform, a single ethnic group. In pre-colonial times they had a warlike reputation, but their adventures consisted of raids for booty, not the subjugation of their neighbors. Chiefs were the principal organizers and beneficiaries of these raids, so that their glory was diminished by colonial pacification. Moreover, chiefs only received tribute; they passed nothing on to any central authority. Indeed, the ethnographer speaks of each of them as a "king" within his own district. Chiefs maintained a few personal bodyguards, and for the rest relied on recruiting young men ready for excitement. There were no age-sets, and no regiments such as Shaka had at his disposal.

Consequently, it is hard to speak of a Bemba state as such. There was no central administration, and chiefs interfered rarely in village affairs. Yet there was an over-arching hierarchy of chiefly positions, acknowledged by all the Bemba. All titles, even those of priests and councilors in provincial courts, were inherited according to explicit rules of matrilineal succession. There were half a dozen, however, that knit the Bemba together into a kind of ritual confederation. Each title was the name of one of the heroes who led the Bemba into their present homeland. The greatest title was Citimukulu. The original Citimukulu traced his ancestry back to the Luba of the Congo region, making his migration another part of the great eastward expansion of the Bantu, like that of the Zulu. Citimukulu set up his capital in a district at the center of the Bemba country and sent close relatives to do the same in the districts around him. These arrangements persisted into the 1940's. The Citimukulu held authority only within his own district, and the other districts remained, undivided, just as they had done for generations.

CORPORATE SOLES

An intriguing aspect of this system is that district chiefs not only assumed the titles of their predecessors, but also their social personalities. They spoke as if there had only ever been one Mwamba or Nkula, or whatever the title was. Moreover, they spoke as if they embodied all the people. So when they recounted the history of the kingdom they said "I came from the Congo, I settled here, I defeated my enemies there," and so on. This is a dramatic example of what is called a *corporate sole* that is an individual representing an entire group or collectivity of people. For the Bemba there was a literal embodiment. The powerful "spirit" (*umupashi*) of a deceased title holder was ritually transferred into his successor. If a candidate had not yet been selected, it was necessary to make sure that the spirit was not lost. So it was temporarily transferred into a child, who was then addressed as "grandfather."

Moreover, the founding ancestors were members of the same royal house, and it is this connection, ritually preserved, that comprised the Bemba polity. This had a further consequence: one man might occupy several different chiefly titles during his lifetime. This came about because the Citimukuluship did not always pass to one of his sisters' sons, but instead to someone in his own generation in a parallel line of descent. Not surprisingly, this made for complicated rules of succession, but the point here is that a man might be selected as Citimukulu who was already "king" in another district. That left his title open for another man, who might already have a title, and so on. The result was that a noble might move from one capital to another, at each place taking on the voice of another ancestral spirit – a remarkable example of shifting social personalities.

THIRD EXAMPLE: AN EGALITARIAN ANARCHY

DEFYING HOBBES

Bemba political organization comes as a surprise to us in the twenty-first century because we take for granted all the familiar administrative apparatus of the nation-state. It is hard now for us to imagine kingdoms whose main function seemed to have been ritual, plus organizing the occasional raid for plunder.

There were, however, more difficult stretches of the imagination in store. Among the Nuer of the southern Sudan, there were no rulers or states of any kind to be found. As described by the English anthropologist Edward Evans-Pritchard in *African Political Systems* and later in several full-length ethnographies, the Nuer presented a major challenge to Western ideas. All of European political theory since the Middle Ages had been founded on the premise that where there was no legitimate government chaos would reign. In the seventeenth century, Thomas Hobbes had no doubt that without strong central government the condition of man would be "a war of everyone against everyone." In the midst of continual fear, peoples' lives would inevitably be, in his famous phrase, "solitary, poor, nasty, brutish, and short."

What Evans-Pritchard had to report, however, was herds of cattle roaming over a grassy plain cared for only by boys, and little villages, each busy with domestic chores. How could this possibly be so? If this was truly anarchy – lack of government – what could possibly be restraining violence and chaos? The simple answer is that people do not need policemen and judges in order to have status and role relationships with one another. Nuer society existed, contra Hobbes, because Nuer people shared norms about what was proper behavior. There was indeed violence from time to time, but everyone distinguished between what was legitimate and what was not. Indeed, they had a strong sense of moral outrage when collective representations were breached, and also the institutions to do something about it.

THE LAW OF SELF-HELP

There were, for instance, conventional payments due to an injured party; so much for a broken limb, so much for theft, and so on.

These fines were stated in terms of cattle, the wealth of a Nuer family. Nuer also made gardens that played an important role in nutrition, but it was cattle that people prized above all else. There was, however, no one to judge whether an offense had been committed, or to collect the fines. Consequently, it was up to every man to assert his rights forcefully, and be ready to back his claims. If he had made his grievance known to the family of the offending party and been rebuffed, if arbitration by a third party had been refused and all routes to a peaceful settlement exhausted, a man had to be ready to go and take the cattle he was owed by force.

Now, helping oneself to one's neighbor's cattle sounds exactly like the war of all against all that Hobbes predicted. But there is an intermediate step: a man could not get away with taking this action unless he had the backing of his kinsmen and fellow villagers. He had to rehearse the details of the crime to them until they agreed about his case. If he was the kind of man who was perpetually getting into arguments, his neighbors might listen him out respectfully and cluck in sympathy, but lifted no finger to help him. Meanwhile, the same process was going on in the village of the offender, where the accused was trying to convince everyone of his innocence. This process is the familiar "court of public opinion." The only difference in Nuerland was that it also governed the most serious matters.

MATTERS GET SERIOUS: A FEUD

The crisis came when an injured party determined that he would seize what he thought was due to him. If the supposed offender resisted, there was a real risk of violence, even homicide. Self-help was a serious step because of the threat of violence it entailed. All Nuer men carried spears, long shafts with iron tips, and stood ready to use them. If either the accuser or the accused caused bloodshed without having the backing of his kinsmen, his position became tenuous. Lacking allies, he would have little choice but to leave the community. If a death occurred during the face-off, the villages of both parties could be plunged into a blood feud. This would result in whole groups of armed men confronting each other, and once again the situation slid towards Hobbes' war of all against all.

What Evans-Pritchard showed was the restraints that kept a feud from getting out of hand. First, all men were armed in the same way. Everyone could see that if a general mêlée ensued, the result could be multiple deaths, leaving both sides weakened. Consequently, there were always people on both sides of a dispute who, while willing to yell defiance with the rest of them, were in fact anxious to see things patched up. Second, a blood feud brought normal life to a halt. After such threats had been exchanged, the fellow villagers of the accused had to draw in their cattle, move around only in groups, and maintain a constant watch against acts of vengeance. Meanwhile, the neighbors of the accuser had to watch for their opponents to let their guard down, and anticipate a pre-emptive counter raid. This situation rapidly became intolerable, so that parties emerged on both sides advocating a negotiated settlement, which would mean the transfer of at least some of the cattle demanded by the injured party.

LIMITS ON THE FEUD: RITUALLY PROHIBITED BLOODSHED

Third, there were means of arbitration available through the person of the "leopard-skin chief" – surely one of the best-known figures in social anthropology. The title is a misnomer since such a "chief" had no authority to order anyone to do anything, nor force to compel them. Instead, his influence came from his sacred association with the earth, marked by wearing a leopard skin over his shoulders. To spill his blood had dire supernatural consequences, so he had personal immunity against violence. Consequently, he could travel back and forth between the warring parties, carrying offers of payment. These would no doubt be rejected with contempt initially, until tempers cooled and moderate voices prevailed. As extra leverage he could threaten to curse those who would not settle, and so provided a face-saving excuse to do so. Meanwhile, the homicide himself could take sanctuary in the house of the leopard-skin chief, but he dared not stir outside.

Put another way, the social role of the leopard-skin chief could only be performed because Nuer shared certain religious beliefs. But if you look back at the Zulu kings and Bemba chiefs, you will see that part of their authority also came from their ritual functions. The only new element in the case of the leopard-skin chief is that his powers were exclusively of this kind. The relation between politics and ritual is a topic to which we will return below.

Meanwhile, the Nuer fear of prohibited bloodshed also controlled violence within communities. If a man were to attack a close relative, the reaction would be, not anger, but horror. Elaborate rituals would be needed to purify the land. If the homicide had been violent before, the only possible reaction was expulsion.

CONTAINMENT OF THE FEUD: BALANCED TRIBAL SECTIONS

The mechanism of the feud was clumsy and slow. Moreover, if feuding villages were a long way apart, everyday life was not sufficiently disturbed for there to be any strong inducement for a settlement. In those cases, feuds could rumble on for years, flaring up every once in a while when the herds converged on permanent water sources during the dry season. The crucial point is, however, that disputes *could* be settled, and consequently Nuer anarchy was not chaos.

Moreover, there were definite limits on how far a feud could spread. In Nuerland, there could be nothing resembling World War Two, in which violence spread like wildfire, each conflict sparking off others. The reason was that in any given feud most Nuer looked on with indifference, favoring neither one party nor the other. Evans-Pritchard explained how this was managed by means of an elegantly simple model. All Nuer were attached to a particular section of a tribe, comprising a handful of villages. If a blood feud broke out, the villages involved would try to recruit support by appealing to the solidarity of fellow members of the same section. If both villages succeeded in making their case, even larger groups of men might confront each other, but a rough balance in numbers would remain. At the same time, there were even more people on both sides pressing for a settlement.

In addition, the smallest tribal sections were grouped into more encompassing ones. Starting with the largest, a Nuer "tribe" was divided into several primary sections, each of which was subdivided into secondary sections, and they into tertiary sections. Every Nuer belonged to a particular tertiary section, and by virtue of that into given secondary and primary sections. Now if a feud broke out between villages not only of different tertiary sections, but also different secondary sections, both parties could appeal for help from all the villages in the secondary section. Even larger opposing forces might be collected, almost certainly including people who had ancient feuds among themselves. But an even greater majority would be pushing for a settlement – that is, after loudly asserting their contempt for those opposing them. Finally, at its greatest extension, a feud might in theory draw in whole primary sections of the tribe in opposition to each other. The tribe was, by definition, the largest population among whom the settlement of a feud was possible. Consequently in this terminology the Nuer constituted not one "tribe," meaning a single ethnic group, but several, in terms of political units. People in different tribes were in a constant state of hostility. Violence between tribes meant war, not law.

KINSHIP AND POLITICS

This simple model of neat boxes, each fitting into larger ones, revealed a political organization that had nothing to do with chiefs and kings. But how did people get into those boxes? The Nuer language did not contain a word that might be translated as "tribal section," let alone "primary," "secondary," and "tertiary" sections. Instead, Nuer themselves viewed the system as a simple conse-quence of kinship relations. Both men and women traced their line of descent through men, as among the Zulu. Beyond the latest couple of generations, the names of wives and sisters were forgotten. What was particularly remembered was a pair of brothers who founded diverging descent lines.

The connection between kinship and politics was that, in any given tribe, the descent lines of a founding clan furnished the polit-ical segments. Figure 4.1 provides an example, a family tree as seen from a person in the Diel lineage. People of Jinaca clan founded the Lou tribe. Jinaca people live also in the Rengyan tribe, but do not give their names to tribal sections there. Three men who lived many generations ago gave their names to primary sections of the Lou tribe: Gaaliek, Rumjok, and Gaatbal. In the descent line of Gaatbal, a pair of brothers founded Nyarkwac and Leng secondary sections. A generation or two later, the descendants of Pual and Dumien separated to form neighboring tertiary tribal segments. Diel, Malual, Kwoth, and Mar were lineages associated with partic-ular villages.

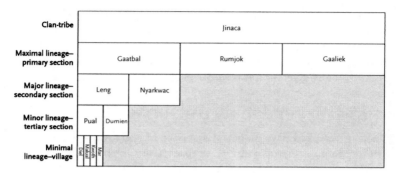

Clan-tribe	Jinaca		
Maximal lineage–primary section	Gaatbal	Rumjok	Gaaliek
Major lineage–secondary section	Leng Nyarkwac		
Minor lineage–tertiary section	Pual Dumien		
Minimal lineage–village	Diel Makal Kwoth Mar		

Figure 4.1 A family tree as seen by a person in the Diel lineage

RESIDENTIAL MOBILITY

At the same time, patrilineages did not constitute residential groups. Nuer felt no restraint in moving from one place to another in search of better grazing or more congenial company. So much was this the case that in any given village only a minority belonged to the founding patrilineage. Moreover, other members of the patrilineage lived elsewhere in the territory of the tribe, and sometimes even in other tribes.

At first glance, this mobility of residence seems to cripple Evans-Pritchard's model of the feud. On average, most cases of violence must have been between people not connected to the patriline of the village where they lived, so how could they mobilize support or be restrained by kinship links that had nothing to do with them? The answer was remarkably simple: for political purposes, everyone in a village behaved *as if* they were members of the founding lineage. This had several consequences. First, most Nuer could recite at least two lines of descent, their own, and that of the founders of their village. Second, if asked about their social identity, people gave the latter. There is indeed a word in Nuer, *buth*, that specifies this kind of "kinship" link. As for their personal "blood lines," villagers not of the local lineage avoided talking about them, so as not to be seen as outsiders. Third, in any confrontation between villages, many of those present were not impassioned by the death or wounding of a close relative. Instead they were displaying the loyalties of *buth* relationship. Indeed, a man might well have close relatives in the *other* village. The risk of spilling a close kinsman's blood, acknowledged by all Nuer as disastrous, which meant that he would be justified in coming unarmed. In these ways, the mobility of Nuer worked to reinforce the mechanism of the feud, by making sure that there was from the start parties on both sides urging a peaceful settlement.

THE PREOCCUPATION WITH KINSHIP

These three examples show the diversity of social organization that ethnographers discovered in Africa. They also share another striking feature, the prominence of ideas of kinship in structuring the entire society. For the Zulu, the state was conceived of as an extension of local kinship relations, incorporating all the complexities of hierarchically organized royal and chiefly clans. Much the same could be said about the Bemba, even though their little kingdoms, and the office of Citimukulu, were unlike anything among the Zulu. Finally, the Nuer extended a principle of lineal descent to create a political system whose very existence defied European political theory.

Under these circumstances, it is not surprising that anthropology in the mid-twentieth century became preoccupied with kinship. It seemed to lie at the heart of everything in societies outside the West. In effect, to study anthropology was to study kinship. The terminology that was elaborated to describe the vast variety of kinship systems became a major professional resource of the discipline, incomprehensible to the uninitiated. Communities across the length and breadth of the African continent were structured by rules of patrilineal or matrilineal descent, but that left plenty of room for variation in status and role relations. Part of the variation came from what exactly it was that descended lineally. Among the Zulu chiefly titles, land ownership, and membership in localized groups were all based on patrilineal descent. None of this was significant for the Nuer, where cattle were the only real wealth. Since this was so, both principles could be at work simultaneously in a system of *double descent*. For instance, rights to land might be inherited through the father, and ownership of movable wealth like cattle through the mother. Magic and ritual knowledge might be handed down through either side, or both. In addition residence rules might vary independently, that is to say matrilineality might be found with patrilocality, or vice versa, and every system created its own complexities. Or couples might routinely set up house on their own, so being *neolocal*.

KINSHIP IN OCEANIA

When this terminology was exported to the Pacific region, deeper complexities were found. In New Zealand, membership in large and warlike local groups called *hapu* could be claimed either through the father or the mother, and ethnographers began to speak of *ambilineality* (from a Latin root *ambi-* meaning "both"). This meant that the potential membership of *hapu* overlapped, so what happened when warfare broke out? In New Zealand, evidently, a man had to make his choice, and then stick by it. But in other parts of the Pacific people could move back and forth. Elsewhere, it was only chiefly lines that bothered with lineages at all, so some kind of mixed system operated. All of these cases required new jargon, until a limiting case was described by Derek Freeman among the Iban of Borneo. For the Iban, all possibilities of communal membership remained permanently available, through parents or grandparents, uncles or cousins, and even through distant in-laws. In short any kinship link at all could be used to join one of the large communities around which Iban life revolved, each housed in a single massive wooden building called a longhouse.

To describe the Iban case, and others like it, a new term came into use: *cognatic*, from the Latin *cognatio* meaning "a kindred". Much ink was then spilled trying to define exactly what constituted a kindred, before it was realized that kindreds only exist around particular individuals. They comprised simply all the relatives that any one person could trace. They might assemble for his or her wedding, but they have no continuity after he or she dies. Consequently, cognatic societies did not have vague or flawed descent rules; they simply had no descent rules. Moreover, as research continued to expand outside Africa, it was found that cognatic societies were not at all rare. This discovery did not invalidate kinship studies, but it brought about a major shift in them, to which we will return below. More importantly, it provided an object lesson to the growing discipline of anthropology against the over-hasty extension of successful models to places where they do not work.

Summary

The goal of this chapter is to show how effectively mid-twentieth-century British anthropology could furnish an understanding of the major features of diverse peoples' social worlds. Even the concise accounts offered in *African Political Systems* allow a European or American reader to imagine what it would be like to live according to radically different understandings of the proper relationships between people. The key point is that eight authors applying the *same* theoretical tools could reveal the tremendous *differences* of social organization among peoples as diverse as the Zulu and the Nuer. In recent years, the criticism has been made that these tools impose alien categories, but this is unfair. Merely using a set of spanners does not imply that all machines are the same machine. On the contrary, the premise of the brand of cultural relativism promoted by these theorists was that all societies had their own modes of politics, law, economics, religion, and so on. It was our job to frame definitions wide enough to exclude nobody.

As it turned out, the most important statuses in many African societies were those related to kinship. Putting that another way, an individual was assigned at birth to groups and categories that would dominate his or her life. The most significant corporate groups were often localized lineages, and the most important categories were dispersed clans. Soon these findings were taken to apply worldwide, among everyone not living in urban environments. It turned out, however, that things worked differently in Oceania, for example. But that only intensified the concern with kinship, and the elaboration of technical jargon. In the process other forms of incorporation dropped out of view, such as those having to do with residence. This was most strikingly demonstrated in the case of the Iban of Borneo, who recruited members in any way they could to longhouse communities numbering hundreds. This undermined the importance of "kinship theory" as it existed in the middle decades of the twentieth century, without invalidating the basic methodology of social anthropology.

FURTHER READING

All of the ethnographers who contributed to *African Political Systems* produced full-length ethnographies, often several. Evans-Pritchard's *The Nuer: A Description of the Modes of Livelihood and*

Political Institutions of a Nilotic People (1969, original 1940) is perhaps the best known of all ethnographies, and is in fact easier to follow than his overly compact essay in the collection. But Evans-Pritchard also wrote an account of Nuer religion (1956), as well as several ethnographies based on fieldwork elsewhere in Africa.

Beyond that, it is hard to know what to recommend, since the ethnography of Africa is now vast, as befits a vast continent. An interesting summary of the state structures is found in Lucy Mair's *African Kingdoms* (1977). An equivalent volume about the stateless societies is the collection *Tribes Without Rulers* (1958), edited by John Middleton and David Tait. The classic account of Iban social organization is Derek Freeman's *Report on the Iban* (1970).

ANTHROPOLOGY, HISTORY AND IMPERIALISM

Much has changed since the appearance of *African Political Systems*, both in anthropology, and in the world at large. In particular, the European empires have been swept away. But in the 1940's and 1950's they were still very much in business. Moreover, in each of the three cases described in the previous chapter there had been major disruption as a result of colonial "annexation." The Zulu were conquered in 1880 in a brief but bloody war. At Isandhlwana, the classic enveloping tactics of the Zulu impis destroyed an English regiment. But firepower eventually won out, and the fourth Zulu king, Cetshawyo, was forced to surrender. The state was dismantled into thirteen chiefdoms. As for the Nuer, punitive raids were still in progress when Evans-Pritchard was doing his fieldwork, and he recounts waking up one morning to discover the village where he was living surrounded by British troops. "I felt that I was in an equivocal position," he says dryly, and he left Nuerland in protest.

By contrast, Bembaland was annexed in the 1890's without bloodshed, mostly because the Bemba were overawed by the use of machine-guns against the Matabele to the south. The British administration was, however, immediately caught up in disputes among Bemba about succession to the most prestigious titles, especially the office of Citimukulu. As we saw above, the details of rights to such titles are complicated and subject to interpretation.

Before annexation, the process would have been worked out by debate and compromise among the Bemba royal houses. But having taken control, the administration felt that it was their job to settle the matter, and they were hard-pressed to work out how to do so.

INDIRECT RULE

This matter was pressing because the British had embarked on a system of "indirect rule" in their African colonies. What that meant was that they would, where possible, rule through indigenous leaders rather than replacing them with a Western-style bureaucracy. This policy was seen by the colonial administrators of the time as progressive, that is, designed for the welfare of indigenous peoples. It was argued that indirect rule minimized the disruption caused by modern technology and economics, and gave indigenous institutions the opportunity to adapt to new circumstances. By the same token, however, indirect rule made it necessary to identify local political structures. The first generation of district officers had no option but to say "take me to your leader," like comic book Martians. It is not surprising that they failed to understand that the Citimukulu was not a king in the European sense. The Nuer were even more frustrating to deal with, since they were unwilling to call any man master. As their experience grew, administrators built up a body of practical experience, a folklore passed to their replacements about how to make day-to-day decisions. Some were remarkably conscientious, and did their best to understand and record local norms. To aid them in their amateur research, the Royal Anthropological Institute published a guide called *Notes and Queries in Anthropology*. But other colonial officers were dismissive of such efforts. A common anecdote, probably apocryphal, tells of a district officer asked to report on the manners and customs of the people under his control. His reply: "manners none and customs abominable."

The existence of *Notes and Queries* makes it clear how deeply British anthropology had become involved in the imperial project. It is no accident that all eight studies reported in *African Political Systems* were made in British colonies, mostly funded by colonial governments or institutes. In the past couple of decades there has been intense debate about the effects of this connection. To what extent were

BOX 5.1 THE BRITISH EMPIRE

The British Empire was by a large margin the biggest empire in history. At its zenith in the early twentieth century it ruled a quarter of the world's population and a fifth of its land area. The English colonies in America were a key part of what is called the "First Empire," but after 1776 Americans thought of themselves as an anti-colonial power.

During World War Two, for instance, President Franklin Roosevelt made it very plain to Prime Minister Winston Churchill that the maintenance of the British Empire was no part of American war aims. This was so well known that the Vietnamese leader Ho Chi Minh expected help from America in his struggle against the French colonial occupiers. He was astonished when the USA backed the French, and, when French forces collapsed, itself assumed responsibility for the war. It is an historical irony that the USA lost its reputation in the Third World as an ally of liberty everywhere, and instead is seen as continuing the legacy of European colonialism. That Americans in general do not understand this change accounts in large part for their support of the invasion of Iraq in 2002.

ethnographers made tools of imperialism, and how did that pervert their findings? Many of the anthropologists of the era held strongly left-wing views, and thought of themselves as allies of indigenous people against their colonial rulers. Evans-Pritchard frankly disliked the clique that ran the Sudan, and withheld from them information about so-called "prophets" who were suspected of stirring up trouble among the Nuer. But hell, we are told, is paved with good intentions. Evans-Pritchard and his colleagues may well have aided colonial exploitation, whatever they imagined they were doing.

FUNCTIONALISM

What makes the anthropology of the epoch suspect is its emphasis on how societies work – in technical terms how they "functioned." There are several brands of anthropology that are described as functionalist, but the British school's notion was strictly sociological, in the tradition of Durkheim. For them the function of an institution was the part it played in supporting other institutions within the same social whole. What that amounted to was accounting for the presence of one set of rules, or norms, or collective representations (the terms are interchangeable, remember) by showing how they interlocked with other ones, and they with others again. You will notice that the reasoning is circular: A is explained by B, which is explained by C, which in turn is explained by A. But this is not disastrous. As we shall see below, most approaches in anthropology share this feature. In effect they do not so much "explain" things, as set them in a context in which they make some kind of sense. That is a more limited goal, but already a tremendous advance towards a culturally relativist understanding of other peoples.

Meanwhile, faced with such a vast variety of indigenous societies across the length and breadth of Africa, colonial regimes could certainly have profited from information about how they "functioned." In an introductory note, the editors of *African Political Systems* say as much: "we hope this book will be of interest and of use to those who have the task of administering African peoples." But the final line of the same paragraph is more tentative: "whether or not an anthropologist's findings can be utilized in the practical tasks of administration must be left to the decision of the administrators themselves." It reflects what was in fact a stormy relationship. Reactionary colonial officials routinely dismissed anthropologists as effete intellectuals spreading dangerous left-wing ideas. They might point for example to the Kenyan leader Jomo Kenyatta, who led an armed struggle for independence and in 1964 became the country's first President. In the 1930's, Kenyatta had studied with Bronislaw Malinowski in London, and wrote an ethnography of his own people entitled *Facing Mount Kenya* (1938).

FUNCTIONALISM AND HISTORY

Nevertheless, the temporal association remains. The approach now clumsily described as *structural-functionalism* arose during the last phase of colonialism. The question is what aspects of the approach are tainted by the connection. At the widest level, the whole practice of fieldwork depends on the existence of some external power that can at least guarantee the ethnographer's physical safety. This was neatly demonstrated in New Guinea, an island tiny by comparison with the continent of Africa, but containing amazing linguistic and ethnic diversity. It was only in the 1920's that it was discovered that the mountainous interior was densely populated. So isolated was the region that its people knew nothing of the use of iron. This discovery sparked tremendous interest among anthropologists, but warfare between local groups made the area dangerous for unarmed anthropologists. Consequently, ethnographers could only follow behind as the Australian administration gradually extended its control into the interior. This process reached its climax in the 1960's when the last remote areas were "pacified."

By the same token, anthropologists had largely worked with people who were, in Eric Wolf's famous phrase, "without history." What that meant literally is that they lacked the kinds of written records that historians study. But there is a broader implication: that such peoples lay outside European accounts of history, and only appeared in them at the moment when they were discovered by Europeans. This readiness to ignore the historical experiences and traditions of other people was another charge laid at the door of structural-functionalism. In concentrating on how societies worked, they discounted the rapid changes occurring in colonial possessions in Africa and elsewhere. They put other cultures under glass, as it were, like exhibits in a museum. Functionalist accounts made African societies appear immutably locked into "custom" rather than seething with unrest and disruption.

There is a great irony in this charge, because the whole point of functionalism in the first place had been to reject previous abuses of history. The terminology of social structure, outlined in Chapter Three, was designed to reveal living cultures, rather than mere relics of prehistory. To understand this contrast, we must look back at anthropology's origins in the nineteenth century.

HIGH IMPERIALISM

Structural-functionalism was associated with an imperialism in decline. Already in the 1920's independence movements were mobilizing, and they had the sympathy of intellectuals in Europe. After World War Two, successive Labour governments in Britain made it their stated policy to encourage developments towards "home-rule." The process began in 1947 with India. In Africa, Ghana was the first to go, in 1960, and the process was virtually over a decade later. Only in South Africa and Southern Rhodesia was the process delayed for a generation, because white settlers refused to accept majority rule. Both declared themselves republics, and left the Commonwealth.

The similar dates of independence mask, however, very different colonial experiences in Asia and Africa. Europeans came to India as early as the sixteenth century in search of trade in valuable items such as spices. British control came about only slowly, and in piece-meal fashion. But from the outset, India provided enormous profits, so that it became known as the "jewel in the crown." By contrast, sub-Saharan Africa was divided up among the European powers in an extraordinarily brief period, and without regard for commercial benefits. Prior to the late nineteenth century, Portuguese and British traders had largely been content to maintain bases on the coast, bartering with independent African kingdoms in the interior. But at the end of the century an intense rivalry erupted between European nations for African colonies. The climax was a conference in Berlin summoned by the German Chancellor Bismarck, and attended by representatives from the USA and the Ottoman Empire in addition to all the major European powers. There were, however, no representatives from Africa. In the space of a few months in 1884–1885, Africa was partitioned without the slightest concern for the boundaries of indigenous ethnic groups and nations.

The event was extraordinary in many respects. Never before had a whole continent been parceled out even before it had been conquered. What allowed such hubris was, of course, the unprece-dented military advantage that Europeans at that moment enjoyed over Africans – machine-guns versus spears. Even nations with no previous dealings with Africa were clamoring for a share. The king of newly established Belgium was allotted the entire watershed of the Congo River simply to avoid a squabble between the French and the British. The results for the people of Congo were disastrous. Germany, as host of the conference, took its own pieces of real estate, so demonstrating its entry into the Great Power club.

The infamous "scramble for Africa" marked the apogee of High Imperialism. Its motives were to fulfill the "manifest destiny" of Europeans to form the vanguard of civilization, and to rule over lesser races. This was the true ideology of imperialism, and sad to tell, the first generation of anthropologists played a role in framing it.

EVOLUTIONISM

That role comprised a theory of social evolution. To speak of evolution calls to mind Charles Darwin and his *On the Origin of Species by Means of Natural Selection* (1859) – surely one of the most influential books of modern times. But Darwinism was a theory of biological evolution, and it is in those terms that we speak of evolution. It now seems strange that evolution was originally mobilized to explain not the differences between species, but the differences between human societies. Specifically, the question was how it happened that some peoples had advanced to civilization, while others remained trapped in varying degrees of primitiveness. It fascinated not only nineteenth-century anthropologists, but also a wide popular audience. Educated Europeans could see all around them the amazing technological advances of the Industrial Revolution, while at the same time they read about peoples in distant colonies who still lived by hunting and gathering, lacking even iron tools. Surely this contrast – never more striking than in the late nineteenth century – called for explanation.

What inspired the social evolutionists was not only the self-evident proposition that more complex forms must have arisen from simpler ones, but also that surviving primitive societies provided direct evidence of what they had looked like. The world became a museum in which were displayed all the stages of evolution that had led to industrial society, that is, the West. The task of anthropologists was to collect all the accounts they could find of non-Western peoples, and then sort those peoples out along a continuum from Savagery (Lower, Middle, and Upper) through Barbarism (ditto), and finally to Civilization. This technique was called the Comparative Method, and I put it in capital letters to distinguish it from other forms of comparativism. What was revealed was nothing less than the whole history of mankind – a breathtaking prospect.

THE ATTRACTIONS OF EVOLUTIONISM

In addition to this exciting intellectual prospect, evolutionism had other attractions. It appealed to the vanity of its European audience, who could see themselves at the summit of an inexorable climb towards civilization, advancing over countless millennia. It made progress seem like a law of nature, promising ever more amazing technological and social advances. Finally, it provided a moral justification for High Imperialism. Clearly it was the duty of the advanced nations to bring Enlightenment to those less fortunate – what the French called "*la mission civilitrice*." To do so was indeed a calling, summed up in Rudyard Kipling's phrase "the white man's burden."

If these attitudes seem merely naïve in the twenty-first century, there was a darker side to evolutionism. Almost inevitably, it became enmeshed in racism. The most ready answer to why Europe had attained such primacy in the world was that Europeans were somehow inherently predisposed to advancement, through superior intelligence or whatever. Arguments against this proposition have already been set out in Chapter Two, and can be summarized in the formula "no gene for culture." Demonstrably, all human beings are capable of being socialized into whatever culture they find themselves. But this was not apparent in the nineteenth century, and racism was all the more insidious for being implicit.

THE ERRORS OF EVOLUTIONISM

There is, however, no necessary connection between social evolutionism and racism. It is possible to argue that innovations occurred because of environmental changes in some places, while they remained unnecessary elsewhere. For example, the development of irrigation in Egypt is attributed to a reduction in rainfall sometime around the fifth millennium bc. This forced more intensive agriculture, as farmers abandoned outlying areas and moved into the already crowded Nile Valley. This hypothesis constitutes a "challenge-response model" of cultural change: an environmental challenge met by a cultural innovation. It can be tested by archeological excavation, revealing differences in residence patterns and land use over the relevant centuries.

The sophisticated techniques of modern archeology were not, however, available in the nineteenth-century. Indeed, the whole strategy of the Comparative Method can be seen as a substitute for direct archeological data from anywhere outside Europe, Egypt, and Mesopotamia. The social evolutionists thought they had found a shortcut: the living museum of primitive peoples. But, like many shortcuts, it turned out to be a blind alley. The basic problem now seems obvious. Cultures do not stand still. None of the societies that the evolutionists classified were in reality relics of some ancient past. On the contrary, each and every one has its own complex history of change and adaptation, of cultural elaboration in one area and simplification in another. Consequently, the societies lumped together in any one "stage" turned out to have very little in common other than the criteria that had been used to put them there. Hunters and gatherers in the Australian outback were totally different in social organization and religion, and even in modes of livelihood, to those in the Kalahari Desert of southwest Africa. Neither looked anything like the people of the Canadian west coast, whose regular supplies of salmon allowed fixed villages and massive houses, all without agriculture. Which, if any, of these resembled the first inhabitants of Europe or China was anybody's guess.

THE FUNCTIONALIST REVOLUTION

The guessing continued into the first decade of the twentieth century, with exponents each passionately defending their own reconstructions. The debates among them became increasingly sterile, however, since there was no independent evidence by which to choose between one and another. By the 1920's it was possible for Bronislaw Malinowski to dismiss the entire enterprise as "projective history." His use of the term "projective" pokes fun at evolutionist thinking by comparing it to the murky contents of what Sigmund Freud had recently called "the unconscious." Instead of discovering the past, they were merely displaying their prejudices.

We have already met Malinowski in Chapter One, at work in the Trobriand Islands developing the techniques of fieldwork. There is indeed a close relationship between his research methods and his anti-historicism. Nineteenth-century evolutionists were able to think of "primitive" societies as relics, as bits and pieces left over from previous epochs, only because they had never experienced one at first hand, let alone participated in it for months at a time. What Malinowski saw was not an ethnographic museum but people getting on with their lives, very much in the here-and-now, and that was what he wanted to describe.

Malinowski was an effective propagandist, and drew many of the new generation of anthropologists to his seminars. His concept of function was in fact slightly different to the one outlined above, but for the present purpose that is a detail we need not pursue. The point is that he led a revolution in the sense that within a generation evolutionism was totally discredited in British and Commonwealth universities, and under siege in its few remaining strongholds in the USA.

FUNCTIONALISM AS SOCIAL ANATOMY

The notion of a "living" society implies that it is an organism of some kind, and indeed functionalism constantly invoked the "organic analogy." It made an appealing contrast to social evolutionism, but paradoxically it also creates a link between the two. The idea of evolution may not have originated in biology, but by the end of the nineteenth century social evolutionists were only too happy to be associated with the scientific prestige of Darwin's theories. In the popular imagination, it was a short step from saying that humans are descended from apes to asserting that "modern" societies were descended from "primitive" ones. The fact that neither is true makes the point even clearer. In the nineteenth century there was almost no direct evidence about hominid evolution, and the wildest ideas were entertained. By the end of the twentieth century paleoarcheologists – those studying the most ancient remains – had a solid grasp of the process, and could show that the remote common ancestors of humans and apes were like neither humans nor apes.

Nevertheless, the analogy still applies. If reconstructing the origins of society is seen as like phylogeny (the origins of species), that functionalism resembles anatomy. As we noted at the beginning of Chapter Four, the brand of relativism that goes with structural-functionalism is nothing more than pointing out that different kinds of animals have brains and bowels. In the same way, different kinds of societies have politics and economics. There are then two analytical tasks. The first is to show how the various organs interact to maintain a healthy social body. The second is to compare equivalent institutions from one organism to another. This is comparativism with a small "c," implying no value judgment about which is more or less evolved.

HISTORY AS PROCESS

The only way that temporal change figures into a functionalist approach is in terms of lifecycles, and here again an organic analogy makes the point. Individual creatures are not of course immutable. On the contrary, they are born, grow to maturity, decline and eventually die. But that does not change the species, which goes through the same processes generation after generation. In the same way, the birth of a human child is socially acknowledged with cigars and congratulations, or whatever is called for in any given culture. The child's physical maturation is accompanied by a process of socialization. As we saw in Chapter One, it is that process that defines culture. Adulthood, marriage, old age and death are all marked by ritual. Consequently, one way to study a society is to describe the stages of peoples' lives, both men and women, prominent and ordinary.

What such a description does not do is consider historical change, that is changes in the whole social organism. Social life remains the same even as individuals arrive, pass through, and depart. Consequently, even in ethnographic accounts that managed to portray a lively sense of unfolding lives, with their crises, trials, and rewards, history itself remained largely outside the view of structural-functionalism.

THE LIMITATIONS OF FUNCTIONALISM

To see this as a flaw is to forget what functionalism was designed to do in the first place. It is absurd to blame a cow for not being a horse. What functionalism can do is show how societies manage to stay the same, and that is a valid question. Not all of history is change, and it is well worth trying to describe what it is that made Trobrianders Trobrianders yesterday, what makes them so today, and what will make them so tomorrow. Continuity is as observable a feature of society as change, and nowadays when anthropologists want to discuss it they speak of "social reproduction."

Nevertheless, if the inability of functionalism to confront historical change is not a flaw, it is a very real limitation. Even in the 1940's and 1950's, Britain's colonies were changing rapidly. The authors of *African Political Systems* were of course not unaware of this, and their reaction was first to reconstruct "traditional" polities, as described by their informants, and then to note the most dramatic changes brought about by the colonial order. The attempt was to produce history as two snapshots. But two images are not enough to capture motion, that is, the movement of history. By degrees, it became obvious that functionalism's rejection of history had been too extreme, and the theoretical pendulum swung back in the opposite direction.

THE HAZARDS OF ANALOGY

At the same time, there really was a flaw in functionalist theorizing, springing directly from the organic analogy. Analogy is a powerful technique for conveying meaning used in all languages. When Shakespeare says "all the world's a stage" we see something about our everyday lives that we might not have seen before. Indeed, the structuralist notion of "role" draws on this metaphor also. Indeed, as we shall see below, theoretical approaches in anthropology often rest on an analogy between culture or society and something else. But there is always a danger that the original insight will harden into dogma by being taken too literally.

Organic analogies are by no means unique to anthropology. In many languages there is identification between the "head" of a body and the "head" of state. True, the metaphor might not appeal to a Nuer. Nevertheless, functionalism can be seen as a systematic elaboration of something that is almost self-evident, at least for people who have states. Other extensions of the metaphor might include "hearts" and perhaps "shoulders." But what would be the "knees" of a society? Moreover, unintended transferences of meaning might occur. Can a society be said to have a skin? That implies that it is bounded and completely distinguishable from other social organisms, and this proposition will not bear examination. Worse, we might imply that foreigners penetrating the "skin" were like dangerous infections, and that way lies fascism. It is necessary to watch out for the loss of insight in literalism.

THE BASIC FLAW OF FUNCTIONALISM

As the organic analogy took hold, the proposition that institutions fulfilled a function ceased to be an hypothesis and became a premise. In the 1930's and 1940's, it was an exciting project to try to work out just how institutions fitted together, and a source of wonderment when they could be seen to do so. That excitement was still apparent when *African Political Systems* was published. There was, however, a fundamental problem. Functionalist theorists had not designed a test that could establish whether a given function was or was not being fulfilled by a given institution. Putting that another way, no room had been left for dysfunction. Lacking such a test, it became simply an assumption that if two institutions co-existed side-by-side in the same society, then each must be supporting the other.

Consequently, by the 1960's, functionalism had become theoretically sterile. It had lost the power to reveal anything new, or worse, it had become an impediment to learning anything new. Not everything was lost, however. The descriptive tools of status and role, group and category, remained useful. The result was that they came to define a classic style of ethnographic description, one that shows how indigenous institutions of politics and law, economics and religion, exist in terms of proper relations between persons. Functionalism faded from the scene, but the enormous amount of research conducted in Africa remained as valuable as ever, a monument to participant-observation fieldwork.

THE POST-COLONIAL WORLD

Meanwhile, a turbulent world made it increasingly difficult to ignore historical change. Independence from colonial rule did not of course mean that "traditional" states took its place. The reality was far more complex than that. Events in the "First World" were every bit as dynamic. Plainly, institutions everywhere could hardly be described in any simple way as "functioning." Many anthropologists continued to be drawn to Marxist theory, which had a very definite notion of the meaning of history, as we shall see in Chapter Eight. Moreover, imperialism in his terms had not at all ceased to exist with the collapse of the European military empires. It had merely been transformed into a later phase of capitalist exploitation, often described as neo-colonialism.

Even anthropologists not drawn to Marxist theory were enraged by new versions of imperialism occurring within the ex-colonies. For example, Indonesia had suffered a vicious war in order to overthrow Dutch control. But that did not stop them from using similar violence to subdue Melanesian claims of independence in the western half of New Guinea. In all of this, anthropology's relations to imperial power remained as complex as ever, and we shall take up different aspects of this in subsequent chapters.

Summary

Throughout the twentieth century, the majority of anthropologists have seen it as their task to escape their own ethnocentrism, and as far as possible to understand how other people experience their worlds. The first generation of anthropologists in the nineteenth century had no such concerns. Their bold strategy was to make use of the primitive peoples as a living museum, showing how humanity had risen to civilization through the various stages of savagery and barbarism. It was a project that captured the popular imagination, just at the moment when the European powers were reaching a crescendo of imperialism. Social evolutionism drew intellectual credibility from the success of Darwin's biological evolution, but the diversity of ethnicities is a very different matter to the diversity of species, as we saw in Chapter Two. Cultural innovations pass freely between populations without any need for genetic change. Consequently, all existing cultures have gone through their own complex historical developments, and there is no reason to believe that any of them resemble our ancient ancestors.

Anthropology's connection with imperialism did not end in the nineteenth century, however. As fieldwork became standard, the majority of ethnographers chose sites in the colonial possessions. The intellectual attractions were obvious: colonial expansion allowed them to work among peoples who had only recently surrendered their independence, and whose indigenous political institutions were relatively intact. This was an exciting prospect, but it meant that they worked within a colonial framework. In particular, it is now often argued that the concept of function directly served colonial administrations. In studying how institutions were linked together to make social wholes, ethnographers provided a guide to ruling them. The extent to which this did in fact happen is debatable, however, if only because ethnographers and senior colonial officers often held each other in mutual contempt. Meanwhile, functionalism was flawed in a more basic way. Since there was no test of whether any one institution did or did not in fact contribute to the vitality of another, functionalism rapidly degenerated from a hypothesis to a platitude.

FURTHER READING

There are many histories of the British Empire. A readable one is Lawrence James' *The Rise and Fall of the British Empire* (1994). The notion of function laid out here derives from the same set of essays by A.R. Radcliffe-Brown (1952) cited at the end of Chapter Three. The phrase from Eric Wolf is quoted from his *Europe and the People Without History* (1982). How ethnographers followed on the heels of "pacification" in New Guinea is interestingly described in a volume edited by Terence Hays, *Ethnographic Presents: Pioneering Anthropologists in the Papua New Guinea Highlands* (1992). Debates among anthropologists about the nature of their colonial involvements are recorded in *Anthropology and the Colonial Encounter* (1973), edited by Talal Asad.

Outside anthropology, a field of "post-colonial studies" has grown up in literary criticism, beginning with Edward Said's *Orientalism* (1979). It enjoyed rapid growth in the 1980's, and its development is summarized in the reader *Colonial Discourse and Post-colonial Theory* (1994), edited by Patrick Williams and Laura Chrisman. It is only marginally concerned with anthropology.

The only sympathetic account of nineteenth-century social evolution that I know of is in the opening seven chapters of Marvin Harris' *The Rise of Anthropological Theory* (1968). Harris' project was to revive the evolutionist program by cleansing it of all its racist associations, but it is now generally judged a failure. The notion of social process is best known through a volume edited by Jack Goody called *The Development Cycle in Domestic Groups* (1962). Finally, it should be noted that one British anthropologist at least made a serious attempt to restore the utility of the notion of function by showing how dysfunction could be detected, that is, cases where institutions clashed with one another. In his study *Bantu Bureaucracy* (1965, original 1956), Lloyd Fallers showed that Basoga chiefs were constantly forced to choose between duties that pulled them in different directions. In the traditional state and even more so in the colonial regime, chiefs had to balance the demands of kinship against those of the state. He labeled this condition "role conflict."

CULTURE AND LANGUAGE

Twentieth-century anthropology took shape as a reaction to the chauvinism of nineteenth-century social evolutionism, but it did not everywhere take the same form. In the USA the intellectual revolution was neither as rapid nor as thorough as in the UK. In part this was because of the far greater number of universities in the USA, leaving room for pockets of conservatism in which the nineteenth-century certitudes continued to circulate. The characteristic form of American cultural anthropology took shape in the course of this struggle, and it developed a broad range of interests. Consequently, British "social anthropology," as described in the previous two chapters, is sometimes contrasted with American "cultural anthropology," which is explored in subsequent chapters. There is, however, no inconsistency between the two. It is entirely possible to weave both approaches together seamlessly in discussing the same data. To avoid any implication of exclusiveness we are sometimes forced to use the clumsy expression "socio-cultural anthropology."

FIRST NATIONS

In addition, American anthropology came to include sub-fields that were treated in Britain as separate disciplines. The historical circumstances that brought this about are not far to seek. From the founding of the first colonies, Americans had been confronted on their own doorstep by indigenous peoples about whom they knew next to nothing. As the area of settlement expanded, so did the necessity to incorporate those peoples within the state. The administrative problems were similar to those the British faced in India, even though the people that Columbus mistook for "Indians" lacked the material wealth and power of the Mogul Empire. One after another the Indian "nations" on the borders of settlement were pacified through "treaties" that acknowledge their status as sovereign powers. As settlers coveted their lands, however, Indians rapidly became subject peoples administered through a system of reservations. In short, American anthropologists were as much implicated in colonial power structures as were the British.

At the same time, the intellectual fascination sparked by the discoveries of new peoples and civilizations in the Americas went far beyond politics. In the seventeenth century, the imaginations of Renaissance philosophers were powerfully stirred by reports coming from the New World. Michel de Montaigne, having met a Brazilian Indian who had been brought to France, speculated about the nature of "savage" society. Needless to say his data were thin, but his attitude was remarkable for its cultural relativism (see Box 6.1). As anthropology moved beyond speculation, it was natural that scholars in the USA would primarily concern themselves with Amerindians. As we saw in Chapter One, pioneers like Morgan and Cushing made experiments with fieldwork in the nineteenth century. Practicing as a lawyer in up-state New York, Morgan could easily visit nearby Iroquois reservations. The expansion of railroads made it possible to make short fieldwork visits across the entire mid- and southwest without requiring elaborate arrangements or any great amount of funding. By contrast, the development of British ethnography was delayed by the need to make long voyages to the far corners of the Empire. In turn, however, that also encouraged longer periods of fieldwork when ethnographers did arrive.

THE "FOUR FIELDS" APPROACH

The same circumstances caused different approaches to archeology in British and American anthropology. Discoveries like the mysterious monuments of the ancient Maya in Central America set off

BOX 6.1 MONTAIGNE AND THE "SAVAGES"

The first American Indians who arrived in France caused a great stir when they were introduced to the court of Charles IX. Montaigne was a courtier, and also an influential writer. In several essays, he insists that there are no absolute standards of morality, and it is not for us to judge exotic customs. Even cannibalism, he argued, might be virtuous, as for instance in a society where it was an act of piety for a son to eat his father. This is a strongly relativist position, and it was one shared by many Renaissance thinkers. Montaigne also attaches a positive meaning to the word "savage." In French, *sauvage* implies simply that something occurs naturally, like fruit on a jungle tree. Perhaps in reaction to the snobberies of the royal court, Montaigne was attracted to the qualities of naturalness and simplicity. It was only in the nineteenth century, when evolutionism became entangled with racism, that "savage" came to mean a state of inhumanity and brutality.

research into the prehistory of peoples whose descendants still occupied the same region. Excavation and ethnology could proceed hand-in-hand, and indeed were often conducted by the same scholars. Meanwhile, in Britain archeologists and social anthropologists were working in different continents. Interest in ancient civilizations was largely directed at Egypt and Mesopotamia. The search for national identities also focused attention on the monuments of the ancient inhabitants of Europe. But in the first half of the twentieth century very little archeological research was carried out in Africa and Oceania. To this day, archeology and anthropology are treated as separate fields in Britain.

Again, American scholars examining prehistoric burials were interested in whether living populations in the same region showed the same physical types. As we saw in Chapter Two, the attempt to sort people into neatly defined races has proved illusory, but the point for now is that this quest caused physical anthropology to become firmly established in the USA. In the twentieth century it developed a whole new range of concerns, as noted in Chapter Two. In Britain physical anthropology was slow to develop, although British and Commonwealth paleoarcheologists have contributed to the exciting discoveries about human origins made in the last half century.

The result in the USA was a synthesis called "the four-field approach," that is: archeology, cultural anthropology, linguistic anthropology, and physical anthropology. Its numerous exponents in the USA argue that it is the only way that humankind can be seen in its entirety, including within one view everything from the evolutionary aptitude for culture to the diverse forms that cultures take. It is a powerful argument, and there is no doubt that at some level these diverse aspects must be integrated. There are disagreements, however, about how that should be done. Without settling these issues, this text is principally concerned with social and cultural anthropology, but reference to the other three fields cannot be avoided without distortion.

OTHER NATIONAL TRADITIONS OF ANTHROPOLOGY

The larger message in this contrast is that the garment of knowledge has no seams. Whatever their nationality, anthropologists are looking at the same world. The way that their discipline becomes defined in universities is not a matter of global realities but historical idiosyncrasies. Consequently, there are more than two anthropologies, and potentially as many as there are nations. For example, different traditions grew up in European countries other than Britain. Nor is anthropology limited to the First World. In India, the government has funded research into minority groups for over a century, and employs a substantial number of ethnographers. Japan has had a research establishment since the 1950's, active particularly in Southeast Asia, and there are other cases that might be cited.

Nevertheless, it must be conceded that a large part of the literature of anthropology is in English. This results from the early development of the field in Britain and America, followed by the emergence of English as a world language. The increasing ease of electronic communication will no doubt reinforce the tendency, at least in the near future, since it encourages a widely international discourse. The trend may perhaps be reversed in the future, as newly emerging nations develop anthropologies that reflect their own interests. For present purposes, however, it is not mere ethnocentrism that, with the important exception of French anthropology, this text is largely concerned with the British and American traditions.

LINGUISTIC ANTHROPOLOGY

Of the "four fields" one remains to be discussed, and it proved particularly crucial for the shaping of American cultural anthropology. The theoretical concern with language in America, as contrasted with Britain, followed in part from a mere accident of fieldwork locations. Many of the languages spoken in sub-Saharan Africa are closely related, belonging to the Bantu sub-group. Their grammar was well known by the mid twentieth century, and even their vocabularies showed wide similarities. Consequently, it was possible to gain a useful competence in only a few months. In Oceania, much the same was true with the numerous and widely distributed Austronesian languages. Moreover, extended fieldwork in the manner of Malinowski rapidly became the norm, involving long stays and communication without interpreters. The result was that British ethnographers thought of language as a fieldwork *tool*, as a way of getting on with fieldwork, rather than as an object of study in itself. Like archeology, linguistics remained a separate discipline.

In the USA, by contrast, Amerindian languages presented the first generation of ethnographers with immediate challenges. To begin with, there was the need to record and classify them – a task that was very far from complete even after four centuries of contact. More importantly, some of the languages they encountered were fiendishly difficult. There is no such thing as a *simple* language, or at least not one occurring naturally. Always they contain subtleties and nuances that can be acquired only with long practice. But some are truly daunting for the beginning adult student because of their complex grammars. As it happens, Amerindian languages include some of the most demanding in the world. This was strikingly demonstrated during World War Two, when American capital ships in the Pacific dispensed with secret codes in communicating with each other. Instead, they simply put native speakers of Navajo on each ship, and they spoke directly to each other without bothering with any kind of code. Such is the complexity of Navajo grammar that the Japanese navy failed to break its "code." The sheer difficulty of Amerindian languages, especially in combination with brief fieldwork visits, made linguistic anthropology essential.

LANGUAGE CONFOUNDS BIOLOGICAL DETERMINISM

There are many reasons why language is a compelling phenomenon for anthropologists, over and above its practical necessity in conducting fieldwork. To begin with, language neatly demonstrates the relationship between biology and culture. That is to say, language is clearly both biological and cultural at the same time, and different logics apply to each aspect.

(1) *Language as a human universal.* No one could now doubt that the aptitude for language is universal in human beings, and that it is the result of hundreds of thousands of years of evolution and of Darwinian selection. The strongest evidence for this is the extraordinary rapidity with which children everywhere acquire their mother tongue, or even multiple mother tongues. Moreover, it is an entirely predictable process, familiar to anyone who has spent time with a small child. A healthy infant first produces cooing noises, but soon begins to experiment with a whole range of vocal play. At somewhere between 25 and 50 weeks the child begins to babble, and care-givers often sense meaning behind the utterances. During the second year, the first recognizable words appear, and then progress towards proper speech is extremely rapid. For an occasional visitor, it seems as if a child learns to speak overnight. Such feats cannot be explained by simple imitation. Instead, a process of maturation triggers an inborn ability to generate original utterances. To use a computer analogy, children come hard-wired for learning whatever language is presented to them. Even the mistakes they make in learning are predictable (see Box 6.2).

This result is confirmed by research in recent decades into the communicative abilities of our nearest living relatives among the primates, particularly chimpanzees. Chimps cannot speak in the obvious sense, since their mouth and throats cannot produce the sounds used in human speech. So experimenters set about teaching them to use other communicative devices, such as colored discs representing words, or even signs on a computer keyboard. It was soon discovered that chimps could acquire a whole vocabulary of signs, and use them to produce messages they had not seen before. Some became so adept that it became increasingly difficult to specify what human speech had that chimpanzee signing lacked. The most remarkable

BOX 6.2 LANGUAGE ACQUISITION: LEARNING THE RULES

The extraordinary linguistic aptitude of infants has been closely studied in recent decades. So much information has to be analyzed from scratch that some researchers describe mastering a language as the greatest intellectual challenge that a person ever faces. Yet children everywhere in the world have effectively completed the process by their fifth year. Moreover, it is clear that what is involved is not mere repetition or copying, but the generation of abstract rules. What most dramatically proves that proposition is that toddlers spontaneously produce incorrect forms that they have never heard spoken by an adult. This occurs in all languages, but a few examples taken from English will serve to make the point. Infants rapidly grasp the idea of plural forms, and so learn to say, for instance, CAT and CATS. But the word HOUSE produces a problem because it already ends with a /s/ sound, until the child hears the plural form HOUSeZ.

Having acquired that plural, it will not be long before he or she produces CATSeZ. What this shows is the child experimenting with grammatical *rules*. The special rule for words like HOUSE has been retroactively extended to construct an incorrect form. So now the child needs to understand that there are two rules at work. That is not all, however. Some forms are simply irregular, and have to be learned case by case. So, presented with singular MAN, most children first acquire the plural MEN. But then they struggle to apply the rules they are finding elsewhere, so they produce MANS. When that is not approved of by adults, they next try MANSeZ or MENSeZ. When these are disapproved, they try MANS again. Only after several weeks or months of deduction do they finally abandon hope of rule-governed behavior for the word MAN, and revert to the plural MEN.

All this fiddling with rules is familiar enough to any adult who has tried to learn the grammar of a new language from a textbook. But infants of course have no access to a guide. Even so they do infinitely better at the task than an adult. Sadly, the aptitudes of a child are mostly lost by the teenage years, and after that learning new languages becomes progressively more difficult. The message is that the time to study languages is now. Do not delay!

case was that of a gorilla taught American Sign Language, as used by hearing-impaired humans (see Box 6.3). Our nearest relatives in the animal kingdom evidently share our communicative predispositions. Exactly where and how in the hominid line these developed into real speech is at present a matter of conjecture. It is hard, after all, to excavate vowels. But it remains the case that only our species spontaneously produces anything remotely resembling the complexity of speech. Until perhaps higher life forms are contacted in other star systems, we remain a uniquely talkative species.

(2) *The diversity of languages.* Having emphasized the universality of human speech, it is time to drop the other shoe. Languages are amazingly diverse. For most people, this fact is disguised by the tendency of those who learn a second language as adults – if ever they do – to study one that is closely related to their mother tongue. For example, an Anglophone American or Briton is far more likely to learn Spanish or French than Mandarin or Maya. True, to learn French requires memorizing new words for things, and even some new tricks of syntax. One cannot translate word-for-word "John's car"; one must say *l'auto de Jean.* But to a comparative linguist, this is trivial.

For Benjamin Whorf, these languages were so alike in fundamental design that he referred to them all simply as "European." The comparisons he drew were with Amerindian languages, where words worked in very different ways.

Since this is not a textbook in linguistics, one example from Whorf must suffice. In the English sentence "he invites people to a feast," several notions are broken up into smaller elements of meaning: "invite," " people" and "feast." In the Nootka language of British Columbia, Whorf says, there are no words corresponding to the English terms. Instead the whole meaning is conveyed in a single Nootka word *tl'imshya'isita'itlma.* (The raised comma indicates a glottal stop. These are not found in most dialects of English, but are conspicuous in Scots or Cockney accents in the middle of words like "bottle" or "water.") This word consists of the stem *tl'imsh-* "boil" with no less than five affixes: *ya-* indicates past tense, i.e. "-ed," *–'is* means "eat," *–ita* is English "-ers," *-'itl* means "go-for," and *–ma* means "he does." The whole word in all its glory might be translated literally "he does something involving going for eaters of something already boiled."

BOX 6.3 KOKO THE TALKING GORILLA

Chimpanzees were used in the first experiments with teaching language to non-human primates, but they become difficult to work with as they mature. By comparison, gorillas remain pacific and gentle. In contrast to their fearsome reputation, observations of gorillas in the wild show that they spend a lot of time together in small groups, and only rarely display any kind of aggression. Koko was born in captivity, and started learning American Sign Language while she was still young. By the time she was half grown she had acquired some hundreds of signs. Consequently, she can "talk" directly to people who use the same system, so achieving the age-old dream of direct communication with animals. Using her signs, Koko produces some strikingly human-like behavior. She displays an understanding of past and future, remembering for instance to demand a promised treat. She uses metaphors by making up compound words for things she has not seen before. Shown the use of a mask, she labeled it an "eye-hat." She teases people, calling them "nut" and "bird." She tells lies. Once she was scolded for jumping on a robust sink in the trailer where she lives, and breaking it away from the wall. Koko promptly pointed to a petite woman far too light to break the sink, and signed: "Kate there bad." For such major misbehavior Koko is banished to the punishment corner, where she faces the wall, hiding her face. After a while she signs that she is sorry, and asks for a hug. When a male gorilla was introduced to keep her company, she promptly set about teaching him signs. Like most male primates he was a slow learner, but they nevertheless do sign to one another, raising the prospect of a spontaneous spread of language among gorillas. Such evidence draws us closer than ever to our nearest primate relatives. For most people, it is comforting to find ourselves incorporated in the world of living things, rather than excluded by some special creation.

A major achievement of modern linguistics has been to describe all the ways that languages vary around the globe, in the sounds they make use of, the ways they assemble words, and the way they build or string words together to convey meaning. The subtleties involved in this are infinite and fascinating, and I cannot do better than refer readers to a companion volume *Language: The Basics*, by R.L. Trask. For present purposes, the point is that a *universal* human aptitude for speech cannot account for the enormous *diversity* of languages as they exist. Instead a separate discipline of comparative linguistics is needed, or linguistic anthropology as it is called in the USA. To imply otherwise is to commit the fallacy of biological reductionism. In the same way, the fact that human beings are fully bipedal, in contrast to all other primates, has a lot to do with how we run and jump. But it would be absurd to argue that biology accounts for the existence of the Olympic Games. Consequently, we have as much need for cultural anthropology as for linguistic anthropology.

LANGUAGE CONFOUNDS SOCIAL EVOLUTIONISM

There is another crucial finding about language: there is no such thing as a primitive language. Presumably there was once, but it must have been a long time ago. In historical times, no one has ever discovered humans talking in grunts and single words, like carica-ture cavemen. In the nineteenth century, however, it was casually assumed that the "primitive" peoples in remote corners of the world spoke "primitive" languages, ones that were somehow infe-rior to "modern" ones. But proponents of the theory took opposite views of what that implied. Some argued that primitive languages lacked abstract categories, citing instances where kinds of trees were named, but there was no word for "tree." Others held that just the reverse was true, that primitive people thought only in terms of supernatural forces, and could not manage a concrete account of the physical such as Western science achieved. So trees and stones were imbued with spirits and behaved in ways that had nothing to do with natural laws. As linguistic anthropologists got to work, both propositions were soon shown to be false. All languages display classifications of the natural world, with both specific and abstract categories.

Moreover, linguistic anthropologists found no correlation what-soever between complexity of language and complexity of technology. As we saw above, some languages are harder than others for begin-ning students. So, for example, Russian is generally counted as more difficult than Italian, but both Russia and Italy are industrial-ized nations. At the other end of the scale, the language of Tikopia is one of the numerous Austronesian languages, which are relatively easy for beginners. In most of them, for instance, verbs do not change (or "inflect" in linguistic jargon) for number or tense. So, the same unmodified verb appears whether the doer is me, you, him, her, us or them, and whether the doing occurred in the past, is occurring now, or will occur in the future. Meanwhile, right next door to the Austronesian languages, those of highland New Guinea are as challenging as Amerindian languages like Nootka.

In short, the Comparative Method produces absurd results if we apply it to language. If we line up languages in order of grammatical complexity, then Italian and Tikopian will appear towards one end, and Russian and Nootka at the other. Clearly, this result forces us to rethink the entire method.

CULTURE AND CULTURES

What is at stake here is whether one language can be described as better than another. We talked above about grammatical complexity, but there is no reason to believe that this variable can be taken as a measure of superiority. One might argue that it enables information to be carried more compactly. So if in English I catch the word "goes" in the middle of an utterance, I know immediately that it refers to a going currently in progress, by a singular person or thing. If this were not true I would have heard "go," "went" or "will go." This is a formidable amount of information to be carried in one word. But, if I hear the whole utterance, as we normally expect to do, then I have already been given the same information with the pronoun "he," "she," or "it." This is a case of linguistic *redundancy*, and highly inflected languages often contain a great deal of redundancy. By contrast, in Malay – the most widely spoken of all Austronesian languages – a whole utterance might consist of one word. For instance, someone might say simply *pergi*, "go." The hearer is now left to deduce who is going, but this is often obvious. If the intensifier "*-lah*" is tagged onto the end, as the speaker stands up, then he or she evidently needs to move on. If the speaker remains seated and lifts his or her chin towards another person, then that person is going or about to go, and so on. Moreover, the Malay speaker is not encumbered as English speakers are with having to indicate the gender of the goer, as I was obliged to do in the last two sentences. It is a stylistic problem in contemporary

English to avoid the boring repetition of "he or she," "him or her," "his or hers." Meanwhile, the Malay speaker can easily specify tense or person if desired simply by adding optional pronouns or tense markers. Then again, vagueness also has its virtues, allowing evasiveness, purposeful ambiguity, or verbal play.

Given all these subtleties, linguists are extremely wary about assessing one language as better than another. What they have concluded in general is that all languages manage to convey the full range of expressible meaning in some way or another, even if sometimes in what seems to an English speaker a roundabout way. It is perfectly reasonable to prefer one language to another, but the choice is one of personal tastes and not science.

Having reached that conclusion with regard to language, it is easy to extend the insight to all things cultural. In the nineteenth century, culture was thought of as something unequally distributed. Educated people were more "cultured" than others, and the same applied to nations. In the twentieth century, culture came to be used in a different way, such that all peoples possessed it in full measure, just as they possessed language. Singular culture became plural cultures. In this usage, saying that one people had "more culture" than another made no more sense than saying one place had "more weather" than another. They just have different weather, and different cultures.

FRANZ BOAS

All of these propositions about language seem so obvious to us now that it is hard to remember that they were radical when first argued in the early twentieth century. A large part of the credit for doing so goes to the American anthropologist Franz Boas.

Boas was born in Germany, where he studied geography. In the 1880's he made an expedition to Baffin Land in Canada to study the effects of an Arctic environment on the Eskimos. His next expedition, to the coast of British Columbia, was entirely ethnographic in purpose, and he returned there many times. In 1899 he was appointed to a chair in anthropology at Columbia University in New York. He soon became a public celebrity, because he was willing to weigh in on all the sensitive social issues of the day. In an America undergoing new waves of immigration from southern and eastern Europe, he attacked the chauvinism and racism that the previous generation of anthropologists had helped to create.

After demolishing social evolutionism, Boas was in no hurry to substitute a new grand theory. The pressing need he thought was for better data. Aware of how rapidly things were changing in the American Northwest, he set about documenting all he could of the diverse cultures of the people in the region. He recorded everything from fishing techniques to seasonal festivals. He was particularly impressed by the arts of people like the Kwakiutl, who built magnificently carved and painted houses, canoes and storage trunks, and elaborate masks used in rituals. He collected thousands of pages of myths, and one thing he noticed about them was that characters and episodes recurred from one community to another, but never in exactly the same way. What he concluded was that the peoples of the region had been borrowing backwards and forwards from each other for centuries. At the same time, however, whatever was borrowed was adapted to fit meaningfully into local traditions. The results, he showed, were complex configurations that existing theories were far too crude to untangle. Boas bequeathed to us a subtle notion of culture, and his students dominated American anthropology for the following half-century.

FROM SOUND SYSTEMS TO CULTURAL STYLES

One of Boas' most outstanding students was Edward Sapir. His overview of the field of linguistics, called simply *Language* (1921), foreshadowed many of the subsequent advances in the discipline. Sapir expanded on the basic insight that the sounds of language form a system at several different levels. At the most fundamental level, any given language makes use of only some of the noises that a human mouth can make. But competence in speaking does not consist of getting noises exactly the same every time, which is not human, but rather of observing certain distinctions between noises. For example, there are languages that make no distinctions between the popping noises that can be made with the lips, what are technically called "plosives." For speakers of those languages it would be hard to even hear the difference between the English words "plot" and "blot." In their own languages a plosive in any particular utterance might vary between /p/ and /b/ without risk of misunderstanding. That is, the *contrast* is not significant. Alternatively, English speakers learning Chinese find it very hard at first to distinguish between the tones that make the same consonant and vowel; /ma/ means both "mother" and "horse." What these examples show is that each language has its own *sound system*, the crucial feature of which is a set of contrasts between sounds. Moreover, as pronunciation gradually changes over time, any modification in one sound has knock-on effects on all the others, transforming it into a new system.

However, orderliness in language goes well beyond sound systems. They also have characteristic grammatical processes and concepts, as in the striking example above from Nootka. But even beyond that, collections of people who share linguistic practices – in technical jargon *speech communities* – also share ways of using language. That is to say, the conventions of conversation, and formal speech making, and telling stories, and so on, constitute particular *genres*. Sapir noticed this in the many Amerindian languages that he studied. But he also had a broad classical education, and in one brilliant section he contrasts the way that the poetry of Latin, Greek, French, and Chinese produces their effects. He argues that each of these rhythmic systems is part of the unconscious habits of the language. In short, Sapir draws together within one framework a broad range of cultural behavior that might be called *semiotic*, or message bearing.

LITTLE WHITE ROOM ETHNOGRAPHY

Sapir's influence directed attention to issues of *semantics*, that is, how languages convey meaning. A logical conclusion of this trend was to provide a whole new way of doing research. After all it is not necessary to go to France to learn French, for instance. All you need is a French speaker to teach you, preferably a native speaker. In the same way, in studying an unrecorded language from, say, the New Guinea highlands, it is often easier to bring the informant to the linguist rather than the reverse. The informant has the adventure of traveling abroad, and the linguist has access to laboratory equipment that can measure sound production, and so on. After World War Two cultural anthropologists began to copy this method, arguing that semantics was at the heart of culture, and all that was necessary to study semantics was a culturally fluent informant and a tape recorder. So radical was this idea to ethnographers raised in the Malinowskian tradition of participant observation that it was labeled "little white room" ethnography.

INDIGENOUS KNOWLEDGES

The results of this kind of research are called *ethnoscience*. Its principal premise is straightforward: indigenous peoples all over the globe, regardless of formal education, have a profound knowledge of their environments. That knowledge, or rather those knowledges, are worth recording both for what they teach us about the world and about culture. In support of their case, they could point to Charles Darwin's experiences in New Zealand during his famous voyage around the world. Despite his knowledge of the natural sciences, Darwin was obviously an innocent in the New Zealand bush. So he hired Maori guides, and he was astonished at their fund of knowledge about the biota of their islands. There were Maori names for everything, and only on a couple of occasions did Darwin find fault with their labeling. In rare cases they mistook the male and female of one species for two different species. Apart from those small lapses, they were expert biologists in their own world. It follows therefore that in parallel with scientific botany, with its standardized Latin names, there exists an indigenous Maori *ethnobotany*. The same applies to *ethnozoology*, and a theory of the heavens that we might call *ethnoastronomy*, and so on.

The goal of ethnoscientists was to collect such indigenous taxonomies, and to work out how categories were distinguished from one another. Not surprisingly, this was seldom explicit. That is to say, it was unconscious, and the researcher's job was to find what *components* of meaning were attached to each category. The methodology for doing this was elaborate, and involved a battery of standardized questions designed to reveal an indigenous taxonomy. Suppose for example a speaker of some dialect of English, someone not trained as a botanist or familiar with Latin names, produces the word "pine." The researcher might ask a whole set of questions about the category, e.g.: is a pine a kind of tree? Is a pitch pine a kind of pine? Is a pineapple a kind of pine? Is a pine a kind of pineapple? Is a fir a kind of pine? The questions need to be asked

BOX 6.4 PART OF AN OJIBWA TAXONOMY OF "LIVING BEINGS"

t.1 /bema.diziwa.d/ "living things"	
t.2 /bema.Diziwa.d/ /anišina.beg/ 'human beings'	t.9 /anišina.beg/ 'Indians' t.10 /gičimokoma.nig/ 'white people' t.11 /makadewiya.sag/ 'Negroes' t.12 /ani.bi.škewininiwag/ 'Asiatics'
t.3 /awesi.yag/ 'large animals'	t.13 /makwa/ 'bear' t.14 /mq.ns/ 'moose' t.15 /atik/ 'caribou' t.16 other
t.4 /manido.weyišag/ 'small animals'	t.17 /žiga.g/ 'skunk' t.18 /agakoji.ši./ 'woodchuck' t.19 /ža.ngweči/ 'mink' t.20 other
t.5 manido.šag/ 'insects'	t.21 /ginebi.g/ 'snake' t.22 /obegomagaki/ 'toad' t.23 /o.ji.ns/ 'fly' t.24 other
t.6 /binešj.yag/ 'birds'	t.25 /migizi/ 'bald eagle' t.26 /go.ko.ko?o/ 'owl' t.27 /wi.na.nge/ 'buzzard' t.28 other
t.8 /adios.ka.nag/ 'spirits'	t.33 /nenabošo/ (culture hero) t.34 /mikiniak/ (great turtle) t.35 /binesiwag/ 'thunderbirds' t.36 /memegwesiwag/ 'paddlers' t.37 /gi.zis/ 'sun' t.38 /no.dino.g/ 'winds' t.39 /ba.na.be/ 'mermaid' t.40 other

This is a simplified version of a taxonomy of "living things" collected by Mary Black from Ojibwa informants in Minnesota. You will note that each English gloss is an attempt to infer the meaning of a specific Ojibwa word from how it was used by native speakers. At the same time, no category is included that is not found in Ojibwa, because the goal is to discover their view of things, not impose ours. Some of the results seem obvious enough. It comes as no surprise that for Ojibwa "Indians," "Negroes," and "white people" are types of "human beings," nor that "bear" and "moose" are types of "large animals." But it is by no means clear why "snakes" and "flies" are grouped together. Presumably, Black glosses *manido.šag* as "insects" because most of the life forms lumped together in that category are insects, but that hardly helps with snakes and toads. Could the category *manido.šag* imply *very small* creatures, or *irritating* small creatures? More research would be necessary, and so the method sparks a new range of questions. Notice also that the categories have no fit with the Linnean classification. *iga.g* might perhaps be synonymous with the genus *Mephitis*, but comparative anatomy has no use for a category of "small animals."

systematically, crosschecking every possibility of categorical inclusion or exclusion. This is not much fun for the informants, who are generally paid for being so relentlessly questioned. In this way, ethnoscientists studied taxonomies of everything from firewood to fast food, in many different languages. For the most part, it was aspects of the physical world that were studied, but the method could be applied to abstract things like spirits or demons.

A REFUGEE IN NEW YORK

In the 1940's, an accidental encounter caused a productive cross-fertilization of Boasian cultural anthropology with an older European tradition of linguistics. Claude Lévi-Strauss was a refugee from the Nazi invasion of France when he was invited to the New School for Social Research in New York. There he met not only Boas and his students, but also Roman Jakobson, who introduced him to the work of the Prague school of linguistics. Meanwhile, he spent many hours in the New York Public Library, immersing himself in ethnographies. His synthesis of these diverse strands produced a very different notion of structure to that current in British anthropology at the same period.

THE UNCONSCIOUS IN CULTURE

Lévi-Strauss' key insight was that what was true of language was true of other domains of culture. One paradox in particular attracted his attention. A native speaker unerringly produces correct sentences, without any awareness of the myriad rules that govern them. It follows that the rules must be stored unconsciously. If you have ever had the experience of helping a non-native speaker improve his or her language skills, you will have discovered this for yourself. Many languages, such as Farsi, the major language of Iran, lack the definite and indefinite articles found in English, "the" and "a." But an Anglophone is often very hard put to explain to an Iranian when one is required, and when the other, and when neither. Consider the old saw: money is the root of all evil. Only one article is used, but how is an Iranian supposed to know that? Try substituting definite and indefinite articles before each noun and see what happens to the sentence. Immediately you notice that you can't say "a money" in any context you can think of, unless in a compound form like "a money problem." So what's going on there? And why can't it be "the evil"? and so on. Unless you're an amateur linguist, you will soon find yourself saying: that's just the way it is. That is, you can *use* the rules without a moment's hesitation, but to *explain* the rules is a very different business.

This is Lévi-Strauss' notion of the unconscious: a part or an aspect of the mind that finds order. One might almost say that it imposes order on a random world, just as unconscious linguistic rules allow chaotic noise to be shaped into meaningful communication. It is not at all like Sigmund Freud's unconscious, with its murky fears and fantasies. Instead, it contains mental *structures* that provide the grammar, as it were, of culture.

BRITISH AND FRENCH NOTIONS OF STRUCTURE

Lévi-Strauss was convinced that his ideas could be applied to any social or cultural domain, so he began boldly with kinship theory – the prevailing obsession of the epoch. This strategy masked the profound difference between his idea of structure and the familiar British version. As we noted in Chapter Three, to study structure for the British was to describe the relationships between persons; how they fit into the groups and categories peculiar to a particular society, and what statuses and roles result from that. All structure was *social* structure. Lévi-Strauss' concept was far more ambitious, and could apply as easily in physics and chemistry as in linguistics and anthropology. For him, structure was evident in any arrangement of elements in an interlocking system, such that changing one meant changing all the others. That is to say, change was not mere accretion, like the accumulation of junk in an attic. Instead it involved all elements simultaneously. In his jargon, structures underwent *transformation* into other forms of what was fundamentally the same structure.

Given the breadth of this concept, it is not surprising that Lévi-Strauss' approach was soon tried in other disciplines. Structuralism grew into an intellectual movement, causing ferment in disciplines as diverse as psychology and literary criticism. Historians were particularly puzzled by the trend, because history seemed to evaporate in the face of transformation. History became nothing more than a series of random *events*, through which structures were preserved or transformed, but never evolved. Meanwhile British structuralism was left far behind, a merely parochial concern of anthropology, so that even to name it required the clumsy formula "structural-functionalism." One might argue that the narrowness, or specificity, of British structuralism was its virtue in the first place. But the British could do very little with the "structure" of a myth, say. Insofar as a story justified the current social *status quo*, then it might be called a *charter myth*. That is a shallow reading, however, of the enormously convoluted plots of myths, in which heroes regularly stand the proper order on its head with impunity. For the study of things other than social persons, Lévi-Strauss structuralism opened doors onto exciting new vistas.

THE *MYTHOLOGIQUES*

Lévi-Strauss' mature work did indeed focus on myth, making use of the vast corpus of Amerindian stories collected by ethnographers working in the Boasian mold. His magnum opus is the four-volume

Mythologiques series, in which he picks up one myth, and then tracks its connections elsewhere in the Americas. In moving from one place to another the myth is transformed, but there is no need to decide which place was the origin. On the contrary, similar structures of the mind are engaged in both places. In this way, Lévi-Strauss pursued the very issue that had so fascinated Boas: how elements of myth were borrowed back and forth, but always modified to suit their local cultural environment. The *Mythologiques* range across the entire continent, examining hundreds of myths – a remarkable fruition of the Boasian project.

MARRIAGE AS GIFT

In his earlier work, Lévi-Strauss pursued issues of classification and totemism, to which we will return in the next chapter. It remains to outline how at the beginning of his career he so upset the applecart in kinship studies. This involved another monumental study drawing on ethnographic data from around the world. Needless to say, Lévi-Strauss did not collect this material himself. In fact, his efforts at fieldwork were not impressive, and he was obviously happier in a library. This gives his work a somewhat nineteenth-century quality, and British ethnographers often accused him of having no feel for what made sense in social terms.

The starting point of Lévi-Strauss' theory of kinship was a famous essay by one of Durkheim's students, Marcel Mauss. In *The Gift*, Mauss argues that simple societies everywhere are brought into being and maintained through a universally understood process of exchange. The process is that you give me something now, and later on I give you something back. For everyone involved, there is an obligation both to give and to receive. Mauss' idea is so simple that it seems to hardly need stating, yet there is a subtle implication. After the rise of capitalism, Westerners had great difficulty in dealing with material goods as anything other than commodities. If a peasant in a market exchanges potatoes for cooking pots, then it is obvious that he has a surplus of potatoes and a need for pots. He makes his bargain and goes home, while the pot-seller moves on to the next market. But what to make of an exchange in which people give each other the same thing, as for instance when an American Indian exchanges bows with another?

Each started with a bow, and ended with one much the same. Mauss' point is that for these two the gift creates a personal bond. The exchange of goods creates relationships, rather than relationships merely being used to obtain goods.

Examples of this kind of gift-giving can be found all over the world, and in his reading of ethnography Lévi-Strauss recognized them in the complex exchanges that often accompany marriage. For Westerners, marriage is a choice of two individuals based on personal attraction, emotional compatibility, and so on. But in many parts of the world a marriage is an *alliance* between whole groups of people related on one side to the bride and on the other to the groom. The importance of an alliance of this kind is marked in gifts – in the jargon of alliance theory, *prestations* – that go back and forth between families for the entire lifetime of bride and groom, and often long afterwards. The nature of these prestations is covered by explicit rules, that is, collective representations. Finally, the best possible outcome is another marriage to renew the alliance. There are then two choices. The rules of marriage may say that a bride should then pass back the other way, so that over several generations the same two groups exchange wives. This is called *restricted exchange*. There is another, less obvious, alternative: the rules may specify that wife-givers cannot become wife-takers. But where then do the wife-givers get women to marry their young men? The answer is from a third group, but there is nothing to stop the third group from seeking wives from the first. In this way, everyone is related as wife-taker to some people, and wife-giver to others. The result is called *generalized exchange*, and potentially it can produce more social solidarity than does the restricted version.

THE MEANING OF WOMEN

Lévi-Strauss' monumental first book *The Elementary Structures of Kinship* spawned a great deal of fascinating research. Ethnographers looked everywhere for cases of positive rules prescribing what categories of people one should marry, in order to test his theories. Negative rules are common enough. Almost everywhere incest rules prohibit marriage with close relatives, such as siblings or parents. But elementary systems are far less common. We will not, however, pursue the results of all the research here. For present

BOX 6.5 RESTRICTED AND GENERALIZED EXCHANGE

A diagram of restricted exchange is very simple: A ◄───► B

In social terms, what this means is that everyone is sorted into one of two categories (or "moieties," in technical parlance, meaning halves), and everyone must find a spouse in the category to which he or she does not belong. From a man's point of view, all women in his own generation are either prospective wives, or they are treated as sisters. A simple rule decides which is which: a parallel cousin is "sister" and a cross cousin is "wife." That is, a father's brother's daughter (FBD) is sister, but so is a mother's sister's daughter (MZD), not to mention a FFBDD or a MMZDD, and so on. Meanwhile, a MBD or a FZD is a cross cousin, as is a MMBDD or a FFZDD, and so on. If you draw a simple genealogy for yourself, you will soon see how everyone gets partitioned between the two groups. From a woman's point of view, all men of her generation are similarly sorted into "brothers" or "husbands."

Generalized exchange allows men to marry only their maternal cross cousins, that is, MBD, MMBDD, MMMBDDD, and so on. But that means his brother-in-law cannot marry his sister, because the sister is FZD to him. So he must seek his wife in another group. At a minimum, there have to be three intermarrying groups, but there could easily be more, allowing more choice for alliances, as these diagrams show:

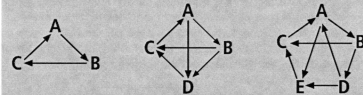

The network can be extended as far as it is practical to maintain alliances.

purposes, the point is that Lévi-Strauss demonstrated the existence of just two elementary structures, each a transformation of the other. Evidence of such structures could be found all over the world, because, he argued, both were universally present in the unconscious, ready to emerge when circumstances were right.

There is another implication coming directly from Lévi-Strauss' application of linguistic methods. In his analysis of alliance, women are in effect messages. Moreover, they are largely sent between political groups dominated by men. Lévi-Strauss is explicit about this. The communications that build social solidarity proceed in three media: gifts of words (i.e. conversation), gifts of things, and gifts of women. Not surprisingly, feminists were not pleased with so blatant a reduction of women to mere objects. Lévi-Strauss found their objections misplaced. He was not dealing with social policy or practical politics but with something much more abstract. If feminists found the notion of men exchanging women distasteful, the whole argument could simply be rephrased in terms of women exchanging men; it came to the same thing.

LANGUAGE AS ANALOGY

The notion of women as messages makes plain the linguistic analogy that lies behind Lévi-Strauss' work. Indeed, he pushes the analogy about as far as it can go. As we saw in the last chapter, however apt an analogy may be it can produce errors if taken too literally. A society may be compared to an organism or a machine, but a society is not an organism or a machine. What is peculiar about the analogy between culture and linguistics is that it compares part with whole. Obviously, language is one of those things that is instilled in children by their parents and teachers. Perhaps that is why the linguistic analogy is particularly suggestive, but not everything in culture has to do with communication. Even Lévi-Strauss himself remarked that the structures found in myth were more "pure," because a narrative has no restraints on it other than pleasing the narrator and his or her audience. By comparison, even the strictest rules of marriage are likely to unravel if complex negotiations about exchanges go wrong, or even if one partner finds the other seriously unattractive.

Consequently, we must maintain some skepticism about the linguistic analogy. Imagine, for example, a Tikopian man building a canoe. The process is surrounded by rules: who may own a canoe; what help he may request, and from whom; what prayers must be said at each stage; and a host of other things. Moreover, there are abstract ideas that have been enculturated in the builder, and that he expresses in the process of building: the place of human beings in creation, on both the land and sea; the mythic place of sea voyages in the stories of ancestor heroes; the protection that the gods may provide on long sea voyages; and at the most basic level what a canoe *is*. In short the whole process is embedded in cultural rules and understandings. Finally, however, there is an accommodation that has to be made with the sea, and that is what we may call ethno-naval architecture, not semiotics.

Summary

The comparative study of languages has been crucial in the development of modern anthropology, particularly in the USA. The first American anthropologists were presented with urgent ethnographic tasks right on their own doorstep. The founding father of modern American anthropology, Franz Boas, made it a priority to record texts in indigenous languages. In this way, he believed, the "genius" of a people could be preserved for future generations. Meanwhile, it turned out that the phenomenon of language neatly demolished both nineteenth-century evolutionism and biological determinism. As regards the former, the Comparative Method produces results that are meaningless. Simply put, there is no relationship whatsoever between technological complexity and language complexity. Regarding the biological basis of language, the demonstration is convincing because all of us know the practical facts of language; how they vary, and how children acquire them. Once they begin, children learn to speak at such an astonishing rate that simple imitation cannot be all that is involved. There must be an inborn aptitude, resulting from a million years or more of biological evolution. At the same time, it would be absurd to imagine that children are genetically programmed to learn one language rather than another. In Britain and the USA we know this very well because we have seen children from all over the world grow up to speak English in exactly the same manner as their school friends. Consequently, we have need of a special discipline of *linguistics* to describe the nature of variation in languages. By the mid-twentieth century, linguistics had achieved spectacular results. It had developed precise methods of writing down and analyzing the sounds made by any type of speech in the world, showing how words were constructed and put together in sentences, and how meaning was conveyed in all manner of speech genres.

This success inspired several attempts to apply the methods of linguistic anthropology in cultural anthropology. A major appeal of this effort was the close analogy between language and culture. Indeed, language *is* culture, since it is learned.

So the analogy should be stated by saying that non-linguistic aspects of culture behave in ways similar to language. This proposition underlies a great deal of the developments in cultural anthropology over the last half-century, as you will notice in subsequent chapters. In this chapter I give two examples. The first is the field of ethnoscience, which tries to discover the meaning of indigenous terms by sorting them rigorously into taxonomies using local informants. These taxonomies can then be compared to those in other languages, or to those in botany and zoology, hence revealing ethnic sciences. The linguistic analogy reaches its ultimate elaboration, however, in the theorizing of Claude Lévi-Strauss. In particular, he mobilizes a notion of structure far more sweeping than the merely *social* structure of the British followers of Durkheim. This technique is most easily understood in his study of myth. In fact, however, he began with the abstract structures of kinship. This was designed to attract the attention of British and American anthropologists, and it succeeded in doing so. But it means that perversely the word "structure" circulated in two very different senses. This caused confusion in the 1950's and 1960's, and still does for the unwary.

FURTHER READING

Boas wrote a great deal, much of it about his fieldwork with the Kwakiutl on the Pacific coast of Canada. He avoided theoretical statements, however. They are best set out in his *The Mind of Primitive Man* (1938, original 1911). An elegant statement of the development of linguistics in Boas' time is Sapir's *Language* (1921), and for a modern overview see Trask (1995). I take my account of Koko's communicative abilities from an article by Francine Patterson (1979), and of language acquisition in children from another by Breyne Moskowitz (1978), both very readable. The best source on the techniques of ethnoscience is found in *Cognitive Anthropology* (1969), edited by Stephen Taylor. The writings of Lévi-Strauss are numerous, and often difficult for a beginner.

Towards the end of his career, however, he wrote a brief, simple account of his ideas called *Myth and Meaning: Cracking the Code of Culture* (1995, original 1978). Many people wish he had written it earlier. His masterwork on kinship is *The Elementary Structures of Kinship* (1969, original 1949), a tome that has daunted generations of graduate students. At one level, it is a vast elaboration of the ideas set out in Marcel Mauss' *The Gift* (1967, original 1924), surely one of the most widely read essays in anthropology.

CULTURE AND NATURE

The linguistic analogy means thinking of cultural domains other than language as behaving in a manner similar to language. That does not imply that cultures are somehow organized for the benefit of anthropologists, so that they can be "read." Instead the "message," to follow the analogy, passes between culture bearers themselves. Putting it another way, every culture provides a way of understanding the world to those who learned it at their mother's knee. Consequently, every culture manifests a unique view of nature. Paradoxically, nature is a construct of culture, and not the other way around.

However radical this proposition may sound, it is far from new. At the beginning of the twentieth century a brilliant young student of Durkheim's named Robert Hertz put it this way: "every social hierarchy claims to be founded on the nature of things ... it thus accords itself eternity, it escapes change and the attacks of innovators. Aristotle justified slavery by the ethnic superiority of the Greeks over barbarians; and today the man who is annoyed by feminist claims alleges that woman is *naturally* inferior." For a hundred years, anthropologists have been accumulating indigenous accounts of what is obvious or self-evident because they invariably take us to the heart of cultural things. Why must these particular people be asserting this? What cultural logic lies behind the claim?

For ethnographers, a casual remark to the effect that something is "only natural" is like the scent of a fox to the hounds, and they are immediately off in full cry.

RIGHT AND LEFT

What prompted Hertz's remarks was nothing more exotic than the widespread tendency for people to favor the right over the left. This preference has two aspects, biological and cultural. The classic biological argument is that we are right-handed because we are left-brained. That is to say the left hemisphere of the brain is usually larger, and since the major nerve fibers are crossed, it controls the muscles on the right side of the body. But could it be the other way around, asks Hertz, namely that we are left-brained because we are right-handed? In support of this idea, he points out that the size of the right cerebral hemisphere can be increased by practice in using the left hand. So, for example, violinists often have to make incredibly rapid and precise movements with the fingers of their left hands in order to play successive chords, while, perversely, the right hand is assigned the easier task of drawing the bow. The result is measurable changes in the brains of accomplished violinists.

Hertz's inversion is striking because it is counter intuitive. That is, it challenges the taken-for-granted knowledge that we call "common sense." In the end he rejects it, however, for the reason that the right hand seems to be dominant in very different cultures all over the world. If it was a cultural preference that produced a biological difference, then we would expect some nations to prefer the left hand and so be right brained and others the reverse. Instead what we find is left-handers everywhere in the minority. Consequently, Hertz concludes that there must be some physical predisposition for the majority of people to be right-handed. That would seem then to be the end of the matter, but for Hertz it is only the beginning.

RIGHT AND WRONG

What Hertz noticed is that there is far more going on with the word "right" than asymmetry in the human body. Isn't it curious, for instance, that right is contrasted not only with left, but also with "wrong." There is no inherent reason for those two meanings to be connected. For the left hand to be less adept is hardly to make it incorrect or immoral. We also speak of "defending our rights," and that concept has nothing to do with not bothering to defend our lefts. Even the word for left is often avoided. The English term "sinister" fell out of usage when it took on overtones going well beyond the left side. Moreover, all these contrasts right/left, right/wrong, right/sinister can be found in several other languages around the world, and not just those related to English. They apply, for example, to the French *droit*, but also to the word *tu'o* in the Berawan language of central Borneo. Hertz summarizes his argument with a famous proposition: "if organic asymmetry had not existed, it would have had to be invented."

We might respond that these usages are simply metaphorical, but that is just Hertz's point. Moreover, there is no reason to identify one meaning as basic. Is the right hand the model for morality, or is morality mapped on the body? Clearly, this is an irresolvable, chicken-and-egg debate. Consequently handedness routinely gets itself involved in anything dyadic (that is, having two parts). Hertz's essay is subtitled "A Study in Religious Polarity" and he assembles an amazing array of examples. A Maori *tohunga*, or priest, for instance, performs a ritual that is simplicity itself: he makes two mounds, one on his left and one on his right. Then he banishes all dangerous and harmful things to the former, and calls down all good things to the latter. This completed, he knocks down the left-hand mound.

Meanwhile, Maori also associate the left side with women. Obviously, there is no biological reason for this. Women are no more predisposed to be left-handed than men. Nevertheless, the male side (*tama tane*) is associated not only with virility and paternity, which seem obvious, but also with the east and creativity, which do not. In Maori thinking, the east is the side of the sunrise, from where comes life, and dyadic logic therefore assigns the reverse to the women's side (*tama vahine*). Sorcery is the women's domain. "All evils, misery, and death," says the Maori proverb, "come from the female element." You will notice that the proverb does not condemn women, but the "female element." Men are capable of sorcery, too. Nevertheless, one does not need to be a feminist to note that we have now wandered a long way from what

BOX 7.1 SYMBOLISM

Nineteenth-century anthropologists were crucially concerned with the evolution of religion, which they saw as a progressive liberation from crude superstition towards "higher" forms of religion, which in turn would fade away with the advance of science. This view was embodied in James Frazer's vast compendium of bizarre beliefs, *The Golden Bough*, which appeared in several volumes between 1890 and 1915, and in an "abridged edition" of 850 pages in 1922. Nevertheless, it was one of the best-selling anthropology books of all time. No doubt, its subject matter was exciting to Victorians, with its instances of primitive ritual, sexuality, and violence. In addition, it seemed to confirm the skepticism of rationalists against the established churches. What weight could be given to "faith," when people were clearly capable of believing just about anything?

In the middle decades of the twentieth century, interest in religion retreated. Wishing to found a mature science of society and culture, anthropologists shied away from the sensationalism of *The Golden Bough*. When interest revived in the 1960's, it took a very different direction, no longer concerned with "the sociology of error." Instead, the goal was to understand indigenous beliefs and practices as a coherent worldview. The key idea in the new approach was symbolism, and the program of symbolic anthropology was first laid out in Victor Turner's *The Forest of Symbols* (1967). By way of definition, Turner quotes the *Oxford English Dictionary*: "a symbol is a thing regarded by general consent as naturally typifying or representing or recalling something by possession of analogous qualities or by association in fact or thought" (1967: 19). A better understanding of what he was after is provided by the example he then gives. During his fieldwork in Zambia, Turner's Ndembu informants told him that the *mudyi* tree was their "flag," or national emblem. It symbolized, they said, the matrilineal principle that lay at the heart of Ndembu society, and the reason for that association was not difficult to discover. If cut the tree exuded a milky sap, and this feature was utilized in rituals. But the meanings of the *mudyi* tree did not stop there. Indeed, Turner produces a whole list of them, beginning with ones that were stated by his informants, and continuing to others that were not. At one level, the *mudyi* represents the customary values that unite people, and so harmony. But it can also stand for the unity of women, and potentially their opposition to their own men folk. In some ritual contexts, it symbolizes the tensions between mothers and daughters, and even the struggles between matrilines. In this way what is *symbolized* goes beyond what is *said*, and so provides a fuller insight into the dynamics of Ndembu society and culture.

Westerners would regard as inherent in nature. On the contrary, we are seeing a very different "nature" under construction.

FROM BODY TO COSMOS: THE ATONI HOUSE

During the period when British anthropologists were obsessed with kinship and social organization, Hertz's essay attracted little attention. But in the 1960's interest in religion revived in both the UK and the USA. Ethnographic accounts of particular symbolic systems became available, and polarity was everywhere in evidence. A famous example came from an account of the spatial symbolism of the Atoni of Timor, an island in eastern Indonesia, provided by Clarke Cunningham. The Atoni make the same symbolic identifications as noted above for the Maori, and moreover build them in, literally, to their houses. In a proper Atoni house, the door should face south, that is, the right-hand side when facing the sunrise. Non-residents approach from the male side, where they are seated on an open veranda. Consequently, the inside of the house is female. A close male relative invited into the house would stay on the right-hand or male side of the house, where there is a raised seating area. You will notice that spaces are male in one context and female in another, and that is a crucial feature of the whole symbolic system. So the right-hand side of the interior of the house is male *only* vis-à-vis the left-hand side; *both* are female relative to the exterior. The back left-hand corner is, so to speak, doubly female. The platform there is used for storing cooking implements, and it is where a woman should give birth.

This account merely scratches at the surface of Atoni house symbolism. There is much more to say about floor plans, let alone the mode of construction, but for present purposes the point is now to extend the view outward. Not surprisingly, the house as a whole

BOX 7.2 ORIENTATION OF THE ATONI HOUSE

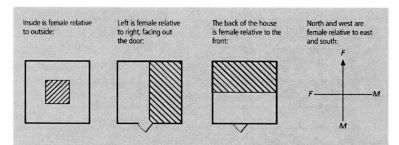

Inside is female relative to outside:

Left is female relative to right, facing out the door:

The back of the house is female relative to the front:

North and west are female relative to east and south:

Visitors approach the house from the south, the side of the door. They are invited to sit on the porch in front of the door (not shown on the diagrams above), men on the right, women on the left. The women of the house converse from the doorway. If kinsmen or women are invited inside, they sit on a raised platform on the right side of the house. They do not go over to the left side of the room, and especially not to the back left-hand corner. Prayers are said on the east side of the house. Note that this is the merest beginning of Atoni house symbolism. The point is to show that space is gendered, but in what manner changes according to context.

is a female domain, surrounded by its four walls. The same model applies ideally to the numerous small Atoni political units. At the cardinal points of each realm are four secular lords, whose job it is to control the movement of people in and out, to collect tribute, to administer justice, and to engage in war. They are called the "male-men." But the most important lord dwells in his palace at the center of the realm, and has no such administrative functions. His job, according to Atoni, is only "to sleep and eat," and in accordance with this passive role, he is called the "female-man." Note that the female-man is never a woman. You can imagine how confused the Dutch were as they tried to extend the administration of their East Indies Empire to the Atoni.

At another level, the whole realm is seen as female in contrast to neighboring ones, where men go to trade or fight. Moreover, the land is seen as female by comparison with the sea, but the shallow sea around the coast where shellfish can be gathered is a female sea, and only men venture offshore to fish in the male sea. Meanwhile, the land is also female in contrast to the sky, which is ruled by the major divinity. In prayer, he is addressed as "Lord of the Sky, the dome-shaped, the protecting, the overshadowing."

Similarly, a lord is ceremonially addressed as "the shadowing one, the shading one." What most obviously shades people is, however, the massive thatch roofs of their houses, which come down almost to the ground, hiding the sidewalls. It replicates both the shape and function of the sky, but on a human scale. And that is the real reason, according to the Atoni, why a door must face south. Since they live below the equator, the sun passes to the north each day. Consequently, its light cannot shine into the windowless house, and become dangerously mixed with the light of the domestic fire that is always kept alight.

RELIGIOUS POLARITY

The remarkable feature of Atoni spatial symbolism is that the same polarities of left and right, inside and out, are replicated in person, house, realm, geography, and cosmos. Presumably, it would be hard for Atoni people to feel the kind of alienation from nature that has been a feature of Western thought for centuries. The same applies to gender. Following Hertz's presentation of left and right, we might say that a biological feature of humans (this time an obviously biological feature) has been projected outward onto the whole world. Or alternatively, as an Atoni might see it, a pervasive quality of the universe is made apparent even in the human body.

The Atoni are not alone in this view of things. Ethnographers have now collected many examples of indigenous religions that divide the world not only into aspects of male and female, right and left, but also blood and bone, sun and moon, domesticated and wild, and many others. In addition there are idiosyncratic pairs that have no self-evident dyadic quality, such as tiger/crocodile or seven/eight. Then again, there are qualities that lend themselves to various arrangements. Red, for instance, might be contrasted with black as life to death, or with white as blood to bone. Or it might be part of a four-color system, as among the Atoni, where east is associated with white, south with red, west with black, and north with yellow. You can see that the possibilities for elaborating symbolic systems of this kind are virtually limitless. One can begin with spatial symbolism, or social organization, or animal species, or colors, and each will lead on to all the others, a complete, self-contained, and consistent rendition of culture and nature, and culture in nature.

THE PREVALENCE OF DUALISM

The tendency to perceive the world in terms of such polarities is called dualism, and examples every bit as complex as the Atoni can be found worldwide. There are, however, several caveats that must be made. Hertz asserted that "dualism marks the entire thought of primitive men," but he overstated his case in both directions. There are many localized indigenous religions that are only weakly dualistic, while to convince yourself that dualism is not unknown in industrial societies you have only to consider the infinite elaborations of "left" and "right" in Western politics. Moreover, it needs to be underlined that worldviews that are dualistic are not for that reason similar to each other in any other way. On the contrary, what ethnographers have discovered is the incredible variety of understandings of nature that can be produced by using different combinations of the very same dyadic elements, not to mention all the idiosyncratic ones, and ones that make sense only in particular natural environments. The sheer creativity of the non-world religions is one of the major discoveries of twentieth-century anthropology. In contrast to the mass of fear-ridden and inchoate superstition imagined by nineteenth-century armchair theorists, we have discovered indigenous philosophies of remarkable sophistication.

A final caveat: the tendency of certain associations to recur – right with correct, moral, legally enforceable, divinity, and so on – does not mean that they inevitably occur. In fact, ethnographers are on the look out for the interesting occasions when they are inverted. It can be safely assumed that any conceivable combination of dyads will occur somewhere, but the most intriguing cases of *symbolic inversion*, to use the technical jargon, often seem to follow as logical consequences from major associations. You may have noticed, for example, an odd consequence of the spatial logic of the Atoni house outlined above. The side of the house that is female is the left side for someone facing out the door. But that is also the side to the east, which is the cardinal point associated with men. So spatial symbolism inside the house is inverted in this respect. Meanwhile, prayers are said by men just beyond the eaves on the eastern side of the house. Does it make them uncomfortable to appeal to the divinity directly next to the most female of all places? On the contrary, the implications of this inversion are elaborated within Atoni notions of sex and gender.

SEX AND GENDER

The crucial feature of the Atoni view is that male and female are not opposites to be kept apart but complementarities to be brought together. You may object that it is hardly an anthropological insight that it takes a man and a woman to make a baby. If that were the end of the story, however, there would be no institutions of marriage. Atoni marriages comprise the kind of alliances between segments of society that we saw in the previous chapter. Consequently, biological reproduction is only the final step, as it were, in a broader process of social reproduction. Meanwhile, the wife-givers, both men and women, take on a female dimension because it is through them that the wife-takers renew themselves. That men pray adjacent to the female side of the house acknowledges this life-giving role.

Another way of putting this is that, according to context, people may be gendered regardless of their sex. This need come as no surprise, since we have seen that even a-sexual things may be gendered. As in many other parts of the world, the moon is seen as female, an identification made stronger by the association of the female menstrual cycle with the monthly waxing and waning of the moon. But the moon cannot literally be sexed because it has no genitalia, and if genitalia are irrelevant then men can be women and women men. More subtly, the process also works in the other direction. The contextual negotiation of gender affects the nature of sex itself. It is as if maleness and femaleness floated around detached from bodies, and it was this that appalled Dutch administrators and missionaries, who saw Atoni views as chaotic and dangerous. What they did not understand was that Atoni ideas did not at all involve categorical confusion. On the contrary, Atoni categories were more rigorously worked out than those of their conquerors.

MEDIATING MALE AND FEMALE

The "female-man" provides a nice example of this. Atoni insist that he really is female, which is to say that his femaleness is as embodied as his maleness. He is usually an old man, past the age when his ability to father children is of much relevance to anybody, but active in roles that promote the fecundity of the entire realm. When Atoni say that his job is only "to eat and sleep," they are saying precisely that he embodies this supreme power; aside from the important ritual functions he performs. He may well have a wife, and like many an old couple they may enjoy an easy familiarity no longer disturbed by the infamous "battle of the sexes." But that does not mean that he is de-sexed, rather he is re-sexed. To elaborate the oxymoron of his title, he assumes an active passivity. In anthropological jargon, the female-man is one of those ritual specialists whose powers come from *mediating* between important aspects of the cosmos.

You will notice that the sexual nature of the "female-man" has nothing to do with sexual activity, homosexual or otherwise. We can, however, find cases where sex acts are involved. Among the Ngaju of southern Borneo, priestesses (*balian*) play a necessary part in many important rites. Their main role is to entertain the assembly with epic songs recounting the exploits of great heroes of the past, but at the end of their performance they sleep with the man who organized the rite. There is nothing furtive about this. It is not an extra service provided by the *balian* in addition to the ritual, it is an essential part of the ritual. Mothers urge on their sons, and the only shame would be in refusing. In addition to the *balian*, there are also transvestite male priests called *basir*, and hosts likewise have sex with them. For the Ngaju, this consummation allows the host entry into the sacred world of the priests and priestesses. The *basir* is particularly effective in this because his dual nature allows him access to both Upperworld and Underworld. This in turn follows from the nature of the divinity, who is both male and female at the same time

GENDER BENDING

In the 1980's, Americans began to speak of "gender bending," particularly in connection with men and women who cross-dressed as the "opposite" sex. Some chose to stay permanently in their new persona, others made it an occasional thing, a kind of hobby. Some were homosexual, others not. All this was deeply disturbing to fundamentalist Christians still reeling from the emergence of "Gay Pride." For historical and theological reasons, Judaism, Christianity, and Islam all share a dread of category confusion. In the ancient Judaic tradition, from which the others spring, to respect God is to maintain purity, that is, to keep apart things that should not be mixed. In the biblical book of Leviticus, it is forbidden to mix two crops in the same field. Better known are the elaborate food rules that require avoidance of all kinds of categorically dubious animals, those neither "fish nor fowl" nor proper cloven-hoofed domestic beasts like cattle and sheep. In becoming a worldwide religion, Christianity abandoned the dietary rules, but the basic premises of purity remained. The reason why the Catholic Church cannot bring itself to allow married priests is that their celibate state confirms the purity that enables them to consecrate the Eucharist. It has been a dilemma for the church in recent decades that this has encouraged the recruitment of gay priests. Meanwhile, some branches of Islam have propagated severe regimes for the segregation of the sexes.

A moment's reflection will show how bizarre this seems to Atoni and Ngaju people, as well as many others around the world. Even Western medicine is implicated in this Puritanism, since doctors do not allow children who are born hermaphrodite to remain in that condition. It is true that such cases are rare, but they are not *as* rare as you might think. The usual practice is to turn such infants into females, since that is easier surgically. No one would suggest that such children might be "special" and valuable. The Ngaju would react with awe – a child bearing the very marks of divinity could become the most powerful of all *basir*. Indeed, gender bending in the West would seem minimal in places where gender is constantly re-positioned. Where is the American equivalent of the female-man? Perhaps it was a mistake by the framers of the constitution that they did not include such a mediator who could restrain the destructive, cut-throat competition of the two-party system.

THE FACTS OF LIFE

Perhaps gender bending is only a matter of "lifestyle," and surely the basic facts of biological reproduction are not negotiable. Even a familiarity with domestic animals is sufficient to confirm them. But the Trobriand islanders, as described by Malinowski (see Chapter One), flatly deny them. Women get pregnant, the Trobrianders insist, by bathing in the sea. It is in this way that the ancestors, who at death fly away to an island far to the east, swim back to be reborn among the living. This does not mean that young girls are at risk every time they bathe. Clearly the ancestors prefer to be reborn to women who are respectably married, although they do apparently make a mistake from time to time. Malinowski describes a man returning from two years of contract labor on a copra plantation, who showed no surprise or distress when his wife handed him a bouncing new baby. It seems impossible that Trobrianders should fail to connect pregnancy with copulation, but who are we to say what they do and do not believe?

Needless to say, this tenet of Trobriand society does not occur at random. On the contrary, it is closely related to its matrilineal structure (using "structure" in the British sense). A child's social person is overwhelmingly determined by the link through his or her mother to a named matrilineage. Consequently, it is in a real sense true that the father is irrelevant to reproduction. For a Trobriander, your father is simply your mother's husband. There is one way, however, that the father may play a role in literally shaping the child. Regular copulation moulds the body and features of the child *in utero*. Consequently, it is a compliment to remark that a child resembles his or her father. Naturally, the contract laborer could not expect such a satisfying outcome, since he had clearly been neglecting his wife.

If Trobrianders manage perversely to eliminate fathers from conception, at least no one could doubt the mother's part. This was the premise on which a great deal of nineteenth-century theory was based. Clearly, they argued, in conditions of "primitive promiscuity" a child might not know who his or her father was, but there could be no possible doubt about who was the mother. Therefore, in the course of social evolution matrilineality must have preceded patrilineality. From this flawed logic a whole mythology of ancient matriarchies was elaborated, and still circulates in some quarters. In fact, both matrilineality and patrilineality are found in very similar societies, often side by side. Moreover, it is possible to reverse the Trobriand formula. Among the Kachin, a child's social identity comes from the father. Correspondingly, conception is seen as the process of implanting his sperm in the womb, just as rice is sown in the ground. The mother contributes nothing of herself to the child, being merely the vehicle of the man's procreative potential. Not surprisingly, accusations of illegitimacy provide most of the political rhetoric among competing noble Kachin families.

DEATH AND TAXES

One last biological certainty remains. When people repeat the old saw that the only inevitable things in life are death and taxes, they are usually sighing about the necessity to prepare their tax returns. The little joke is that taxes are not really inevitable, and those repeating it know very well that wealthy individuals and corporations that can afford to hire tax lawyers routinely get out of paying them. But death really is certain, and no one would believe an anthropologist who claimed to have discovered a people who thought themselves immortal. Even so, I shall make the claim that death is, in the current jargon, "socially constructed."

To show what this means, let me take an example from the USA. If an elderly man walking down the street suddenly clutches his heart and collapses, passers-by readily diagnose a heart attack. When the ambulance arrives, the paramedics may look for life signs, but will in any case rush him to the nearest emergency room. Arriving there the doctor on call makes a fuller exam, and may declare the patient Dead On Arrival (DOA). Studies in Los Angeles public hospitals show that those declared DOA are almost invariably dirty or shabbily dressed. Men arriving in business suits are almost never declared DOA. Whatever their life signs, or lack of them, an attempt is made to resuscitate them using electric shocks to stimulate the heart, and other procedures. Why all this is so is not hard to figure out. But if death is a biological fact, how can it be that whether someone is dead or not depends on the clothes he's wearing?

In Western medicine, there has been an on-going debate about what constitutes death. Technical advances allow patients seriously injured in car crashes, for instance, to be kept alive with machinery that performs bodily functions for them while they have a chance to recover, even such basic functions as breathing. But in several cases, they have not recovered, but fallen into what is evocatively called a "vegetative" state. In what sense is such a person "alive"? The medical answer is that if any brain function persists, in terms of electrical activity in the cortex, the patient is, if not exactly alive, at least not dead. Only an appeal by relatives, followed by a court order, allows doctors legally to turn off the machines. You will notice how complicated the definition is, and what a large amount of equipment is needed to confirm so ordinary a thing as death. Clearly such quibbles are beyond the resources of most people in Third World countries, but that does not mean that their definitions of death are any less "socially constructed."

PRODUCING ANCESTORS

Many Polynesian languages share a word *mati* that early ethnographers readily translated as "dead." They soon discovered, however, that it was possible for someone, usually a senior man, to be alive and also *mati*. How could this be? Surely his neighbors could see that he was still breathing? The situation came about when a chief ordered his followers to stop feeding him. Such a man could not feed himself, but had to be fed, because of his great *mana*. (Exactly how to translate the concept of *mana* is an ancient conundrum of Polynesian ethnography, but for now I will gloss it as "spiritual power.")

Suicide is known in Polynesia. For instance, a young man caught in a shameful act such as incest with his sister might climb a tall coconut palm and then plunge to his death. The chief's act was not suicide, however, and his motives were usually to defend the prestige of his chiefly line, his ancestors. When the emaciated chief finally "died" he would be given a funeral in accordance with his standing, but he became *mati* at the moment when he issued his order. What comprised death for Polynesians was not the malfunction of the body as machine, but severance from the society of the living.

Elsewhere in the Austronesian world, in Borneo, Sulawesi and Madagascar, death is not seen as an incident at all, but as a process spread out over months or years. Those who have died according to Western medicine are spoken of as having "lost breath" or some such euphemism. After the funeral they are stored temporarily to complete the process of rotting away, so freeing themselves of the bonds of the flesh. This process is not attractive, but it is necessary.

Until the bones are dry, the souls of the recently deceased are volatile and malevolent, liable to kill others in their jealousy of the living. It is only at the end of this transition, often marked with a communal festival, that the dying individual is admitted to the company of the dead. As the mortal remains are stored in a final vault, he or she becomes one of those ancestors who are the principal defenders of the community. The deceased is not dead until all this is finished, and the elaborate rituals constitute a kind of ancestor factory.

RESPONDING TO AFFLICTION

Not only do understandings vary as to what death is, so do the explanations for what brings it about. In many parts of the world, death is never a matter of statistical chances, an unpredictable visit by the Grim Reaper. Except in the case of very old people, it always indicates the machinations of enemies. Such is the case among the Azande of Kenya, as described in another of Evans-Pritchard's celebrated ethnographies. For the Azande, any kind of serious misfortune is caused by the activity of witches. This misfortune could be a serious or persistent illness, or it could be an accident, either of which might cause death. To cover both, anthropologists speak of affliction. The response to affliction among the Azande is first to try to turn it around, so that it bounces back on the sender. If that does not work, professional diviners are summoned to locate the witch, who is then confronted and urged to desist. This is less absurd than it sounds because witchcraft may act without the witch's volition. He or she has inherited the witchcraft substance, which is attached to the liver. Any kind of jealousy or rivalry may activate it. Everyone who is accused remains convinced of their own innocence, but they are equally convinced that there are witches among their neighbors. How else to explain recent deaths? Consequently, they perform the little rites designed to stop the effects of witchcraft, just to show that they are willing to cooperate responsibly. People who are repeatedly accused – usually the socially marginal – are subject to expulsion from the community, or worse.

In many parts of Africa affliction is seen as arising from social tensions, but that does not always imply witchcraft. In Victor

Turner's several ethnographies of the Ndembu of Tanzania, he portrays a society prone to constant disruption. Leaders compete to swell the size of their own villages by drawing people away from neighboring ones. Individuals are tugged this way and that by different kinship obligations, and tensions are bound to arise. Turner describes an entire battery of elaborate rituals designed to restore harmony, each directed to particular kinds of problems. Often they constitute a kind of initiation, so that those who perform the rites are those who have needed them previously. Consequently, Turner calls them "cults of affliction."

CURING SYSTEMS

We might note that Ndembu notions contain more than a little truth. People who are depressed or under stress do indeed have a tendency to grow sick more easily than others, and to suffer longer from whatever illnesses they contract. Consequently, with a slight shift in focus what Turner studied as ritual and religion could equally well be seen as a system of curing, and that would extend our vision outward to all kinds of everyday practices that are less spectacular than the cults of affliction but equally engrained in Ndembu life. Like people elsewhere, the Ndembu make use of all kinds of plants in their environment to provide cures, and some people are a veritable fund of knowledge on the local fauna and flora. As we saw in the previous chapter, ethnoscientists had already noticed this, but not in the context of curing.

Indigenous curing systems are worth pursuing for at least three reasons. First, they are worth study in their own right. They raise all the theoretical questions of belief and rationality that have exercised anthropological studies of religion since the nineteenth century. That is to say, when people seek cures they embrace an understanding of nature in which the "treatments" make sense, whether that means swallowing a potion, or summoning a shaman (see Box 7.3), or choosing from a host of other techniques. It is then for the anthropologist to try to figure out just how they "make sense" to those people, and that raises deep philosophical issues of epistemology, of how things can be known. Moreover, in many places indigenous curing techniques persist and thrive long after conversion to world religions. In many parts of South America, people of Indian descent who are sincere Catholics in their weekly religious observances would not hesitate to consult healers whose practices relate directly to pre-European religions. Consequently healing practices provide a fascinating avenue of exploration into them. Research in this area, under the label medical anthropology, has become a dynamic field in contemporary anthropology.

USEFUL KNOWLEDGE

A second compelling reason to study indigenous curing systems is that they provide useful knowledge. As we noted in the last chapter, an outsider, even a trained botanist, cannot possibly know as much about local biota as local people. He or she must learn from them. By the same token, local people have been conducting experiments, perhaps for centuries, on what helps with what medical conditions. It is a given that ethnographers will respect the knowledge of their informants, but so do international pharmaceutical corporations. For instance, a great number of modern drugs were refined from plants pointed out to scientists by Indian people living in the vast Amazon rainforest, home to one of the largest range of species to be found anywhere on the earth. Perhaps only a third of these species have been described by botanists and zoologists, and the forests stand to provide a cornucopia of useful chemicals – unless of course human beings destroy them first.

In addition, there are long-standing literate traditions of medicine that demand respect. The first Westerners to reach Asia were impressed with the healing arts that they found there, and it was only in the twentieth century that Western medicine gained such prestige as to leave them in the shade. Consequently, when China became accessible again after the Maoist era, American and European doctors scoffed at such techniques as acupuncture. It seemed absurd to imagine that a needle inserted in the right place would allow a patient to undergo surgery painlessly without anesthetic. Nevertheless it did, and demonstrably so. Not many doctors took the logical step of consulting the ancient Chinese texts, however, with their strange diagrams. That would have been difficult for them because the texts presented an entirely different view of the human body to the one they had struggled to master in medical school.

BOX 7.3 SHAMANISM

The word shaman is borrowed from the Tungus languages of Siberia. Shamans are the most powerful people in Tungus society because they have the ability to gain access to spirit realms, while in a self-induced trance. As anthropologists discovered similar kinds of practitioners in other cultures, so the term was extended, and cases are now reported from every continent. Shamans are often curers, and they heal by recovering the lost souls of their patients. To do this they make long and dangerous spirit journeys. While their own souls are away, the shamans' familiars enter their bodies, and that is what the audience witnesses during the trance. Beyond these basic features, there are a thousand different variations on shamanic procedure. Indeed, since his or her own spirits individually inspire each shaman, there are in theory as many styles of shamanism as there are shamans. It follows that shamans cannot be trained; they have to wait for the spirits to seize them. Experienced shamans may, however, assist novices during their first few encounters. It is often the case that people do not want to be shamans because the process of being seized by a spirit is exhausting and dangerous. They are forced into it to relieve the chronic illnesses, often involving emotional disturbance, that are imposed by their spirits. Shamans can be men or women, but worldwide there is a preponderance of women adepts. Note that the plural of shaman is shamans, not shamen.

Indian concepts have had a greater impact on American practice, even though there was no single revelation as dramatic as acupuncture. The great contribution of Indian medicine has been its emphasis on the health of the whole person, rather than treating medical problems in isolation. The latter tendency comes basically from the notion of the body as machine – if the brakes on your car are not working, there is no point fixing the carburetor. In addition, elite status in the medical profession is reserved for specialists, and they are trained to focus on only one type of medical problem. It is often remarked that an experienced GP (general practitioner) is more likely to cure you than a team of specialists. In addition specialists tend always to look to the same kinds of intervention.

Infamously, surgeons recommend surgery, and all doctors prefer a specific pill aimed at specific symptoms. Meanwhile, many conditions, including such life-threatening problems as heart disease, are better treated with diet, supervised exercise, and a changed attitude to life – to the whole person. Never more than today have Westerners needed to hear the message that health is not a matter of first making yourself ill, and then expecting doctors to fix it.

THE REFLEXIVE ROLE OF MEDICAL ANTHROPOLOGY

This last point reveals a third reason to study medicine comparatively. Having approached non-Western traditions of healing as systems of knowledge we are in a better position to look back at Western medicine in its social and cultural contexts. This is a major development in medical anthropology because in the beginning its main role was seen as simply aiding "modern" medicine. The key phrase was "health care delivery," and it expressed an obvious necessity. Throughout the world, there were many people suffering from health problems that Western medicine could cure. This much was clear. Surprisingly, however, people did not always cooperate with their prescribed treatments. It was the job of anthropologists to work out what was getting in the way, and remove the obstacles. This task was of the type then described as "applied anthropology," that is, ethnographic knowledge put to some good use. But the pioneers in medical anthropology soon discovered that things were not so simple. They began to doubt the absolute contrast between rational scientific medicine versus quackery and superstition. On the one hand, the applied role hampered their ability to understand other healing systems in their own right, as they wished to do. On the other, they began to question the transparent rationality of Western medicine.

In fact, these two insights go hand-in-hand. If indigenous healing practices could be studied as belief systems, each supported by specific social institutions and cultural concepts, then why should the same approach not be applied to Western medicine? With this shift, medical anthropology came of age. It made what is called a "reflexive" move, which is to say that medical anthropologists turned the insights gained from studying other people back onto the culture in which they themselves were raised. The results have been fascinating, and we shall return to them in the final chapter. For the moment, one example must suffice. In the nineteenth century, learned practitioners detected a disabling condition of emotional agitation among women that they labeled hysteria. The term soon made its way into everyday language as in the phrase "don't get hysterical," or "she had hysterics." Meanwhile the medical profession accumulated dossiers of confirmed cases, and set about in proper scientific fashion to locate causes. Many techniques of treatment were tried, including some extremely radical ones. At one point it was fashionable to "cure" hysteria by surgically removing the uterus, that is to perform a hysterectomy. What logic was followed here is hard to imagine, other than the shared Latin root *hystericus*, meaning "related to the womb." But in its epoch it passed as reasonable and scientifically valid. Nowadays, there is no medical practitioner who would give it the slightest credence. At this distance in time it seems very clear that the emotional agitation that these women felt was a perfectly reasonable – I am tempted to say "natural" – response to the stultifying narrowness of the lives imposed on many upper-class women.

The point of this narrative is not to deny the value of medicine or science, but to point out that scientists are human beings, as fallible as anyone else. They have their places within particular societies, and they are bound to reflect its preconceptions and prejudices. There is simply no telling how these prejudices might insinuate themselves into scientific work, while the scientist is all the while congratulating himself (or herself, but mostly himself) for his total objectivity. This might occur in even the most abstract science, but it has been particularly obvious in medicine, which is so intimately involved with our own lives and bodies. A comparative approach has the potential to expose such traps, to encourage a proper humility, and so to advance science.

OUR PLACE IN NATURE

In this chapter, I have taken my examples of how cultures construct nature, or rather natures, from our own bodily experiences. Conception, birth, illness, and death really are biological phenomena. All animals undergo them. Nevertheless, as Hertz showed, they are not only biological phenomena. In contrast to other animals – or so we assume – humans seek to place them in some kind of overarching order, within which it is possible to say what birth and death *are*, rather than simply what happens when somebody is born or dies.

There is a great deal more to say on this topic. We have not, for instance, dealt with what non-human species are, in these diverse views of nature. To illustrate where this discussion might go, let me take a few examples from the Amazon basin. Many peoples in the region see themselves as having complex relations with animal species, which replicate their dealings with other human groups. Some animals are related as in-laws, for instance, and hunting them is a kind of marriage exchange in which animals give meat in return for gifts, often things that the animals can in turn use to marry and procreate. In this way the exchange benefits all parties. What is remarkable about this idea is that it mirrors the notion in Western biology of an eco-niche, in which all species are connected together in a constant re-circulation of the materials of life. Contemporary environmentalist activists constantly try to dun this idea into the heads of Westerners who can only see the world in terms of resources to be exploited. If we cannot see ourselves as part of a system that must remain in proper balance, then disaster will follow. Among Amazonian Indians, this modern understanding of the world is already in place, and it is often underlined by another remarkable concept. Other species, it is said, only look like birds and animals to us. That is the appearance they wear for *us*. What they see when they look at their own kind is the human form, just as we do. Moreover, in their societies, hidden from us by feathers and fur, there are chiefs and followers, rituals and rhetoric, just as there are in ours. What we look like to *them* is a mystery. What is plain, however, is that human beings are not unique, the only beings with souls, as we are in the Jewish, Christian and Muslim view. Instead of being alone in Creation, we are part of an expanding family of beings with whom we would do well to maintain proper relationships.

REFINING THE CULTURE CONCEPT

A final word on the cultural construction of nature. When the influential Chicago anthropologist David Schneider set about studying American kinship, he turned away from the classic British

approach. As described in Chapter Three, the study of social structure meant describing statuses and the roles that went with them.
So the questions were framed in this way: among such-and-such a
people, what are the rights that a father has over his children, and
what are his responsibilities? These questions are repeated for all
the other kinship statuses, mother, aunt, uncle, and so on. Schneider
asked white, middle-class Americans similar questions, but not
surprisingly he found their answers predictable and boring. So
instead he asked informants to explain what kinship is, that is, what
it was that knits people together in the deep bonds of family. What
he found was an indigenous theory of "blood," as in the mysterious
maxim: "blood is thicker than water." This revision of kinship
theory paralleled shifts in emphasis elsewhere in anthropology, as
illustrated throughout this chapter. The effect was to move interest
away from social structure and towards what is sometimes called
"worldview," that is a people's fundamental perceptions of the
world and their place in it.

These developments refocused attention on the concept of
culture that was the mainspring of American anthropology. As we
have seen, it had always been a broad concept, accommodating to a
wide range of interests. Schneider's proposal was to bring more
focus to the concept by specifically excluding from it everything to
do with status and role, that is, all the collective representations
bearing on interpersonal relations. You will notice that this makes
necessary a revision of the definition of culture given in Chapter
One, because the rules of proper behavior clearly are among those
things learned at the mother's knee. Nevertheless, it is in
Schneider's sense that most anthropologists now use the term, and
towards it that they direct their research. The only terminological
adjustment necessary is that social and cultural anthropology
become different things – though still complementary – rather than
the former being a component of the latter.

Summary
In the last chapter, we saw that human language was both natural and
cultural: found everywhere, but everywhere different. Hertz's classic
essay (original 1909) extends that argument from language to
symbolism. To remark that human beings, being bipedal, have two

hands, is trivial but significant. If we had three arms, or three eyes, we would certainly "see" the world differently. But there is another biologically determined feature: in all human populations, it seems, there is a preponderance of right-handed people. If that were not so, we would not find that the "right" is everywhere given preference over the left, a preference "embodied" in language. But from this slight asymmetry, cultural meanings expand in every direction, involving things that have no logical connection with laterality at all, such as male and female, good and evil, sun and fire, or deep sea and shallow sea. In this way, symbolic universes are built up that are as diverse as languages.

Sex and gender are particularly interesting examples, since no culture can fail to invest them with meaning. Gender may be extended to things that have no sex, such as sun and moon. But even sex itself has to be constructed. Are men and women so inherently different that they should be kept rigidly apart? Or is that absurd, since sexuality appears and disappears, or reverses itself, in all manner of different social contexts? Would it in fact be calamitous to try to separate what only makes sense as one? Again, childbirth is surely a biological fact, the same for animals. But that does not remove the necessity for humans to construe its meaning. The issue of what exactly has been reproduced, and how, is answered very differently in different parts of the world. Finally, that most human of conditions, our common mortality, is dealt with and understood in remarkably varied ways.

What we conclude is that, paradoxically, nature is culturally constructed. This finding has consequences for all of anthropology. For instance, in the expanding field of medical anthropology there is more to do than facilitate the delivery of Western medicine to Third World countries. Indigenous medical systems are worth study in their own right, and they also cause us to look back at Western medicine to see what cultural assumptions have been unthinkingly incorporated in it. Meanwhile, the general impact of the finding has been to sharpen our notion of culture. Its crucial dimension is how people understand the things that make up the world they live in. The goal of understanding culture in these terms provides the modern understanding of "cultural relativism." It is more profound than the relativism of British social anthropologists of the 1940's and 1950's, as described in Chapter Four.

FURTHER READING

Hertz's essay is reprinted in translation in *Right and Left: Essays in Dual Symbolic Classification* (1973), edited by Rodney Needham. The same volume contains the article on "Order in the Atoni House," by Clark Cunningham, that provides the details quoted here. There is now a large literature in anthropology on the issues of sex, gender and reproduction. A good starting point is *Nature, Culture, and Gender* (1980), edited by Carol MacCormack and Marilyn Strathern. Another interesting collection edited by Strathern is *Dealing with Inequality: Analysing Gender Relations in Melanesia and Beyond* (1987). For an account of the diversity of death rites and their meanings see Metcalf and Huntington *Celebrations of Death* (1991). The concept of "affliction" is laid out in Victor Turner's *The Drums of Affliction* (1968). Turner also played a major part in developing what became known as "symbolic anthropology." For a statement of his ideas see *The Forest of Symbols* (1967). An overview of medical anthropology is provided in *Medical Anthropology: A Handbook of Theory and Method* (1990), edited by T. Johnson and C. Sargent. For a theoretical discussion see Byron Good's *Medicine, Rationality, and Experience* (1994). The cultural perception of animals is discussed in several essays in *Nature and Society* (1996), edited by Philippe Descola and Gisli Palsson. Finally, David Schneider's more focused notion of culture is explained in his widely influential study *American Kinship* (1968).

8

THE END OF THE TRIBES

When graduate students in anthropology tell friends and relatives what they are studying, they often get a skeptical response, along the following lines: "surely, there isn't much call for that anymore. Aren't the tribes just about all gone by now?" It is a question that is hard to answer briefly. On the one hand, no one contests that there are very few people left anywhere, even in the deepest jungles and most remote mountains, who are self-sufficient, beyond the reach of the global economy, and unaware of the outside world. On the other hand, humans continue to display a strong tendency to fragment into different cultures and sub-cultures in the face of universalizing forces. Though re-orientation has been needed, anthropology shows no sign of running out of material to study. On the contrary, it has learned to thrive in new environments. To explain how that occurred let us go back to the beginning.

SAVAGES AND BARBARIANS

In the nineteenth century, when anthropology emerged as a named discipline, it was inspired by the vast accumulation of travel literature over the previous centuries of European expansion. It told of glittering civilizations, like the China of the Great Khan, and wild peoples who knew nothing of agriculture or iron. This was so striking that it raised urgent questions. How could such diversity exist side-by-side? What did it mean? The answer that the first generation of anthropologists provided came directly from the dominant mode of thinking of the nineteenth century: evolutionism. Its great apparatus was the Comparative Method, which made use precisely of cultural diversity to reconstruct the entire history of mankind. For nineteenth-century anthropologists, the simplest peoples were the most fascinating because they gave evidence of the most remote epochs – a veritable time machine.

In this framework, it is clear why anthropology was concerned with people who were "tribal," in the sense of living beyond the borders of civilization. This is still the general impression of what anthropology is about, and that is largely because of the tremendous public interest stirred up by the evolutionary anthropologists. They also bequeathed a technical lexicon that is still with us. The three great stages of human technical advancement they proposed were: savagery, barbarism, and civilization, and examples of each still existed. When the first European explorers entered the Pacific they encountered people who had no knowledge of iron. Their tools were made only of stone and shell, and other materials available in their island habitats. Consequently, Cook, Tasman, Bougainville and others literally sailed into the Stone Age, and the drama of their adventures echoed around Europe. The Pacific islanders were by definition "savages," but that was not meant to imply that they lived like wild beasts. On the contrary, a notion came back to Europe of island paradises, where food literally dropped from the trees, leaving healthy, clean-limbed people to engage freely in the arts of love. To this day, you can make an Englishman's eyes go dreamy just by mentioning "the South Seas." The Latin root of the word savage does not in fact imply "violent," as we now normally use it, but the more sympathetic notion of simplicity and wildness, and those were characteristics that many Europeans admired.

As for "barbarian," that was taken from the term Romans used to describe the Germanic tribes that they encountered north of the Alps. These people had beautifully made iron tools, often superior to Roman ones. What they lacked militarily was the central organization and practiced discipline of the legions. They had chiefs certainly, who could temporarily mobilize an army of warriors. But they had no on-going organization that justified the title of "civilization." In the nineteenth century the fateful decision was made to associate civilization with writing – key, it was thought, to rational organization. In addition, however, the writing had to employ phonetic scripts. That excluded ways of writing using signs for concepts rather than noises. The effect, indeed the intention, was to put the urban complexes of Central America, and the trading states of central and Eastern Africa, outside civilization.

TABU WORDS

To sum up, nineteenth-century anthropology left us with a vocabulary that has made its way into everyday English, but is carefully avoided by most anthropologists. In the twenty-first century it will not do to describe people as savages or barbarians. First of all, those people are nowadays likely to read what you have to say about them, and will not appreciate these labels, whatever technical spin you try to put on them. They are plainly derogatory. Secondly, to use any of the vocabulary of social evolutionism is to become trapped in its mode of thinking. Lumping together peoples from all over the globe under one term implies that they have something important in common, that they share the same stage of development. But this obscures more than it reveals. Differences far outweigh any single shared trait. Indeed the possession of iron may reveal nothing more fundamental than having iron-using neighbors. That the people of Hawai'i and Tahiti lacked iron hardly negates the splendor of their cultures. The term "primitive" must likewise be abandoned. It can have a harmless meaning, and we sometimes circumlocute it by saying "small scale, technologically simple societies." But there is no way to salvage a word that is now thoroughly pejorative. Oddly enough, we have also to stop talking about "modern" societies, unless that means all contemporary societies. There are none somehow stuck in time. (We can, however, speak of "modernization" without ambiguity.) "Civilization" is a word we can hardly avoid. The best we can do is to abandon any technical definition, and use it in the broad sense in which it occurs in everyday speech.

Finally, even the word at the head of this chapter, "tribes," is normally too loaded to be useful. It is still sometimes employed to mean people with mid-range social organization – having chiefs but not kings – but the nineteenth-century overtones persist. Consequently, one simple answer to what happened to the tribes is that we stopped calling them that. If that seems trivial, try imagining how condescending it sounds to an American Indian or an Australian Aborigine to be asked to name his or her tribe. It is always the *other* people that have tribes, not *us*.

STUDYING "SIMPLE" SOCIETIES

In the twentieth century mainstream anthropology abandoned the framework of social evolutionism, but remained fixated on remote places. As anthropologists began to undertake first-hand research, they went off to far corners of the world. There were at least two reasons for this:

First, it was argued that simpler societies revealed fundamental features that were hidden in more complex ones. In the British terminology, there were far fewer important social statuses, so that they could reasonably be studied in their entirety. By contrast, it would take whole teams of sociologists, with armies of interviewers, to even begin to describe the salient roles of an industrialized society. By the mid-twentieth century this was a reasonable distinction. In contrast to sociologists, anthropologists worked alone in uncomfortable conditions, or at least ones lacking urban facilities. It soon became obvious, however, that the distinction would not hold up for long. Anthropologists were soon working in African cities because, even in the 1950's, villagers were migrating there in ever increasing numbers. In addition, the societies that had seemed "simple" at first glance turned out to be not so simple when studied in depth. The classic example of this was the Australian Aborigines, who had been treated in the nineteenth century as a kind of base line of primitiveness. But as study of Aborigine culture deepened, an amazing complexity was revealed in such things as kinship and ritual. For a scholar to become expert in them is now the work of a lifetime, and many mysteries remain. Not surprisingly, given their historical experience of repression, those Aborigine peoples who retain something of their indigenous religions are very careful about what they reveal, and to whom.

ANTHROPOLOGY'S ACHIEVEMENT

There was a second and more compelling reason to seek out peoples relatively remote from industrial societies. Whether simple or otherwise, they were likely to be the most different, both from the West, and from each other. That is to say, they provided evidence of the extremes of human cultural diversity, and consequently of the plasticity of human "nature." Aside from any of the strategies of social evolutionism, that remained an important goal, one that inspired ethnographers throughout the twentieth century. It was apparent that if the job was to be done, it needed to be done soon. When Boas set about recording the myths and rituals of northwest coast American Indians, he was very clear about the urgency of his task. Analysis and theorizing could come later. At different times in different places, in Oceania and Africa and elsewhere, the same urgency became apparent, as historical circumstances conspired to bring indigenous cultures to the brink of extinction.

There were ludicrous aspects to this hunt for the disappearing exotic. Sometimes it took on an air of prospecting. The most extreme case occurred in the New Guinea highlands, which were only "pacified" in the mid-twentieth century, between, say, 1930 and 1960. As we noted in Chapter Five, anthropologists tended to follow closely behind the colonial advance, and there was a gold-rush atmosphere as would-be ethnographers staked out their claims. As more arrived, ethnic groups that had already received attention were found, luckily, to comprise several sub-ethnicities each deserving documentation.

Nevertheless – and I need to say this very plainly – the enterprise was a noble one. The worldwide ethnographic record that was produced in the twentieth century stands as an amazing historical archive. Much of what is to be found there can never again be observed. Scholars will be studying it for centuries to come, and future generations will turn to it with wonderment.

THE FATE OF INDIGENOUS MINORITIES

Having said this, we have many issues to untangle. First of all, to talk of cultures coming to the brink of extinction is not at all the same as a people suffering the same fate. There have indeed been cases where it *was* the same thing. Infamously, the Aborigine population of the island of Tasmania, south of Australia, was hunted to extinction in a direct policy of genocide. The most striking example in all of history is, however, the wholesale destruction of American Indian peoples in the centuries after first contact by Westerners. By some estimates, the indigenous population of the Americas, North and South, was reduced by 90% in those centuries – a vast human calamity. Most of the death toll was caused by the sudden introduction of diseases to which Indians had no resistance. For the most part this was unintentional, though there were cases where settlers deliberately infected local Indians with smallpox by giving them infected clothes. In South America, untold numbers of Indians were worked to death in the silver mines of Peru, which provided the wealth of Spain during the seventeenth and eighteenth centuries.

At a later date, Indians were subjected to direct attempts to extinguish their cultures, what we might call "ethnocide." Indian children were forcibly removed from their homes and put into schools where they were forbidden to speak their own languages, and subjected to a strict Christian upbringing. The promoters of these schemes saw themselves as acting in the Indians' own best interests. Clearly they were sinking deeper and deeper into lethargy and poverty on the reservations. To have any hope of improving their lot, they needed to make a clean break with the past and work for assimilation into the white community. The same approach was tried in Australia, and left the same legacy of bitterness.

INDIGENOUS RESILIENCE

To such cultural repression the Maori people of New Zealand have a simple response. Assimilation, they remark, is what the shark said to the fish. Early in the twentieth century it looked as if the Maori were dying out. In the dispiriting period after their defeat in colonial wars, fertility rates plummeted. Missionaries spoke of "smoothing the pillow of a dying race." But Maori people responded by founding their own churches and seeking their own political representation. In the second half of the twentieth century, the Maori population began to recover, and is now growing at a rapid rate. If current demographic trends continue, New Zealand will in a few decades once again have a majority Polynesian population. Along with this has come a new confidence. Much of Maori tradition is gone, in the sense that it cannot be made relevant to the lives of young Maori. The Maori language itself remains threatened, even in country areas. Nevertheless, many Maori have retained or revived connections with their home communities, and community festivals routinely welcome guests from far and wide. Most importantly, urban, English-speaking Maoris are working out new ways to express their cultural distinctiveness.

BOX 8.1 THE MAORI WARS

The first Europeans to stay any length of time in New Zealand were from whaling ships stopping for repairs and supplies. The whaling bases soon gained a reputation for lawlessness and debauchery, and mission organizations encouraged the British government to establish order there. In 1840 a treaty was signed at Waitangi between British representatives and a number of Maori chiefs in the Bay of Islands region in the north. One of these, Hongi Hika, was invited to England to meet Queen Victoria, and took the opportunity to equip himself with a large number of muskets. When he got back to New Zealand he wreaked havoc on the Maori tribes to the south. By depopulating whole regions, he opened the way for the first English settlers. As their numbers increased, pressure grew for more land to be annexed, even though the rights of the Maori to their land had been guaranteed in the treaty of Waitangi. In 1858, the Maori elected a king from among their chiefs, and adopted a general policy of not selling land to the settlers. The policy and its breaches caused anger on both sides, and war broke out in 1860. The fighting was not as unequal as in other colonial possessions. The Maori had a strong warrior tradition, and they had learned the lesson that Hongi Hika had taught them. Even regular troops from Britain found it difficult to dislodge the well-armed Maori from their strongholds in the middle of the north island. The first war ended in truce, but the causes of friction had not been removed, and fighting soon broke out again. The settlers then recruited their own forces, promising rewards to those who served from confiscated Maori land. After organized Maori resistance collapsed, a bitter guerrilla war dragged on until 1872, when resistance finally ceased. After the wars Maori still retained considerable amounts of land, but claims to alienated land remain a hot political issue to this day.

This trend is not unique to New Zealand. Sadly, it is too late for the Tasmanians, but not for Aborigines on the mainland, or for American Indians. In many parts of the world where indigenous minorities once seemed all but gone, they are bouncing back vigorously, both in terms of population and cultural assertiveness.

INVERTING THE PROPOSITION: *PLUS ÇA CHANGE*

This hopeful news brings us to another persistent anthropological theme, one that parallels and inverts that of cultural loss. Time and again, ethnographers have been impressed by the way that people somehow manage to go on being themselves in the midst of the most tempestuous circumstances. To those who are familiar with it, Maoriness seems immediately recognizable, whether found in town or country, or indeed abroad. If you think about the ethnicities that are familiar to you, no doubt you will be able to say the same thing. But what exactly is it that is always "the same"? In many ways, anthropological theory is an attempt to capture what it is that is so basic in a culture that it can survive all kinds of drastic changes. British ethnographers of the 1950's saw it in interpersonal behavior, including the appropriate body postures, gestures, and conversational modes that children learned at a young age, and practiced all their lives. Lévi-Strauss saw it in terms of unconscious structures, which were subject to all kinds of disruptive historical events, but often managed to put themselves back together again afterwards. The American notion of culture is broad enough to have several answers, or perhaps too vague to have any. Schneider's refined version of the concept, however, points clearly to the kinds of perceptions of the world that we saw in the last chapter.

Between the two great themes of cultural loss and cultural persistence, contemporary anthropologists must pick their way with care. We feel vindicated when we find cultural continuity. A cynical observer once characterized the convoluted history of nineteenth-century France as *plus ça change, plus c'est la même chose*, "the more things change, the more they stay the same." He meant that the same cliques seemed always to be in power, but he was also remarking on the famous resilience of French culture. At the same time, change, real change, is everywhere about us in the modern world. In order to keep their methods relevant to that world, anthropologists will have to be enterprising and innovative.

MARX AND MODERNITY

Meanwhile, Karl Marx was already theorizing about the forces of modernization in the nineteenth century. He also saw a world around him that was seething with change, after the massive technological innovations of the Industrial Revolution. The most dramatic of those changes were then occurring in Europe itself, where ancient rural communities, each with its own folklore and traditions, were being torn apart by a new kind of industrial farming. Agricultural production was organized around "rational" economic criteria, while millions of "inefficient" subsistence farmers were forced off the land into the abysmal slums that surrounded factory towns. At the same time an ever-expanding European imperialism was creating new markets to soak up the surplus production of the same factories. It was Marx's genius to see that the entire world was caught up in the same processes of modernization.

The irony is that Marx was in many ways an orthodox social evolutionist. He was a strong proponent of technological progress, in which he saw the future liberation of humanity from the grinding struggle to satisfy material needs. He also had a schema of development through successive stages of evolution, beginning with a kind of primitive communism, in which people were egalitarian but materially poor, passing through stages of exploitation under feudalism and then capitalism, and finally emerging into socialism, from which in time could grow a communism in which people would once again enjoy egalitarian relations but now enriched by the amazing productivity of industrialization.

There was, however, an important difference between Marx and other evolutionists: he did not trap himself in any kind of explicit or implicit racial determinism. The road that he saw was open to anyone and everyone, and he would have laughed to scorn the claim that those who had seized hold of the means of production under capitalism were somehow inherently superior.

WORLD ECONOMIES

Not surprisingly, there have always been anthropologists who were attracted to Marx, and over the years they have made an important contribution to the discipline by repeatedly criticizing mainstream theorizing. That this continues to be the case may seem strange. After all, communism has been virtually abandoned by all those countries that used to advocate it. The Soviet Union is gone; China looks more and more capitalist every day. Third World countries that used to see socialism as their way of breaking the colonial grip on their economies have quietly dropped it. It is only academics, it seems, who still take Marx seriously. Are they so far behind the times? The answer is simple: Marx was the first theorist to see the global economy in its entirety, and he devised much of our basic vocabulary. On these topics it would be as impossible to ignore Marx, as it would be to ignore Freud in psychiatry.

This brings us back to the issue of the disappearing tribes. At the beginning of this chapter I characterized the sort of thing that people have in mind when they say "tribe" as follows: self-sufficient, beyond the reach of the global economy, and unaware of the outside world. What Marx would respond is that throughout history very few peoples have ever fitted this description, and that the process of drawing peoples into broader economic formations has been going on for millennia – certainly since long before anthropologists came on the scene. In recent decades, anthropologists have tried to put this insight to work in understanding cultural variation. In the process they have drawn on the terminology of the Marxist historian Immanuel Wallerstein. His key term is "world economy" and what he means by that is not an economy that includes the whole world, but instead one that creates a world of its own, whether large or small. By way of illustration, consider an island that lies at the center of the Southeast Asian archipelago.

WILD MEN AND BEZOAR STONES

At the beginning of the twentieth century Borneo had the reputation of being one of the wildest places on earth, a vast island (bigger than France or Texas) covered with dense rainforest, and inhabited by fierce headhunters. At that time it drew the attention of explorers from all the major European countries. But in the 1920's Borneo was suddenly upstaged by New Guinea. The first flights over the island revealed that the high mountains, previously thought empty, had dense populations of uncontacted stone-age people. Thereafter Borneo became a sideshow – literally. When the American showman P.T. Barnum "discovered" in Minnesota a pair of strong but mentally retarded dwarves, he immediately seized on a stage name to promote their act: "The Wild Men of Borneo." With such a reputation, nowhere, one might imagine, is more likely than Borneo to contain the primitive tribes of the popular imagination.

Needless to say, the truth is very different, and far more inter-esting. Interior Borneo has for a thousand years been part of a world economy that stretched from Cairo to Canton. That is to say, trade in rare and valuable jungle products drew on commodities from all over the island, even the far interior. The nature of these products seems nowadays unbelievably exotic, but they were for centuries items in high demand in China. Many had medicinal uses, and the first European traders to arrive in the seventeenth century were only too happy to tap into these profitable markets. A couple of examples will make the point. Bezoar is made from the kidney stones of monkeys. In Chinese medicine it was renowned as an antidote to poisons of all kinds, and was so valuable that it was used as tribute to the Emperor. Meanwhile, monkeys suffering from kidney stones are about as common, or rare, as humans with the same problem. No one found it profitable to go hunting monkeys for the occasional bezoar stone, but monkeys are frequently killed, using a blow gun dart tipped with poison, both for meat and to stop them damaging crops. Every time a monkey was shot it was checked for stones, and any lucky finds were gradually traded down river to the coast. Again, aloes is a resinous substance sometimes found in diseased trees of the genus *Aquilaria*. It provided the most prestigious form of incense in China, and was always in high demand. People who stumbled on such a tree in the forest promptly stopped to inspect for aloes. Whatever they found was carefully hoarded until an opportunity arose to exchange it downriver.

BEADS AND BRASSWARE

Arriving at the coast, these products were traded to ships' captains who came from coastal cities all over Southeast Asia, cities that were also connected by Indian shipping and Arab dhows to places as far away as Cairo. When European ships arrived, the key port for Borneo products was Canton in southern China. In earlier centuries, however, the links to India had been more frequent. Indeed, the oldest Hindu monuments in Southeast Asia are found in Borneo. Sanskrit words occur in most indigenous languages, especially in connection with religion.

This then was the world economy of which Borneo was a link, if only a small one, and it shaped the entire history of its people. To see the impact of ancient trade it is only necessary to look at the valuables traded upriver in exchange for jungle produce. The most sought after items in the interior were beads, brassware, and porcelain jars. The only jars valuable enough to be traded over long distances came of course from China, famous for centuries for its fine ceramics. Beads are hard to track, but it seems that most of them were made by Indian craftsmen, either in India itself or at production sites set up in the archipelago. A few, however, came from as far away as Venice. Finally, the brassware that made its way upriver – cannon, elaborately decorated trays and containers – was produced in the Islamic states that grew up around the coast, especially in Brunei.

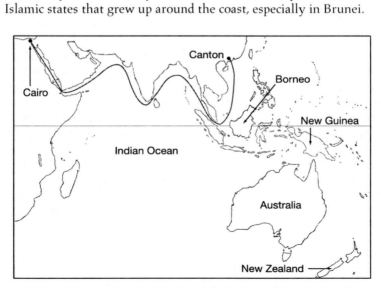

Figure 8.1 Map showing the Asian global economy in relation to Borneo. Also showing New Guinea, Australia and New Zealand

Note that the nature of this exchange still characterizes Third World trade with the First: raw materials for manufactured goods. The difference is of course that the volume of products being moved about in the pre-modern era was tiny. Even so, the significance of this trade cannot be overstated. The valuables that went upriver were the very mark of elite status. Moreover, it was the elite who organized trade, and kept the bulk of the profits from it. In turn, they needed lots of followers in order to hope to accumulate any reasonable stocks of the most valuable jungle produce, but clearly they could not afford to support workers to do the job. These requirements underlie the characteristic form of communities in central Borneo: longhouses containing hundreds of people under one roof; inhabitants engaged in subsistence farming by cutting new clearings in the forest each year; and every community having its leaders, who gave themselves considerable aristocratic airs.

WORLDS WORLDWIDE

The twentieth century saw the emergence of something new in world economies, something that is called, somewhat redundantly, the global world economy. For brevity, I will say simply global economy. But before we consider that, let us glance rapidly at pre-modern trading systems in other parts of the world where "tribes" are supposed to be found. In the nineteenth century, the whole vast area of sub-Saharan Africa was viewed in much the same way as interior Borneo. It did not take long to discover that it contained savannah as well as forest, and also substantial kingdoms with ancient pedigrees. It took longer for scholars to be convinced that elaborate trading systems connected people over wide areas. The best known is the one in East Africa that for centuries connected inland kingdoms like Zimbabwe to the coast, and from there to Arabia. Along these routes flowed, amongst other things, the iron tools which are essential to African agriculture.

In the New World and Oceania there may have been no iron, but plenty of other things were circulating. Archeological finds make it clear that maritime products such as necklaces made out of seashells made their way into the center of North America. To communicate between different language areas, Indians worked out sign languages that were widely known and used. The early ethnographer Lewis Henry Morgan was so struck by them that he theorized that such codes were the origin of language. Turning to New Guinea, the first ethnographers were fascinated by ritualized systems of exchange that connected people over wide areas. In the archipelago on the western end of the island was the famous *kula* ring, described in Malinowski's *Argonauts of the Western Pacific*. In the highlands, pigs and shell valuables were exchanged in a series of great feasts that brought together neighbors from adjacent valleys, even hostile neighbors, all dressed in their finery. Wily old men speculated on exchanges, and gained prestige when their investments paid off, like so many Wall Street brokers. As for the islands of the Pacific, they were settled by people who were surely among the most intrepid and persistent explorers in history. Their sailing and navigating skills amazed the first Europeans who met them. Even the Tikopians, who we met in Chapter Three, though living in about as remote a place as can be imagined, still remembered their migrations, and still made trading voyages to islands hundreds of miles away.

In sum, there has been a marked tendency to underestimate the mobility of "tribal" peoples, the range of their contacts with the "outside" world, and their sophistication. No doubt the global economy intrudes ever more forcefully on the lives of people everywhere, but it is important to note that these circumstances constitute an intensification of processes long at work, and not something utterly unprecedented. It is for this reason that we need not expect the world to somehow become culturally homogeneous, simply because we are all watching the same sitcoms.

THE BOUNDEDNESS OF CULTURES

This perspective frees us from the notion that anthropologists are doomed to go on hunting for lost tribes in rapidly diminishing rainforests. Instead what we have to deal with is people in various degrees of self-sufficiency, integration in the global economy, and innocence about the outside world, both now and in the past. However, it introduces a whole range of new problems – not new in the sense that anthropologists never noticed them before, but newly pressing in the face of the global economy.

The issue is this: if we are to pay attention to connections that draw peoples together, how can we simultaneously see them as separate societies and cultures? And if we cannot do that, where is the subject matter of social and cultural anthropology? If this statement of the problem seems overly dramatic, let us take it a step at a time. Firth had no problems speaking of Tikopian society, since it was so neatly bounded. That allowed him also to speak of Tikopian culture, religion, and so on. As we saw in Chapter Three, even in this case there were necessary caveats: by the time Firth arrived a substantial number of Tikopians were Christian. Nevertheless, Tikopia approximates the popular ideal of the tribe. If we turn now to interior Borneo, the obvious thing to do is treat every longhouse as a little island in a sea of jungle, especially as the populations of some longhouses approach that of the whole of Tikopia. Moreover, longhouses have exactly that feel about them. But longhouses always had important interconnections of marriage and alliance, not to mention the trade in jungle produce described above. So, when an ethnographer picks one longhouse in which to conduct research by participant observation, as described in Chapter One, the premise surely is that the results will tell something about a larger population. But how large a population? Are there not tribes to which individual communities belong? Now this is where the fun begins. Ever since the beginning of the colonial era, foreigners have been struggling to make maps of where the different tribes live. Their efforts have been a failure because interior people do not sit still the way self-respecting tribes are supposed to do. Instead they fragment and migrate in different directions. In their new homes they make alliances with their neighbors and exchange all kinds of cultural items, everything from vocabulary to rituals, to the point where they resemble their neighbors more than their supposed co-tribesmen. In this situation Westerners usually have recourse to language: one language, one nation. But all the languages of the region are Austronesian, and closely related. So which can be treated as "mere" dialects, and which are "real" languages? To further complicate matters, many longhouse communities incorporate minorities with different backgrounds, so that not even a single longhouse can be relied on to share the same language. The result is that the closer you look, the more "tribes" you find. How then to delineate particular "cultures"?

THE CULTURIST ILLUSION

You will note that my example from Borneo, which could be replicated in other parts of the world, has nothing to do with current political turmoil or the ever-tightening grip of the global economy. When we include them in, things of course get even more complicated. But first let us pause to note the implications of what we have seen so far.

In recent decades, a forceful critique has been made of the whole concept of culture, on the grounds that it imposes an unreal uniformity on whole populations. This in turn produces a politically conservative vision of the world, in which everyone has their own little culture, which they share with those around them. Everyone feels cozily at home, provided no political activists come along to disturb them with radical ideas. The most commonly cited example of this view comes from the American anthropologist Clifford Geertz, whose writings were widely influential in the 1970's. One of Geertz's famous maxims was that cultures are to be treated as texts. He was of course extending a metaphor – yet another to add to our collection – of cultural things as like books to be "read" by the savant. But as always, metaphors can easily lead us astray. Cultures do not come neatly bound between two covers, nor does one author write them.

Parenthetically, we must pause to note that the British notion of function is even more damned by this critique, to the point where it becomes useless. Institutions can only prop each other up if they are all working together in a neatly bounded "structure." Oddly enough, however, the underlying British concept of "society" is not implicated. It consists of links between people, links that can extend outward without any logical termination. Indeed, a social description of interior Borneo could be managed, provided we did not once again get caught up in naming tribes. It might for instance take the form of a description of pre-modern trading networks.

MARXISTS, POSTMODERNISTS, AND SEAMSTRESSES

The critique of the culture concept comes from two different viewpoints, which differ from one another on just about every other issue. I shall characterize them as Marxist on the one hand, and postmodern on the other, although neither represents a unified school of thought. To illustrate the difference, let's take another example where it is not easy to apply the concept of culture, but this time from a situation characteristic of the latest phase of development in the global economy. If you have ever looked at the labels in your clothes, you will have noticed that they are mostly made outside Europe and America, often in Indonesia, Malaysia, Sri Lanka, or China. On the island of Mauritius in the southern Indian Ocean, huge garment factories have been established. Since the local population is small and unwilling to do the repetitive work of sewing, young women are brought from India under contract to do the work. They are housed in dormitories, where they are strictly supervised, supposedly to preserve their reputation for when they go home to get married with the dowry they earned themselves. In this way, a few years' work holds the promise of an improved life back in India.

So now the question is to what culture these young women belong. Certainly they are all Indian nationals, but how important is that given the enormous internal diversity of India's population? Are their primary loyalties then to their caste or ethnicity back home? If so, they are surely straining the links by being away for so long alone. Is it really likely that when they get back they will slide neatly into their old cultural niche without a ripple? What if their fathers decide they will pocket the young women's earnings, won't they then put up a most untraditional fight? Meanwhile, they can hardly be called Mauritians, even on a temporary basis, since their contacts with local people are limited by the long hours they work and their segregated living arrangement. So then the final question: do these young women somehow create a culture of their own? What could it comprise, and how would we know it was there? They are, after all, not learning it "at their mother's knee," to repeat the definition offered in Chapter One.

FIRST ALTERNATIVE: CLASS-CONSCIOUSNESS

What a Marxist would immediately see in this situation is that capitalists have invented yet another way to exploit the workers, skimming off the enormous profits of selling clothes in Europe and

America while paying their laborers a pittance. All over the Third World, corporations prefer the labor of young women because they are docile. Their eyes are on their individual chances of a successful marriage, and they are not about to wreck them by making trouble. Unionizing such workers is nearly hopeless, especially as the women are supervised so that no "trouble makers" can get in. Young women also have good eyes and nimble fingers, just what is needed not only for sewing but also for such tasks as assembling computers. Finally, the employers never have to worry about old workers or pensions or anything of that kind, because the women take care of that themselves, leaving space for new recruits. As for the government of Mauritius, they play along because they are cut in on the profits. Corruption aside, this provides the only income that they have in this dog-eat-dog world with which to improve the lives of their own people. Having made this extremely damaging critique of the global economy, what, in Marx's famous clarion call, is to be done? The answer of classical Marxism is that only an emerging class-consciousness can save the workers. They have to ignore or overcome those things that make them different – their cultures – and come together in a common worldwide struggle against their oppressors.

SECOND ALTERNATIVE: DISJUNCTURE, INCOHERENCE, PASTICHE

This proposition postmodernists regard with contempt. To them it is obvious that Indian seamstresses in Mauritius are simply another example of the condition that assails all of us in this epoch. We are creatures of a mass consumption society in which any sense of identity that may once have been provided by the "tribes" is long since gone. Every seamstress in Mauritius has her CD player, and she listens to Ravi Shankar and Elvis Presley one after the other. Perhaps she dreams of somehow meeting an American, one of the bosses perhaps, and going to America. Or maybe she stumbles on to West African club music, and cultivates that as her personal taste. The inescapable point is that her sense of self floats around amid whatever signifiers the global economy presents to her, and she is permanently alienated from the communal cultures of her homeland. But everyone in the West has already gone through this process. Despite our struggles and affectations, we add up to nothing more than the labels in our clothes and the fantasies presented to us in television commercials. Everything – love, family, the companionship of friends – starts to seem inadequate if it does not resemble the images presented in the media. Identity disappears into a sea of anxiety, narcissism, and schizophrenia.

Having heard this chilling portrayal of our lives, it is difficult to escape it. Once you begin to take notice, it is obvious that we are bombarded by messages telling us what to be and what to buy so we can be seen by others as being that thing. Is there any possibility of opposing this vision of disjuncture (unconnectedness), incoherence (senselessness), and pastiche (images made from random bits and pieces), using the homely and now antiquated notion of "culture"?

A POINT OF AGREEMENT: CULTURE VS. CULTURAL

As a first move, let us note that the adjectival form is still secure. Even if bounding cultures is a tricky business, no one is about to deny that what governs our behavior and our understanding most of the time are things learned, primarily as a child but also later in life. That is, cultural things. Marx did not use the word culture, since it was only available to him in the sense of "high" culture, as in a "cultured" person. But he did of course make space for things learned, under the category of "ideology." In his sense, ideology meant the ideas circulated within an economic formation – feudalism, capitalism – that masked the real nature of class exploitation, whether of peasants or proletarians. So, for instance, organized religion was, in his famous phrase, "the opium of the masses." As Hertz also pointed out, those on top always propagate the notion that they are "naturally" superior.

Postmodernists would take an even stronger position. Skeptical of all Western positivism, they would reject the claims of science, or of Marx's science of society, to uncover fundamental truths that underlie the surface of everyday reality. Science is for them no better and no worse than Christian tent revivalism. Consequently, there is nothing *else* but cultural things, and no reality beyond them.

RESOLUTION: FINDING CULTURAL NICHES

This point of agreement among diverse rhetorics indicates not less work for anthropology to do, but more. The concept of culture must be made to serve us, not imprison us. In the case of the Indian seamstresses, it will not do to assume that they must have a culture of their own just because they seem to be locked out of anyone else's. Instead, we must treat it as an empirical question: are there ways in which these women, against all the odds, manage to construct cultural resources of their own with which to confront their situation? The question is not a philosophical issue, it is a call for someone to go and see – assuming the government of Mauritius will let her in (the project is obviously more feasible for a woman anthropologist). The results could be fascinating. Given that the young women spend a lot of time together, how do they strike up friendships? Are there groups along the lines of religion and caste? Under what circumstances are these barriers overcome? How do women socialize, and what do they talk about? Are there musical or clothing fads that sweep the factory, and what cultural sense do they make? Do the women ever cooperate, for instance to defend one another from unwanted sexual advances from the few men in the factory? Is there in fact any understanding of their own place in the world order? These and a thousand other questions would keep an ethnographer busy for months or years.

One advantage of this situation for an ethnographer is that there would be clear sites for participant observation: the factories and dormitories. In other projects these might prove more elusive. How to begin for instance to study immigrants in New York, from, say, Senegal? There is no reason to believe they would live in the same neighborhood. They might be scattered all over the city, so that it was a figment of the imagination to speak of "the Senegalese community," as politicians like to do. On the other hand, it is frequently the case that people come to a major metropolis because they have kinsmen and friends to help them out when they get there. So there might be buildings where everyone was from "back home" and knew each other. They might even get each other jobs, and then a particular kind of work might be associated with them. For instance, West Africans are widely known in New York for braiding hair, a fashion style that has now spread to mainstream

America. Again, in all the myriad ethnic institutions in New York there might be a Senegalese "cultural center" somewhere. There must surely be a website for Senegalese, where they keep up with each other in America and back home. It would be fascinating to know how the migrants' visions of America change over the months or years of their stays, and how their relatives in Senegal receive that vision.

There is of course no need for the search to be limited to Third World peoples. Anthropologists have in recent years worked in scientific laboratories, studying their stratified social organization and elaborate culture of work. The same could be said of corporations, which often make a point of claiming their own special "corporate culture." In the infamous collapse of the Enron corporation that ruined so many investors, the failure was widely attributed in the media to a cavalier corporate culture in which advancement came from taking absurd risks and then covering up the failures.

In sum, the challenge for contemporary ethnographers is to discover niches within the complexity of the contemporary world in which new cultural forms – that is, cultures – are emerging. Where this does occur, in the midst of migration and mixing, and all the disruptions of modernity and postmodernity, it is the unstructured research methods of anthropology that will reveal them. As an example, let us return to Borneo.

TELEVISION IN REMOTE PLACES

In the 1980's, television sets began to appear in longhouses in the interior. It was inevitable, you might say, showing simply the advance of modernity even in the most remote places. Nevertheless, it did not just happen by itself. There were particular historical circumstances, of which the most crucial was the wholesale clearing of ancient rainforests that previously covered a large part of the island. As cutting operations approached their villages, interior people were employed to do the hardest and most dangerous labor around the massive machinery used in felling and moving the enormous trees. Consequently, money became available in longhouse communities in amounts never known before, even though pay rates were tiny compared to the enormous profits involved.

Longhouses were "modernized" with formica and linoleum, generators were installed allowing electric lighting in the evenings – and televisions arrived. Needless to say, they transformed the sociality of the longhouse. Evening gatherings and their modes of entertainment, including familiar genres of storytelling, disappeared overnight as people sat glued to the family television.

The story, however, is not one simply of loss, of the abandonment of cultural independence in the face of modernity. Longhouse dwellers had always been insatiably curious about the outside world, and now they began to learn all manner of new things. They also began to develop their own viewing tastes, reflecting their outlook on the world. Regular broadcasting struck them as boring because it was full of government propaganda and Islamic teaching. So they bought CD players, and found disks in shops on the coast. Savvy Chinese shopkeepers noted their tastes, which were entirely different to those of coastal people, and set about satisfying them. In the interior disks passed from hand to hand, in and between longhouse communities.

The most dramatic example of their preferences was a voracious interest in professional wrestling. At first glance, this seemed absurd. The posturing of wrestlers when interviewed before bouts, their violent gestures and boasting, were all completely foreign to longhouse manners. Anyone who behaved in that way would be shunned. On second thoughts, however, these strange-looking men, blonde or bizarrely masked, with their huge bodies, resembled nothing so much as the unruly heroes of longhouse myth. These characters also had massive bodies and were capable of amazing feats of strength. But they were not always wise: they defied social conventions and even picked fights with the gods. With this parallel in mind, the fad for watching wrestling was not some disjunct, incoherent, consumption of whatever Hollywood had to hand out. On the contrary, there was a cultural logic. What most impressed longhouse people was not the wrestlers' ability to hand out appalling blows, but to take them. Time and again, the hero would crash to the floor in a way that would break the bones of ordinary men. But at last he would struggle to his feet, and turn on his tormentors. Like the heroes of mythology, the wrestlers may have been impetuous, even foolish, but they were not quitters. They displayed that ultimate virtue of a martial people: stoicism.

Meanwhile, as local supplies of timber were used up, logging companies moved on and the jobs with them. Young men either followed the companies, or migrated with their families down the logging roads to the coast. As the longhouses emptied out, urban slums expanded. People from different longhouses were thrown together, and a new sense of cultural identity began to grow up among them. They became a self-conscious minority, inhabitants of the "Fourth World" like American Indians and Australian Aborigines. Under these circumstances, they have need of new heroes, and the examples they offer of stoicism and persistence.

Summary

In the twentieth century, anthropology achieved a remarkable feat of documentation that will only grow more valuable in centuries to come. Armed with the techniques of participant observation research, ethnographers fanned out across the world, studying cultures that were imminently about to undergo massive changes as they were drawn into the global economy created by the Industrial Revolution and European expansion. It is not easy to find an appropriate label for these cultures. "Savage," "barbarian" and "primitive" are all clearly pejorative. Moreover, they immediately invoke the discredited "Comparative Method." Nor can we contrast them with "modern" societies without implying that they are somehow stuck in some "archaic" period, with the same result. The terminological difficulty points to the diversity of the peoples involved, and their reactions to change. Counter to their "savage" stereotype, people in central Borneo had been involved in an expansive Asian economy for at least a millennium. True, their place in this trading network was marginal, but everything about their societies was shaped by the flow of high-value commodities upriver and down. The same could not be said for the Polynesian peoples of the central Pacific, even though they must be judged among the greatest navigators in all of history. In Melanesia there were elaborate ritual exchange systems, but their social effects were unlike the commodity trade in central Borneo. In sub-Saharan Africa, some regions were hooked into Swahili trade networks, and others remote from it.

Meanwhile, ways of life were changing everywhere. The peoples of Europe and North America were the first to experience the disruptions of the Industrial Revolution, and suffered their own traumas. Increasingly, all the continents were bound up in the processes that Marx first identified. Traditional societies became divided between rich and poor, and the latter migrated in search of work. This process is now most evident in the Third World, and it means that "cultures" and "societies" – our units of study – are ever more difficult to identify. But this is only an intensification of a problem that ethnographers have always encountered. There is no simple way out of the problem; instead anthropologists must be enterprising in locating cultural niches, and wary of all ethnic categories.

FURTHER READING

To convince yourself of the complexity of Australian Aborigine social organization, you need only look at the diagrams in Part One of Lévi-Strauss' *The Elementary Structures of Kinship* (1969, original 1949). For a description of how Maori people have maintained their traditions see Anne Salmond's *Hui* (1975). For a general account of the fate of "tribal" peoples in the modern world, see *Victims of Progress* (1990), by John Bodley. Marx's writings are voluminous and not easy for beginners. There are numerous guides for beginners, including cartoon versions. Concerning globalization, a brief and readable modern adaptation is provided in Immanuel Wallerstein's *Historical Capitalism* (1983). An influential study of exchange systems in Melanesia, employing Marxist categories, is Chris Gregory's *Gifts and Commodities* (1982). The standard work on Polynesian migrations is *Man's Conquest of the Pacific* (1979), by Peter Bellwood. For more about the enthusiasm for professional wrestling in central Borneo, see Metcalf (2003). For an intriguing reflection on the difficulties of locating "cultures," see *The Predicament of Culture* (1988), by James Clifford.

9

CULTURE AND THE INDIVIDUAL

The difficulties of discovering "tribes" in the contemporary world is not a matter of searching in obscure places, but of seeing what is going on before our eyes. There is nothing unprecedented in what is happening, but there is a difference in scale. Never have cultural influences been transmitted so rapidly, and at such great distances. Consequently, it becomes increasingly difficult to designate cultures that are bounded in any simple way. In fact, cultures in this sense always were a heuristic device, that is to say, an approximation of reality allowing us to get on with business. Nowadays anthropologists are under pressure to justify every such casual claim. This has been, and remains, a serious challenge. But it has also had a stimulating effect on research, causing ethnographers to pursue cultures in all manner of social niches. The point is neatly made when ethnographers are tempted to refer to the "tribes" of Chief Executive Officers, or of scientific specialists, or even of anthropologists themselves, who share an elaborate international culture, full of rituals, alliances and feuds.

Meanwhile, insofar as the notion of "cultures" has been destabilized, attention turns once again to how individuals react to the cultural influences tugging at them. I say "once again" because issues of individual and group psychology have always been important in American cultural anthropology. We approach them, however, with two premises in place.

BIOLOGY, PSYCHOLOGY, CULTURE

First, there has been no retreat from the insistence on the pervasiveness of the cultural. On the contrary, it has advanced. The domain of the cultural includes everything that is neither at one extreme unique to particular individuals, like the contents of dreams, nor at the other common to the whole species, like bipedalism. In fact even these things can easily take on a cultural dynamic. According to neurologists, dreams are like other mental processes in that they result from electronic impulses passing through synapses in the brain. What distinguishes them is that they are not the result of sensory stimulation from the outside world, but are apparently random neural impulses. Nevertheless, they were for Freud a direct avenue into the unconscious, in which lurked sublimated desires and fears. Anyone nowadays reading Freud's analyses of dreams, however, is bound to notice echoes of the Vienna of Freud's time, with its particular social urges and anxieties. Consequently, we are left with several levels of reality. In order to remember a dream, let alone recount it, the dreamer must have placed meaning on random patterns of color. Next, these meanings are made, if you believe Freud, to fit things buried deep in the unconscious. Finally they have to be presented in terms of things we know in the real world, in whatever bizarre ways they are put together. That is, they are passed through a cultural lens. The comparative study of dreaming has yet to be attempted, but we know that peoples vary greatly in the attention they pay to it. Some people report elaborate dreams, even if radically different to anything a Westerner would dream. Others have a stilted repertoire, classifying all dreams under a handful of stereotyped narratives. In either event, the universal human propensity to dream, which produces totally inward experiences unique to each individual, can only be reported in culturally appropriate terms.

What this shows is the mediation of human biology and individual psychology through cultural perception. Starting from the other end of the spectrum, walking on two legs is a characteristic of the hominid line of evolution, and no one since the Middle Ages has doubted that it is the universal mode of locomotion in all *Homo sapiens* populations. At the same time, however, peoples' individual gaits are subtly different. It is amazing how one can recognize friends and family without seeing their faces, even at a long distance, simply from the way they walk. But it is also the case that people move differently according to their ethnic background. Even a casual observer notices hand gestures, ways of standing while talking to others, and so on, that are part of a culturally transmitted "body language." For example, Westerners in Borneo longhouses make themselves conspicuous by walking around as if they were out in the jungle. Proper longhouse etiquette requires that someone approaching people indoors roll their shoulders inwards, and bend their knees, so as not to tower threateningly over those seated on the floor – there being no furniture. Westerners find the resulting shuffling gait embarrassingly effeminate, which is odd considering the warrior traditions of their hosts. To longhouse people, meanwhile, Westerners seem ill-mannered and childishly assertive.

CULTURAL IMPOVERISHMENT

There is a second premise, which follows from the twentieth-century notion of culture. If you think back to the Indian seamstresses in their factory dormitories, the temptation is to see them as culturally deprived. But we have rejected any definition of culture that conceives of some people having more culture than others. These women are almost invariably multilingual, so how could they be said to "lack culture"? Moreover, we must take into account that the young women are being exposed to all kinds of new cultural influences. Rather than industrial servitude, they may experience their jobs as liberation from pre-modern patriarchy. That is certainly what their bosses would have us believe – modernity on the march!

There are, however, more dramatic cases. When American Indian and Australian Aborigine children were taken away from their families, it was to give them a chance to escape a poverty that was more than material. The policy is now in disrepute, but there was more than a grain of truth in the argument. For example, in rural areas of Australia where white farmers control the land, ethnographers have reported very little activity among Aborigines that might be connected to traditional matters: gatherings, rituals, or anything of that kind. Some Aborigines are "integrated" in the sense that they work with white stockmen, and drink alongside them in the pub. But many others live lives that are in every sense marginal, housed in shacks on the outskirts of small towns, eking out an existence on government allowances, and appearing to do nothing day after day. They seem caught between cultures, unable to move either backwards or forwards. Frustrated policymakers confront anthropologists, who are supposed to know about these things, demanding to be told forthrightly what should be done. They are usually disappointed. Often, the best ethnographers can do is explain why all the proposed new interventions will do more harm than good.

The point is, of course, that it is no more the ethnographer's job to tell Aborigines what they must be than it is the government's. Nor can we participate in the rhetoric of cultural impoverishment without risking all that was gained by the twentieth-century re-definition of culture. If Aborigines are culturally impoverished, what about working-class Australians reading the sports page of the newspaper rather than the international news? Clearly we are on a slippery slope here. Before long anyone without a college degree will be diagnosed as culturally impoverished, and culture will be what it was in the nineteenth century. Meanwhile, how is an ethnographer to describe the apparent vacuum that is "the culture" of displaced Aborigines? Could we make a start with narratives of displacement, such as encounters with missionaries and landowners? Or perhaps with the Aborigine enthusiasm for "westerns," Blue Grass music, and everything to do with cowboys? Or is there in Aborigine passiveness still an echo of the hunting and gathering lifestyle? Are we missing something that our own cultural premises make invisible? If so, it will take an ethnographer of exceptional talents to show us what it is we are not seeing – most likely an Aborigine anthropologist.

CULTURE AND PERSONALITY

Long before these terminological difficulties became acute, however, American anthropologists were dealing with similar issues of cultural worth using ideas borrowed from psychology. It was an easy step, since Freud's ideas had been received more enthusiastically in the New World than they were in the Old. In the New York of the 1920's and 1930's psychiatry was fashionable (see Box 9.1). As active participants in the intellectual ferment of the times, Boas and his students mixed socially with practicing psychiatrists, and interacted with them at conferences and seminars. Some of Boas' students underwent psychoanalysis, a process that requires a considerable investment of time and energy. It is not surprising that there would be a cross fertilization of ideas. The result is that psychology has had an impact on American anthropology second only to linguistics.

BOX 9.1 PSYCHOLOGY, PSYCHIATRY, AND SOCIAL PSYCHOLOGY

The use of these words is often confusing, so a word of clarification is called for. Psychology is the broadest term, and refers to the study of the mind and mental processes. Psychiatry is a branch of medicine, concerned with treating mental disorders, including psychoses and neuroses. In Europe and North America a practicing psychiatrist must also be trained as a doctor, that is, hold an MD degree. But there are other kinds of therapists who treat mentally disturbed people and, somewhat confusingly, they are often referred to as psychologists. In general, psychiatry has drawn on the concepts of Sigmund Freud, including that of the unconscious. Freud described his technique as "the talking cure," because it involves the patient reflecting on his or her problems. The most extended form of treatment is psychoanalysis, which can last for years. Psychotherapists ("psychologists") working in other traditions use a variety of techniques from drugs to mental exercises, designed to alleviate symptoms rather than delve into the unconscious. Finally, social psychology is a branch of psychology dealing with how the reactions of individuals are affected by interactions with other people. Experiments in social psychology often involved creating a controlled social context in laboratory conditions and then monitoring the responses of a subject. For instance, a famous experiment demonstrated just how hard people will work to agree with their fellows. The result was obtained in this way. The subject is asked to join a panel that is asked to rank objects in various ways. The subject does not know that all the other members of the panel are actors, whose job it is to reach some evidently unreasonable opinion. Invariably, the test subject will go to great lengths to avoid being a minority of one.

The bridge between anthropology and psychology was made through the concept of "personality." The immediate reference of the word is, of course, to something entirely individual. If asked to describe someone's personality you might say that he or she is warm, or shy, or arrogant, or a thousand other possible attributes. You will remember, however, that the "person," in the technical jargon of Chapter Three, is not the same as the individual. In an analogous fashion, whatever is inherent in individual personalities is also molded to some extent at least by their upbringing and experience. In pursuit of this cultural aspect of personality, students of Boas elaborated the idea of a "modal personality," that is, one that is particularly admired and held up for emulation. In different societies, it was argued, different traits were valued or condemned.

MODAL PERSONALITY IN DOBU

An obvious place from which to take an example is Ruth Benedict's *Patterns of Culture* (1934). The book was written for a popular audience, and also taught to a whole generation of undergraduates in liberal arts colleges. It was such a success that it is often credited with bringing the new Boasian meaning of the word culture into general circulation. The core of Benedict's book consists of portraits of three indigenous cultures, described in terms of modal personalities. The Pueblo peoples of New Mexico respect a person who is gentle, self-effacing, and knowledgeable about a complex spirit world and the rituals it requires. She characterizes them as Apollonian, that is having the rational attributes of the Roman god Apollo. By contrast, the Kwakiutl of British Columbia were impetuous and boastful. She describes them as Dionysian, after the Roman god Dionysus, whose ecstatic cult involved drunkenness and sexual excesses. The Kwakiutl were fiercely competitive. In showy festivals chiefs tried to outdo each other in destruction of wealth. Shamans gained power by contact with dangerous and unpredictable spirits, using remains of the dead.

The ethnographic material for these portraits came from the fieldwork of Boas himself, and his students who had worked among American Indians. Her third case, however, is based on the account by the New Zealand anthropologist Reo Fortune in his *Sorcerers of*

Dobu (1932). Dobu is a small island off the eastern tip of New Guinea, not far from where Malinowski did his pioneering field-work. Drawing on Fortune's data, Benedict portrays a society sunk deep in paranoia. Everyone lives in constant fear of sorcery by their neighbors, and even slight misfortunes are attributed to it. Magic is needed for everything from growing crops to evading the attacks of sorcerers, and everyone jealously guards their own spells. You can imagine that marriage under these circumstances is not easy. A man seeks a bride from exactly those neighboring villages that house his enemies, and mutual distrust is so great that the couple is never allowed to set up house permanently in either village. Instead they shuttle back and forth every year, taking it in turns to be the object of contempt and suspicion in the village of their in-laws, where they are seldom well fed. Should either partner die away from home charges of murder will fly, and ordinary hostility may well escalate to violence. Even between husband and wife there is little trust or affection, at least not until the marriage has endured for several years, and everyone has settled into a grudging acceptance. Benedict repeats an anecdote about a man who declines an invitation to socialize with friends, on the grounds that his wife will accuse him of having had a good time.

MADNESS AND DEVIANCE

The success of Benedict's book shows that her portraits are convincing. In addition, her technique of giving labels to cultures makes it easy to grasp her argument and remember it. But it involves some worrying implications. When Benedict labels Dobu culture as paranoid, she is taking a diagnosis applied by psychiatrists to mentally ill patients, and applying it to a whole population. But mental illness is usually defined in terms of social functioning: the troubled individual is unable to live an ordinary life. By Benedict's own account, being paranoid is exactly the way to function in Dobu. Could a Dobuan psychiatrist then diagnose non-paranoia as a mental illness? If not, what could it possibly mean to say that a whole society is mentally ill? The proposition comes close to chauvinism. The project of anthropology is clearly cancelled if we allow the familiar claim that the foreigners are all mad, and there is nothing more to say about them.

This shows the dangers of mixing the jargons of psychology and anthropology. Benedict does not confront the issue directly, but she is careful to avoid the implication that peoples' temperaments are mechanically produced by their cultures, like nails in a nail factory. There might indeed be individuals living in a pueblo who, despite all the pressures of socialization, remain assertive and quarrelsome. In Benedict's terms they are "deviants." The same is true, however, of a Kwakiutl or Dobu person who is easygoing and likes to get on with everybody. Such misfits are likely to be miserable, and their lives difficult. This is a good moment to reflect on your own culture or cultures. What are their modal personalities? What temperament is rewarded and how? How well do you fit in, and what penalties do you suffer when you do not?

There is a feature of Benedict's notion that seems odd at first glance, but turns out to be useful. When politicians speak of social deviants, they usually mean those inclined to crime or sexual irregularities. But there is everywhere a movement back and forth between mere unpopularity and outright criminality. Consider, for instance, the change in attitudes in the West concerning homosexuality. A few decades ago active homosexuals could be thrown in jail, and so lived fearfully "in the closet." They were also, according to the American Medical Association, mentally ill. Now those legal threats and diagnostic claims have largely been swept away. But, despite Gay Pride parades, homosexuality remains for many Americans deviant in Benedict's sense. Consequently her notion of deviance provided a way to think about the various ways in which people are made marginal in their own societies.

PSYCHIC UNITY

In Benedict's argument, every society must have its deviants because the raw material on which different cultures work is everywhere the same. This doctrine is called the Psychic Unity of Humankind, and its import is sufficiently profound to merit capital letters. It can be seen as the American equivalent of the British proposition, described in Chapter Three, that all societies have institutions of law, politics, economics, and so on, however diverse they may be. Each provides the basis of a relativism that runs counter to nineteenth-century evolutionism, but reflecting different national traditions. Moreover, both constitute an assertion of faith, rather than a testable hypothesis. Certainly, it would be odd for an anthropologist to claim that there were people anywhere in the world who did not feel love or hatred, grief or joy. To do so would surely be worse than racism. Yet it would be a ticklish problem to isolate "love" in every culture, and there is no reason why that particular bundle of ideas should be part of everyone's worldview. In Europe and America, a marriage is supposed to be the result of "falling" in love, but that notion is far from a universal, as we saw in Chapter Six. Moreover, it would not be possible in most languages to say that you "love" chocolate as opposed to simply liking it, let alone "loving" God. Consequently, the doctrine of psychic unity is best understood simply as a broad assertion of common humanity.

DANGERS OF STEREOTYPING

Benedict's diagnosis of Dobu culture as paranoid raises another problem, which also applies to the labels Apollonian and Dionysian. Insightful and convincing as Benedict's portraits are, her labels come dangerously close to stereotypes. Indeed in the case of Dobu she admits as much:

> The Dobuans are known to all the white recruiters as easy marks in the area. Risking hunger at home, they sign up readily for indentured labor; being used to coarse fare, the rations they receive as work-boys do not cause mutiny among them. The reputation of the Dobuans in the neighboring islands, however, does not turn on their poverty. They are noted rather for their dangerousness. They are said to be magicians who have diabolical power and warriors who halt at no treachery. A couple of generations ago, before white intervention, they were cannibals and that in an area where people eat no human flesh. They are the feared and distrusted savages of the islands surrounding them.
>
> (Benedict 1934: 131)

In other words, Benedict is repeating what the neighbors of the Dobuans say about them. But when we hear people describing their neighbors as cannibals, or werewolves, or inverted people, it will hardly do to take their word for it. Moreover, stereotypes are invariably phrased in negative terms. When Americans describe the

British as cold, and the British describe Americans as brash, both are saying the same thing but evaluating it in reverse terms. Even if we eliminate the negativity, and say instead that the modal American personality is outgoing and friendly, while the British is polite and modest, we have gained little. Stereotypes flatten a complex reality. Some Americans are retiring, and some Britons are friendly. The interesting questions are how do friendliness and reserve vary by region, class, and context? What signals are sent out to indicate a willingness to be friendly, or the appropriateness of reserve? Stereotypes may hint at something, but they routinely hide more than they reveal.

To check the truth of this, consider for a moment the stereotypes that you have of others. What value are they? What do they reveal, and what do they hide? What about those that others have of you, how much do they bother you, and why? Can you make a joke about them, or take a joke, or are they too explosive for that? What historical experiences shaped those stereotypes, and how can they be revised?

THE WIND IN THE PALM TREES

Benedict's book was influential and controversial. In both respects, however, it was outdone by Margaret Mead's *Coming of Age in Samoa* (1928). Mead was also a student of Boas, though somewhat younger than Benedict. In this, her first of many books, she set out immediately to be provocative, and to make a strong cultural-relativist argument in the manner of her teacher. She also struck out in a new direction by working outside continental America, even though the eastern half of the mid-Pacific island of Samoa was a protectorate with an American naval base.

Mead's goal was to show that the problems of teenagers, which adults in the USA had come to see as a "natural" and inescapable part of growing up, were in fact produced by cultural arrangements that were subject to change. Mead intended to influence public opinion about how American school systems should deal with unresponsive students and juvenile delinquents – and she succeeded. Consequently, her book not only attracted a wide readership, but also sharp criticism from within anthropology. The British were not impressed with her fieldwork, which they found flimsy and impressionistic. They suspected that in her haste to make an unambiguous case she had suppressed inconvenient data. They were also suspicious of a picture of Samoa that fulfilled everyone's dream of a tranquil South Seas paradise, where vigorous and happy young men and women danced away the moonlit night, and made love without guilt. In his review, Evans-Pritchard characterized Mead's description as "the wind in the palm trees" ethnography.

A far more aggressive attack came in the 1970's, when the Australian anthropologist Derek Freeman set out to reverse Mead's relativist argument, and show that biological maturation was as fraught with problems in Samoa as it was in America. He conducted further fieldwork in Samoa, including reading police reports about teenage crime. He paints a very different picture of Samoan teenagers, including psychic stress and routine violence against women. He discredits the information that Mead had collected from Samoan girls, arguing that they had motives to gossip with an American woman not much older than they were, and to wildly romanticize their own lives. Freeman, however, goes on to make the same mistake, asserting in effect that he really does know about the sex lives of Samoans. This is equally unsupportable. The simple truth of the matter is that you cannot study sexuality by participant observation. Not only is it unethical to exploit sexual opportunities, it is also ineffective. If the ethnographer is one participant in a sex act how could it possibly be representative of local practices? Consequently, fieldworkers have no means of checking what "informants" tell them about the most obvious subject for lying imaginable. Even where people tease constantly about sexual matters, the ethnographer is almost always in the dark about what really happened, and this must simply be accepted as a limitation of our methods. Consequently, the controversy about Mead's findings will never be settled. The majority opinion among anthropologists is that Mead over-simplified Samoan life, but they are even more skeptical about Freeman's biological reductionism. In short, cultural relativism survives, but no thanks to Mead.

CHILD REARING

When British anthropologists criticized Benedict and Mead as impressionistic, they were contrasting their methods with their own. It seemed clear to them that the systematic collection of social norms concerning particular named statuses and roles went far deeper than mere stereotypes, and discovered things that were new and surprising. In response to this criticism, the American school of Culture and Personality moved to develop a more rigorous methodology of its own, and it involved the observation of techniques of child rearing. This development was already under way when Mead went to Samoa, and that was why she focused on young girls. Indeed, she provided the metaphor that underlay the method: as the twig is bent, she said, so grows the tree. In other words, if you want to understand how the adults of a particular culture end up with their characteristic personality traits, then look at how they reproduce them in their children.

For example, Mead made a brief study of child rearing in Bali, a small island in Indonesia, designed to shed light on why Balinese culture is so rich in artistic expression and dramatic ritual. She and her then husband, Gregory Bateson, concluded that Balinese children were subjected to constant teasing by their parents, including being shown desirable things that were promptly whisked away. Parents seemed deliberately to provoke tears of frustration, and this contributed to unstable and temperamental adult personalities, just the kind that, according to Freud, produced artists. In their research, Mead and Bateson made use of film to catch fleeting interactions between parent and child, and Mead went on later to make films contrasting French, English, and American child-rearing practices.

After World War Two, specialists like the Harvard anthropologists John and Beatrice Whiting refined these methods. For instance, they borrowed from child psychologists techniques for recording in detail the interactions of children, using a score card and a stopwatch. In this way, they could quantify such things as the frequency of acts of aggression, cooperation, or withdrawal. They similarly measured in cultures all over the globe the age of children when they were weaned, the frequency of co-sleeping with one or both parents, and many other things. What was produced was a remarkable demonstration of just how differently young children were raised in different cultures. This in turn lent credence to the proposition that adult personalities, in all their diversity, were shaped by cultural practices.

CULTURE AND EMOTION

Note that the argument goes from child rearing to personality, that is *from* culture *to* psychology. Consequently, it is not guilty of psychological reductionism, as described in Chapter Three. This is not easy to grasp in connection with something that seems so, well, personal as personality. The effort to avoid reductionist arguments is even harder in connection with emotions. It is impossible to doubt that powerful emotions well up from within us unbidden, and take control of us. Surely they are as interior an experience as can be imagined. But cultural relativism does not imply otherwise. The only requirement is that cultural things are not explained, or explained away, in terms of emotions.

The classic example of this particular battle between common sense and cultural relativism concerns funerals. Surely, no one could deny that the death of those close to us can be a devastating experience. This is a case when Psychic Unity must clearly be invoked. What then could be more natural than to cancel the normal routines of everyday life and, with the help of friends and neighbors, take the time to deal with the shock, and at least begin the process of mourning. This is a funeral, and the fact that they occur all over the world proves only the impact of our common mortality.

It is at this point that Durkheim takes up the issue in *The Elementary Forms of the Religious Life* (1912). He begins by quoting at length from a description by two early travelers in central Australia of arriving at an Aborigine camp just as a death occurred. People cried and howled inconsolably, flinging themselves about dangerously. Some took sharp sticks and stabbed them into their skulls until blood flowed down their faces and necks. Others cut themselves with stone tools, and one man went so far as to sever the muscles of his calf, inflicting on himself such damage that he would probably never walk properly again. Such a display may be shocking to us, but there is no doubting the sincerity of the emotions displayed. But now Durkheim plays his trump card: it was not just anybody who cut his leg in this way. It was the dead man's mother's brother. It was always the mother's brother. It was part of his assigned role.

Consequently, strong emotions co-exist with culturally appropriate ways of expressing them. It is true that no society lacks death rituals. No one puts corpses out with the trash, and gets on with everyday affairs. But there are some very simple rituals. Kalahari Bushmen leave a corpse where it lies, but immediately abandon the campsite, not returning for years. Without burial, it is left to corruption and wild animals to dispose of the corpse. At the other end of the spectrum, there are mortuary rites found in Borneo and elsewhere that last for months or even years, and involve moving corpses from a place of temporary storage to a final grand mausoleum. At various points in this long process there are loud and abandoned displays of grief, but these occur at predictable moments in the ritual sequence. Moreover, women are specially invited who are good at singing moving dirges. An outsider – the ethnographer for instance – might be inclined to conclude that the emotions shown on these occasions are false, mere performances. But who are we to say what emotions other people are feeling? There is simply no way to know that for sure, even in one's own culture. Maybe no one really cared much for the dead person in the first place. On the other hand, almost every adult has suffered real, heartfelt loss, and on occasions of mourning the remembrance easily comes back, and then tears well up. The truth of the matter is that there is no fixed relationship between ritual and emotions, even at funerals. While some are still in shock, others are busy hiding their indifference. Consequently, an appeal to Psychic Unity cannot begin to account for the huge diversity of mortuary rituals. As always, things cultural can only be understood in terms of others the same.

CULTURE AND MOTIVE

There is a parallel argument to be made concerning individual motivation. In the 1960's an attempt was made to salvage British social anthropology from the circular arguments in which functionalism had trapped it (see Chapter Five). The problem, as some critics saw it, was that the focus had been so firmly set on the abstraction "society" that the individual actor had disappeared from view. You will notice that this is the same problem that we saw in the last chapter: the slipperiness of bounded units of analysis, either societies or cultures. Meanwhile, it was argued, social outcomes were obviously the result of individual choices. So the objective of "actor-centered approaches" was to understand the social situations that individuals confronted in everyday life, and how they chose to invest their limited resources of time, energy, wealth and influence.

The classic ethnography in this mode was by Fredrik Barth, a British-trained Norwegian anthropologist, who studied the Swat valley in Eastern Afghanistan (1959). Swat society was infamously unstable. Petty lords, or *khan*, were constantly at war, and the nominal king of Swat could not control them. There were noble lineages and clans, but they fought among themselves as vigorously as with outsiders, so that the models that British ethnographers had applied in Africa, as described in Chapter Four, did not apply. Instead, Barth sets about explaining how the game of being a khan was played. Each had personal followers, who spent much of their time in his men's house. He protected them from other khans, who were liable to harass unprotected farmers by theft or abuse of their women. On the other hand, the khan had to exploit his own followers by taking a large part of their crops in order to have resources to run elaborate feasts and so impress other khans. Without allies, he was doomed. Consequently, a delicate balance had to be maintained between attracting and driving away followers. Another resource that a khan had at his disposal was a reputation for violence, which gained both allies and followers. But the reputation had to be maintained, and neighboring khans were always probing his defenses by making casual insults to his followers. If he was seen to back down, he soon lost ground. But if he got involved in an all-out feud, he might be so badly mauled as to be powerless against the next rival to appear. Meanwhile, of course, every follower was carefully calculating his own profits and losses, and switching allegiances accordingly. Barth's book makes it plain why Soviet forces could not control Afghanistan in the 1980's and just what problems lie in store for the current American-appointed government.

ECONOMIC MAN

Ethnographies in this style make lively reading, as one identifies first with one actor and then another. Moreover, the metaphor that underlies the approach is easy to grasp: that of the marketplace. Some people come to it poor, others rich, but everyone has their own deals to make. That is to say, everyone is involved in social transactions. Consequently, the approach is often called "transactionalism." As we have learned, however, even vivid analogies lead us astray if taken too literally. The problem here is that transactionalism suffers from the same limitations as the liberal economics from which it takes its jargon of resources, management, investment, profit and loss. Mainstream economic theory works by making assumptions about what a rational person would do if offered choices, say, spending money on a new car or putting it in a pension scheme. This mythic person is called Economic Man. By aggregating the decisions of whole populations of the same, theorists arrive at models of how a market economy will respond. These projections make economists enormously influential in democracies because the state of the economy has a large impact on how people vote. But even a casual reading of the newspaper shows that fashions come and go in economics, such as the infamous theory that corporate profits would somehow "trickle down" to employees. Moreover, no one is surprised to find that the experts have totally misread the economic tea leaves. Indeed, economists close to governments resemble nothing so much as the court diviners of a Bemba king (see Chapter Four). Always something comes along to upset the neat models: a political scandal, an oil shortage, or merely a change in buying habits.

What destabilized Barth's model of the tricky but predictable transactions of political life in the Swat valley was religious fervor. Every generation or so, a new Islamic teacher succeeded in rousing the common people against outside threats and internal decadence. Then a great cultural movement overwhelmed rational calculations of marginal gains, and the khans were swept aside. The result is that Barth's model, however intriguing and insightful, can never provide the whole picture of politics in Swat, but only an aspect of it. The same is true in Europe and America. The petty haggling between political parties over influence and spoils is occasionally pushed aside by issues that arouse popular feeling. Real politics has to do with the latter and not the former. In the same way, econometrics – the mathematically precise modeling of economies – can be useful under controlled conditions. But "the market" of which economists speak, with its supposedly iron laws, operates only in niches provided by a social and political system whose historical origins lie

elsewhere. As we saw in the last chapter, this is why Marx's terminology still circulates, even though the systems he himself designed
proved unworkable.

INDIVIDUALISM AS IDEOLOGY

At this point, we come back to the same conclusion as was reached
in Chapter Three, and again in Chapter Six. It is a mistake to
imagine that we are somehow imprisoned in the norms or collective
representations of our individual societies. On the contrary, they
provide us with ways of existing without which we could not be
human at all. Nineteenth-century anthropologists tried to imagine
savage (that is, "wild") peoples who completely lacked rules or
customs, but in the end they could not manage it. There is no
evidence that such humans ever existed. We are social animals, and
so were our pre-human ancestors. Again, it became fashionable in
the 1970's to speak of the "prison house" of language, but this is a
thoroughly perverse notion. Could we be human without language?
Finally, when Benedict popularized the notion of individuals
embedded in cultures, the same cry was raised. Do we not lose our
individuality if we allow that we are in part the creatures of our
own cultural upbringing?

This is, for the most part, an American concern. Europeans are
not bothered by the notion that they are partly shaped by their
national cultures – indeed they are proud of it. But in America,
Individualism *is* the national culture. Americans are in fact remarkably conformist about their individualism. There are no doubt
many reasons for this, but some are easy to see: the rejection of
Europe, with its suffocating "culture" embroiled in a vicious class
system; the tradition of town meeting politics, where everyone had
his or her say; the doctrine that everyone can get ahead if they put
their shoulders to the wheel. Perhaps the most influential of all was
the self-help ethic of the frontier. But the seemingly endless plains
are settled now, and John Wayne may not be the best modal personality for contemporary America. Meanwhile, the ethic persists as a
kind of internal frontier. Ever since the appearance of Dale
Carnegie's *How to Win Friends and Influence People* (1936),
American bookstores have been filled with self-help books on
everything from how to lose weight to how to improve your

marriage. For better or worse, Europeans generally feel less optimism about remaking themselves overnight by sheer willpower, and they are more comfortable with the proposition that we do not create ourselves out of thin air.

Summary

A central issue in anthropology has always been the relationship of individuals to their own societies and cultures. In Chapters Three and Four, we saw that British social anthropology gained its power from setting aside the psychic peculiarities of the individual in favor of social person. In Chapter Six we followed the consequences of the linguistic analogy. From that point of view, cultures do not tell people what to say, but they do provide them with a way of saying things. In Chapter Seven we saw culture as a set of premises about what constitutes the nature of things, everything from conception to cosmology. In large part, this last is the significance that the term "culture" usually invokes in anthropology today. But from its beginning in the work of Boas, American anthropology has had a hankering somehow to forge a link with individual psychology. This is entirely possible, provided psychological reductionism is avoided. That is to say, psychic phenomena – or some psychic phenomena, it can never be all of them – are to be explained in terms of cultural features, but not the reverse. For example, human emotions are about as volatile and individually variable as anything one could imagine. Yet we can only *name* them through cultural categories. In the performance of ritual, powerful emotions may be aroused. But we can never know what individuals are actually experiencing from moment to moment.

To deal with these variables, the generation of students trained by Boas developed a notion of personality as something shaped by culture. Specifically, each culture held up a modal personality for emulation, and treated those who could not conform to it as deviants. The work of the "culture and personality" school made a large impact on the American public, and helped to propagate Boas' relativistic (i.e. non-judgmental) notion of multiple cultures. It was criticized, however, for producing little more than bromides that came dangerously close to stereotypes. To deal with this, the second generation of American anthropologists interested in these issues focused on careful observation of child-rearing techniques worldwide, and documented their remarkable variation. Meanwhile, the collapse of functionalism left British anthropologists scrambling for new ways to account for individual behavior, and so they turned their attention to motivation. But these transactional analyses only smuggled psychological assumptions in through the back door, and unsubtle ones at that, to the effect that everyone was constantly seeking to maximize his or her power or wealth, in complete contrast to what Mauss had argued in *The Gift*.

FURTHER READING

The most popular books produced by the culture and personality school were Ruth Benedict's *Patterns of Culture* (1934) and Margaret Mead's *Coming of Age in Samoa* (1928). The controversy over the latter continues to this day. The most strident attack is by Derek Freeman (1983). For a more measured assessment see Lowell Holmes' *Quest for the Real Samoa* (1987). The most influential research about child-rearing techniques worldwide was by John Whiting, for instance in his *Child Training and Personality* (1953), co-authored with Irvin Child. The cultural conditioning of emotion remains a lively area of research, for example in Catherine Lutz's *Unnatural Emotions* (1988). During the two decades when transactionalism was popular it produced some engrossing ethnographies, full of the deviousness of politicians great and small. The best known of these was Fredrik Barth's study of *Political Leadership Among Swat Pathans* (1959). It was criticized, however, by Akbar Ahmed in his *Millennium and Charisma among Pathans* (1976) for not taking account of the depth of Islamic fervor in the region. The terminology of transactionalism was elaborated in Frederick Bailey's charming and readable *Stratagems and Spoils* (1969).

CRITICAL ANTHROPOLOGY

You will have noticed that, throughout the book, we have repeat-edly approached topics that have political significance. During the twentieth century, anthropology was often associated with left-wing causes. But it is important to note that there is nothing in the subject matter of the discipline that makes this inevitable. In the 1930's Hitler employed anthropologists, drawn from the most pres-tigious German universities, to find the limits of the Aryan master race, and define the perfect physical types of Silesians and Westphalians, and so on. To guard against threats to racial purity, it was also necessary to assess the degrees of inferiority of other peoples, and all of this was presented in the most solemn possible language of hard science. The irony is that the term Aryan was made up in the eighteenth century, not to separate "races," but to join them together. It was the English linguist William Jones, studying the ancient languages of India, who first noticed that there were words in classical Greek that closely resembled ones with similar meanings in Sanskrit. This happened frequently enough that it could not be an accident. Slowly, Jones came to realize that the only possible explanation was that Sanskrit and Greek derived from a common ancestor. With this amazing discovery, the field of historical linguistics was founded, and its first achievement was to demonstrate a vast family of related languages spreading from Ireland to India. These were the Indo-European languages. The ancestral language, labeled proto-Indo-European, was evidently spoken somewhere in the Caucasus region about five millennia ago, too recently for biological evolution to have had any but superficial effects. If Hitler had followed his own logic, he would have had to include at least Gaels, Slavs, Persians, and north Indians in his Aryan race.

REPORTING FROM THE DISEMPOWERED

Given such extreme forms of anthropological theorizing as Hitler's master race, the only proper principle to follow is *caveat emptor*, "buyer beware." This applies, for instance, to the travel and history programs on television that routinely present the results of "anthropology" to sensationalize "primitive" peoples. They are the modern equivalent of the fantasy travelogues of previous centuries. Nor are academics exempt; the discipline has accommodated its share of cranks and charlatans. And finally, of course, even the most careful ethnography is subject to scrutiny and re-interpretation. It is for these reasons that most contemporary anthropologists prefer to avoid claims of practicing a science. There is, after all, nothing esoteric about our methods. Our motives are unusual, but anyone might find reasons to go to live among other people, and to learn their language and customs. Some have had no choice but to do so. It has happened throughout history; it is a familiar part of human experience.

Nevertheless, it remains the case that anthropologists get out and about in the world in ways that other scholars do not. We have things to report. Moreover, throughout the twentieth century anthropologists tended to work with disempowered people, Fourth World minorities and colonial subjects. A cynic might remark that those were exactly the people who were defenseless against our uninvited intrusions. But even if that is true, it has caused anthropologists repeatedly to look at power structures in the way that their hosts see them, from the bottom up. This, finally, is the reason why anthropologists nowadays tend to be skeptical of the self-satisfied homilies handed out by politicians, and often become outspoken critics of the *status quo*.

"CRITICAL" ANTHROPOLOGY

These are the roots of critical anthropology, but the word "critical" needs defining. Right-wingers like to describe liberal rhetoric as a constant guilt-laden whining about the injustices of the world, both boring and useless. But we can put a more precise meaning on the term. What characterizes critical anthropology is not negativism, but reflexivity. That is to say, insofar as anthropologists manage to enter into other peoples' worlds, they have the ability to look back at their own with new eyes. This freshness of vision is what critical anthropology has to offer, and it is a positive contribution. When policymakers and activists debate planning on all sorts of social matters, they always invoke "common sense" – that is, what seems obvious to them. But, as we saw in Chapter Seven, these are just the kinds of propositions that anthropologists scrutinize, trying to make out what social and cultural arrangements underlie them. In any particular case, this may or may not produce useful insights. There are people who become impatient when their own cherished version of common sense is challenged, and they wave aside all attempts at rethinking as a waste of times, an impediment to action. But in such cases there is often a deadlock between opposing view-points that have been debated over and over again. What is needed is something new, and anything that can move the discussion forward is valuable. If critical anthropology plays such a role, does that constitute tinkering in politics? Perhaps. But as we shall see below, the findings of anthropology have always taken on political significance. Moreover, one of the things that we learned from the British anthropology of the 1950's was that politics was inseparable from other social activities.

POLITICS AND CULTURE

In Chapter Four, we saw that the Nuer of southern Sudan lacked any institutions of governance; no chiefs or councils of elders, no armies or law enforcement. From the point of view of Western political science, they simply lacked politics. Yet their anarchy (lack of government) demonstrably did not result in chaos (total disorder). Consequently, anthropologists argued, there was nothing dysfunctional about Nuer society. Instead there was something wrong with our terminology. Needless to say, the European notion of politics does not translate into Nuer. When Nuer discuss "politics," it turns out, they talk in terms of kinship, of the solidarity and rivalry of groups related as brothers. This discovery in turn requires us to rethink what we mean by "kinship." In another part of Africa, it was the duty of the chiefs of the Bemba of Zambia to perform rites that made the land fertile and the rains come on time. In short, Bemba politics was entangled in Bemba religion. Nor are these findings limited to "tribal" peoples. Across the full range of political systems, what constitutes politics is not something apart, but merely an aspect, a way of looking at the whole range of institutions.

Simply put, anything can be, or become, political. There were moments during the 1960's when the most significant political issue in the USA was where African-American people in Birmingham, Alabama were planning to have lunch. It was on such details that the abstractions of the Civil Rights movement became reality. The Democratic President and his party were obliged to back their stated convictions with action, and the reaction among southern whites eliminated what had previously been for Democrats the "solid south." During the same epoch, long hair came to be a political statement, indicating sympathy with the appropriately named "counter culture." What began then as the "culture wars" continues in the political activities of the "Christian right," which in turn puts pressure on the doctrine of Separation of Church and State. Consequently, while one segment of the American public tries to assert their own "traditional values," another responds with a different set of values, those hammered out by the framers of the Constitution.

Meanwhile, academics have generally maintained their image as unkempt and ill-dressed, marking an outsider status that pre-dates the 1960's. This includes anthropologists, of course, many of whom sympathized with the critical stance of the "counter culture," without embracing all its issues and fashions. It remains after all a culture, with its own premises, however "counter" they may be.

UNCRITICAL ANTHROPOLOGY

Back in the late nineteenth century, when anthropology first emerged as a discipline, it was already embroiled in politics. Indeed, it has never since been so deeply politicized. It provided the "scientific" underpinnings for a social ideology that was enormously influential at the time, and remains implicit in much political discourse to this day. It is, however, anything but critical. It was not framed by people who had ever tried to look at the world from anybody else's point of view, let alone the poor or disempowered. Instead, it is flatly chauvinist. It provided a rationale for the stark social contrasts that resulted from the Industrial Revolution, by making them seem an inevitable fact of nature rather than the result of cultural arrangements.

This ideology was a Frankenstein largely created by anthropology. Consequently, any introductory text is obligated to point out how it was created, how to recognize it, and how to defeat it. Moreover, the anthropology of the twentieth century was to a large extent a reaction to that of the nineteenth. To understand the former it is necessary to know something about the latter. Nor is this a matter of transient intellectual fads; it was and remains politics at its most basic – raw politics.

THE MISNOMER OF "SOCIAL DARWINISM"

This ideology is called Social Darwinism, because it comprises a mixture of social evolutionism and biological determinism. The implication is that the ideas of Darwin concerning the processes of speciation (that is, the *Origin of Species*) were applied to cultural diversity within the human species. Just the reverse is true. Theorizing in evolutionary terms about cultural variation predates Darwin by a century at least, and arguably much longer. Meanwhile, both Alfred Wallace and Charles Darwin arrived at the same novel theory of biological evolution in the 1840's and 1850's. As we all know, it was a stunning intellectual success. For the first time, Western science had an account of the entire spectrum of life. All the strange animals in medieval bestiaries no longer represented the whims of an inscrutable Creator, but made sense in terms of progressive adaptation to particular ecological niches. After Darwin, our sense of being in the world could never be the same again, and that indeed is why it so alarmed the established churches at the time, and continues to alarm those who adhere to a literal reading of Genesis.

Meanwhile, theorists of *social* evolution basked in Darwin's reflected glory, and exploited it to assume equal scientific credentials. The most influential of these was the English social theorist Herbert Spencer. To understand the parallels and differences between the views of Darwin and Spencer, let us compare their own statements. Here is Darwin summing up in the last paragraph of the *Origin of Species* with a sublime view of the wonderful diversity of the natural world:

> Thus from the war of nature, from famine and death, the most exalted object of which we are capable of conceiving, namely the production of the higher animals, directly follows. There is grandeur in this view of life, with its several powers, having been originally breathed by the Creator into a few forms or into one; and that while this planet has gone cycling on according to the fixed laws of gravity, from so simple a beginning endless forms most beautiful and wonderful have been, and are being evolved.
>
> (Darwin [1958: 449], quoted in Harris 1968: 118)

PROGRESS THROUGH STRUGGLE

In this paragraph, Darwin manages to fuse two seemingly irreconcilable positions that had warred with each other ever since the Enlightenment. The first was that humankind had the power to free itself from its ancient miseries by the application of Reason. The second was that catastrophe awaited those so arrogant as to imagine that Perfectibility was in their reach. The Marquis de Condorcet argued that freedom from ignorance and superstition held the key to Progress. As a nobleman, he was soon arrested after the French Revolution, but even from his jail cell continued to praise the goals of the Revolution. His intellectual rival Thomas Malthus sneered at such optimism. In the Revolution he saw only "such a fermentation of disgusting passions, of fear, cruelty, malice, revenge, ambition, madness and folly as would have disgraced the most savage nations in the most barbarous age." Malthus' view of history was much darker, an incessant struggle to survive caused by constant tendency for populations to outgrow their food supply. Technical improvements might increase food production occasionally by small increments, but whatever gains were made were soon swallowed up by rates of reproduction that could rapidly double the population and double it again. In making this argument Malthus invented the discipline of demography, but of more importance for the moment is that he provided a key element in Darwin's theory of evolution.

Darwin's insight was that the constant struggle both within and between species was what drove evolution forward. In the process, those creatures best fitted to secure food in any particular eco-niche leave behind more offspring than less successful members of their own species. That species was then better equipped to drive other species to extinction. This is the idea captured in the first of Darwin's sentences quoted above. Progress (or Perfectibility) was not defeated by Struggle; on the contrary, it was *brought about* by Struggle. This remarkable resolution of an old dilemma is what made evolution so irresistible a concept. The values of the Enlightenment were vindicated. Humans (or enlightened ones, anyway) understood the world with renewed confidence.

SPENCER'S VERSION OF STRUGGLE

The stage is now set for the success of Spencer's theories. Here he is writing in very similar terms to Darwin – if less elegantly – seven years before the publication of *Origin of Species*:

> Those to whom this increasing difficulty of getting a living which excess of fertility entails, does not stimulate improvements in production – that is, to greater mental activity – are on the high road to extinction; and must ultimately be supplanted by those whom the pressure dies so stimulate ... And here, indeed, without further illustration, it will be seen that premature death under all its forms, and from all its causes, cannot fail to work in the same direction. For as those prematurely carried off must, in the average of cases, be those in whom the power of self-preservation is the least, it unavoidably follows that those left behind to continue the race are those in whom the power of self-preservation is the greatest – are the select of their generation. So that, whether the dangers to existence be of the kind produced by excess of fertility, or of any other kind, it is clear, that by the ceaseless exercise of the faculties needed to contend with them successfully, there is ensured a constant progress towards a higher

degree of skill, intelligence, and self-regulation – a better coordination of actions – a more complete life.

(1852: 495–6)

This is Spencer's idea of the Survival of the Fittest – a phrase he devised, as Darwin acknowledges. His talk of premature death may disturb those of a sentimental temperament, but it is no more severe than Darwin's "famine and death." The truth, it appears, is not for the faint-hearted.

THE POLITICS OF THE "PRACTICAL MAN"

While Spencer was at the height of his influence, there was already criticism of his views. But it was phrased it terms of moral objections, and the appalling contradiction that he presented to Christian values. Churchmen were, however, already reeling from the blows that Darwin had delivered to orthodoxy, and could do little more than wring their hands as solid, respectable parishioners became convinced Spencerians. Meanwhile, no one in that era had the tools to confront Spencerism on its own ground. So gradually it became the accepted truth of "practical men," those who understood the hard nature of the world, and planned to take care of their own families whatever effeminate simpering they might encounter. This is how it was that Spencerism, or Social Darwinism, became "common sense" for many in the West. In that form it persists to this day among practical men who have never heard of Herbert Spencer.

Now let us look at the political implications of Social Darwinism. In the crowded and unsanitary slums of nineteenth-century industrial cities, smallpox was a scourge that carried off children by the thousands. When it was discovered that a simple process of vaccination could protect children, there was an immediate appeal by philanthropists to make it freely available. The technique seemed a miracle; all that was involved was a little scratch on the arm, and the application of lymph from an animal infected with a milder form of the disease. After that, the child's own immune system would take care of future exposures to smallpox. The technique was quick and cheap, and required no second visit. But Spencer roundly denounced any public subsidy for such a project. It amounted to cruelty, he argued, because those unfit children would be saved from one natural death only to encounter another, probably worse, like starvation. To go against the laws of nature could bring only harm, not to mention the tax money used on the project made British industry less competitive with its rivals, and might in the end bring ruin to the whole society.

By a similar logic, Spencer opposed free public schooling, libraries, and hospitals. Their services were expensive to maintain, and wasted on those clearly unable to profit from them. He was opposed to the licensing of doctors and nurses, because intelligent people could work out for themselves what services they needed, and pay for them. The poor could be left to their quacks and home remedies. Most vehemently of all, he was opposed to the "poor laws" that provided very minimal housing and subsistence to the destitute, in the grim and appropriately named "work houses." He opposed all kinds of public welfare systems whatsoever, and the only role that he considered proper for the state was the protection of private property, enforcement of contracts, and defense of the state. This policy constitutes what is called *laissez-faire* economics, "let them (the capitalists) do as they please."

THE TWENTIETH-CENTURY CRITIQUE

What is wrong with Spencer's logic now seems absurdly obvious: it takes no account of the things that people learn as they grow, as opposed to the traits they were born with. That is, it makes no room for cultural things. There are two reasons why no one seemed able to point this out in the late nineteenth century. First, the twentieth-century notion of cultures in the plural did not exist. Culture in the singular meant appreciation of good wines, painting, and music, and perhaps knowing a little Greek or Latin, and these were indeed attributes of the superior people that Spencer saw as the "select of their generation." The fact that factory workers had no chance to acquire these attributes, especially where there were no public schools or libraries, does not seem to have occurred to him. Meanwhile, as we saw in detail in Chapter Three, all humans are capable of acquiring any culture to which they are exposed. Nowadays, no one would deny that a bright child from a working-class family has every bit as much chance of learning Latin – or wine tasting – as a peer from the upper classes. The experiment has been tried too many times for anyone to doubt the result.

Second, neither Spencer nor Darwin had any idea of the mechanisms of genetic inheritance of biological traits. It was not until the findings of an obscure Austrian monk became generally known that this missing piece in evolutionary theory was finally put in place. Through a series of elegant experiments with crossing different varieties of peas, Gregor Mendel showed that there were particles – genes – that controlled characteristics like color and size, and passed in predictable ways from generation to generation. These mechanisms, together with Darwin's notion of natural selection, are what make up the modern synthetic (i.e. "combined") theory of evolution. The great achievement of twentieth-century biology has been to reveal exactly how genes are constituted and reconstituted, and even the chemicals that make up their immensely complex chains. In short, we know the mechanisms by which evolution proceeds. With the wisdom of hindsight, the propositions that seemed irrefutable in Spencer's lifetime now seem merely bizarre.

One example neatly makes the point. During Spencer's wildly successful tour of the USA, where wealthy patrons greeted him as a hero, he happened to see Buffalo Bill's Wild West Show. In a re-enactment of an attack on a wagon train, he saw Indians display remarkable acts of horsemanship, including riding sideways and shooting under the horse's neck. All this neatly fitted his theory that "savages" had innate abilities suited to their stage of evolution, ones that might even make them superior to "modern" men in physical skills. There is a problem with this account, however. There were no horses in the Americas until the Spanish brought them. Plains Indians acquired horses only a couple of generations before the first settlers arrived, hardly enough time for natural selection to occur. They did not have a *gene* for horse riding; instead they had gained their skills by imitation and practice; they had *learned* them.

Once the distinction is in place between what is innate and what is learned, the edifice of Social Darwinism collapses. When Spencer makes it seem a great insight that those who suffer "premature death" must be those "in whom the power of self-preservation is the least," all he is really saying is that the losers lose. For this, we do not need Darwinian evolution. If we translate his proposition into the terminology of synthetic evolution, he must be arguing that those who have wealth are genetically superior to those who do not. This proposition may retain its appeal for some, but they have hardly proved themselves "fit" in a struggle for survival in which every newborn starts equal, as animals do. Meanwhile, how many potential entrepreneurs, not to mention scientists and poets, died of smallpox for want of a simple vaccination? The nation that invests in education does not ruin itself; on the contrary, it profits from the abilities of all its citizens.

ACTIVISM AND CRITIQUE

In the twentieth century, anthropology had a clear duty to show the errors of Social Darwinism. Everyone who understood the operation of genetics and the concept of culture(s) could only come to the same conclusion, and oppose the simplistic policy of *laissez faire*. But that was not the end of anthropology's involvement with politics. On the contrary, the data of anthropology proved relevant to all kinds of controversial issues.

Twentieth-century feminism provides a good example. Agitation for women's suffrage (that is, the right to vote) began in America and Britain in the mid-nineteenth century and had triumphed by 1928. In the 1970's a "second wave" of feminism aimed at securing the equality that, disappointingly, had not been achieved through the ballot box. What "women's liberation" required, it appeared, was more than formal recognition. Instead, it required a change in pervasive attitudes among men and women, nothing short of a cultural revolution. After the activism stirred up by the Vietnam War and the "counter culture" this seemed attainable but not without a struggle. Anthropologists were drawn into it, just like everyone else. As it happened, there had been distinguished women anthropologists throughout the twentieth century, such as Margaret Mead and Ruth Benedict (see Chapter Nine). Despite their fame, however, or perhaps because of it, neither was offered a post in any of the elite Ivy League schools. In Britain, women in the generation of Monica Wilson and Audrey Richards (see Chapter Four) had written well-respected ethnographies, but Africanist anthropology remained a male-dominated field. Women students were common, but they were less likely to be hired than their male peers, and were paid less if they were. Consequently, women anthropologists had their own fish to fry during the 1970's. Since then, they have achieved better representation in the discipline, and there is no doubt that they have had a great impact on its development.

Beyond career concerns, women anthropologists often found their expertise summoned by feminists outside academe. This turned out to be less easy to provide than might have been expected. Women anthropologists could not always confirm the claims activists wanted to make about women in other regions and eras. Moreover, they disagreed among themselves about what the accumulated data of anthropology implied. What followed was two decades of ferment, with all kinds of theoretical positions being advanced and criticized. Space does not allow a full review of them all, but a couple of examples will make the point.

THE PRE-MODERN FAMILY

Obviously, feminism contains an inherent cultural relativism. That is to say, it must argue that relations between the sexes are not immutable, the result of some "natural" inequality (see Chapter Seven). Instead, they reflect cultural premises that are contingent on particular historical circumstances. This is exactly what Marx had argued a century before. Marx had based his ideas on the work of Lewis Henry Morgan, whose pioneering fieldwork among the Iroquois of upstate New York had first revealed the nature of matrilineal families (see Chapters One and Four). Marx's closest colleague and sponsor, Frederick Engels, published their interpretation under the title *Origins of the Family, Private Property, and the State* (1884). Briefly, he argued that the subjugation of women had emerged only after the emergence of private property and institutionalized social stratification. This idea was appealing because it suggested that sexism was something "new" in the whole history of humankind, and indeed transient, as the contradictions of capitalism were overcome.

This is where anthropologists were summoned to provide confirmation. Is it in point of fact true that in "tribal" societies women are not subject to domination and exploitation? It took a decade of research and reanalysis by Marxist scholars to come to the disappointingly indecisive conclusion that the answer was yes and no. A great deal, however, was learned along the way. There were indeed places where women enjoyed high status and real political power. But there were as many where the male dominance existed in even more severe forms than it did in Europe, even in Victorian times. Let us take care to note what this means. First, the proposition that the relations between the sexes are variable from place to place, and therefore culturally contingent, is confirmed. What was discredited was the notion of some lost Eden in which humans existed without property and in egalitarian harmony. For instance, in the New Guinea Highlands, a region as close as could be imagined to a stone-age paradise, women were symbolically inferior to men in every respect, and wives were subject to serious violence, while "big men" competed ruthlessly for property, and warfare was endemic.

MOON RHYTHMS AND GODDESSES

In fact, feminist anthropologists were from the start ambivalent about Marx's notions of the pre-modern. They were, after all, derived from the same discredited social evolutionism as those of the Social Darwinists, even though his politics were the reverse of theirs (see Chapters Five and Eight). The ambivalence of feminist anthropologists turned to embarrassment, however, when they were confronted with another hoary nineteenth-century shibboleth. Misunderstanding the difference between matrilineal and patri-lineal descent systems, the evolutionists had argued that what they called "matriarchy" had pre-dated "patriarchy." The next step was to fantasize a grand cataclysm in which men rose up and overthrew a previous order of female control. This idea lingers on forever it seems, like so much of the sensationalism of nineteenth-century anthropology. In the 1920's the émigré English novelist Robert Graves wrote a fictional account of an island in the Mediterranean ruled by an order of priestesses. Once a year they allowed the men out of their crude huts and into the sanctuary, where an orgy ensued. The women brought up the resulting children within its precincts, expelling the boys when they were old enough to go to work in the fields. The novel enjoyed a revival in the 1980's, when various brands of mystical feminist essentialism grew up that sought to reverse the primal revolution of men. Here is an example of their propaganda:

For woman, with her inexplicable moon rhythms and power of creating new life, was the most sacred symbol of the tribe. So miraculous, so powerful, she had to be more than man – more than human. As primitive man [sic] began to think symbolically, there was only one explanation. Woman was the primary symbol, the greatest entity of all – a goddess, no less.

(Quoted in di Leonardo 1991: 27)

With such diverse schools of thought converging in feminist activism, you can see that the position of feminist anthropologists is not a simple one. Certainly feminist critical anthropology remains directed at "the establishment," pointing out what implicit cultural assumptions underlie debates about gender. But it also has a role in scrutinizing where feminist activism itself is going. In this way, it manages to achieve reflexivity twice over.

THE FEMINIST CONUNDRUM

There were further complications for the feminist anthropologists of the 1970's, this time in connection with fieldwork. As we saw above, many could not report that the people with whom they worked were models of gender equality. On the contrary, the reverse was often the case. They were then faced with what Micaela di Leonardo calls the feminist conundrum: "how could we analyze critically instances of male domination and oppression in precisely those societies whose customs anthropology was traditionally pledged to advocate?" (1991: 10). In other words, how could someone morally invested in cultural relativism, immediately set about criticizing his or her hosts? Keep in mind that women often accept the same values as their men, and teach them to their children, even in circumstances in which they are denigrated and abused. Must a feminist anthropologist simply see this as just another cultural system, as good as any other? Even if the temptation is resisted to "raise the consciousness" of local women, can the ethnographer legitimately describe the situation in terms of a conflict of which his or her informants are unaware?

This dilemma was further complicated by the reactions of Third World feminists. They were quick to point out that the issues of feminism had been framed by middle-class American activists, who they labeled White Western Women. The interests of Third World women, they argued, had more to do with poverty than career fulfillment. What they needed was protection from a rapacious global economy, rather than gender warfare. The Indian seamstresses we discussed in Chapter Eight provide a case in point. The criticisms of Third World feminists converged with those of postcolonial theorists, who were suspicious of all forms of "liberalization." As they saw it, this constituted the continuing imposition of Western ideologies on developing countries, in the interests of the former rather than the latter. Anthropology came in for its share of criticism from the same quarter, as we saw in Chapter Five, emphasizing anthropology's complicity in colonialism. None of this invalidated the role of critical feminist anthropology, but it certainly complicated the project.

THE ACHIEVEMENTS OF FEMINIST ANTHROPOLOGY

In the midst of all this ferment, however, much was achieved. The first stage was to inaugurate what was called the anthropology of women. Its objective was simply to put women into the ethnographic picture. Re-examining the Africanist ethnographies of the 1950's, it was remarkable how little many of them had to say about women, as if half the population had been put under erasure. This motivated a whole new wave of research putting women at center stage, not to mention re-analysis of old sources to see how their accounts needed to be qualified. Gradually, this obvious correction to the literature broadened into what became gender studies, which sought to understand how the social construction of gender impacted everyone's lives, female, male, and otherwise. As we saw in Chapter Seven, this goes beyond gender roles to what gender is in itself understood to be. This development moved feminist anthropology to the mainstream, since issues of gender obviously cut across all other aspects, political, economic, and so on. It is now an essential part of graduate education, for men as much as women.

At same time, feminist anthropology has made real contributions to international debates about the status of women. One of the most dramatic achievements of activists worldwide has been the recognition of the crucial role of women in Third World development. This brought together both First and Third World feminists, and it showcased the kinds of local knowledge that ethnographers achieve. It is now generally agreed that resources spent on educating women and improving their health are more cost effective than focusing attention on men. In the first place, efforts at population control largely depend on reaching women. Men are often indifferent, being just as glad to have as many children as possible. If many die, that is only a reason to have more. But women bear the burdens of pregnancy and child rearing, and they are usually enthusiastic about taking control of their reproductive lives. With fewer children, they can give more attention to each, passing on what they have learned. The same often applies to literacy campaigns, and even to economic development. Women are the main customers of banks that offer tiny loans without security ("micro-credit") to the poorest people in Third World countries, and they have an amazing record of paying back their loans.

BROADENING THE CONUNDRUM

After these developments, the feminist conundrum can be put into perspective. First, it is not unique to feminists. From the earliest experiments with fieldwork, ethnographers have agonized over their mixed reactions to their hosts' worlds. What if local leaders whose cooperation is essential happen to be slaveholders? There are parts of the world where governments embrace United Nations conventions about slavery, but do not actively prosecute respected men in rural areas who follow "traditional" patterns of debt slavery. Should an ethnographer turn in his or her host to the police? How to treat the slaves themselves? To be too friendly, out of guilt, will confuse everyone, especially the poor slaves. Or should one set about bringing change by persuasion? But what right does the ethnographer have to go around sermonizing? It should be pointed out that the professional associations of anthropologists in both the USA and the UK have carefully considered all the issues of ethics in fieldwork, and issued clear guidelines. As a broad approximation, an ethnographer operates under rules similar to those of a journalist. Short of knowing in advance of some shocking crime, the ethnographer is obligated not to reveal information that might bring harm or embarrassment to an informant.

This raises a second issue: what if an ethnographer cannot bring him or herself honestly to like his or her hosts? There are certainly cases where this has happened. What are we to make of ethnographies that flatly announce that such-and-such a people are mean, cruel, and abuse their own children? Are we not back to the stereotypes that we discussed in Chapter Nine, with a vengeance? On the other hand, we know perfectly well that all ethnographers undergo culture shock, as described in Chapter One, and find their hosts unbearable from time to time. Consequently, we would be equally suspicious of an ethnography that viewed everything with rosy-tinted glasses, and expressed delight over each and every feature of someone else's culture. This is simply chauvinism in reverse. How to balance these contrary tendencies between being ethnocentrically judgmental on the one hand, or blindly enthusiastic on the other?

DEALING WITH THE CONUNDRUM

For most contemporary anthropologists, the most important thing *not* to do is claim scientific objectivity. A half-century ago such claims were often implied, but the author's opinions and reactions always peeked out from behind the most sober language. Nowadays it is widely conceded that the ethnographer cannot be kept out of the picture, as if he or she were observing by telescope from the moon. We need to know how exactly fieldworkers participated in other peoples' lives, and what they found trying or agreeable about the experience. Indeed, in the 1980's there was a brief fashion for ethnographies that reported exclusively what the ethnographer experienced or felt, as being the only things the ethnographer really knew. The genre came to be called "navel gazing," since such relentless autobiography rapidly becomes boring. We want to hear what the ethnographer learned about *other* people. So once again, we must seek a balance.

Coming back then to di Leonardo's conundrum, she offers the alternatives of criticism, or continuing simply to describe "the customs anthropology was traditionally pledged to advocate." But this is an overstatement of what anthropology "traditionally" practiced: cultural relativism does not require advocating other peoples' customs. I may, for instance, study former practices of headhunting without advocating them. (One hopes the practices are "former," or the dilemmas of fieldwork really would be impossible.)

Cultural relativism requires only that judgment be suspended, while the effort is made to make sense of a belief or a practice within a total worldview. Many ethnographers do in fact find things to admire in their hosts' way of life. Time and again, students report that they will never again feel comfortable with the materialism, waste, and lack of social support that is so characteristic of the West in modern times. Consequently, they have made the reflexive move. When they write their ethnographies, they are immediately engaged in critical anthropology.

CRITICAL STUDIES OF SCIENCE

Consequently, there are ways in which most twentieth-century anthropology was critical anthropology. Nevertheless, the term is usually reserved for studies explicitly focused on aspects of the West, and of modernity as it is experienced worldwide. One of the most obvious aspects of modernity has been the enormous prestige of the natural sciences, as a result of the technological advances that they have enabled. Consequently, it is appropriate to ask what kind of cultural phenomenon science is. This may sound contradictory, since a major goal of science is to escape subjective opinions and prejudices and achieve an understanding of natural phenomena that is universally applicable. Nevertheless, science is conducted by humans, not robots, and humans are fallible. Even scientists were children once, and as adults can no more step into some cultural vacuum than anyone else. In short, all knowledge is cultural knowledge, and this applies as much to science as to those indigenous forms of knowledge discussed in Chapter Six that anthropologists call ethnosciences.

Consequently, there is work for ethnographers. Some have studied the social organization of science. Scientific research can be expensive. Decisions about which projects are to be funded are therefore economic decisions, which in turn means that they are political decisions. First, they reflect the priorities of political figures or corporations. In the 1960's the "space race" between the USA and the USSR had more to do with national pride than science, but even so, fabulous sums of money became available for scientists who could contribute something to the effort. Second, scientists must jostle among themselves for attention, forming elaborate alliances, and trying to scoop sensational new discoveries. Finally, they set up institutions that are invariably organized hierarchically according to seniority and reputation. Note that there is nothing cynical in saying this: the scientists genuinely want to get on with science, but they have no choice but to work within a social system. In most fields, the time is long past when scientists working alone in their basements had any chance of making useful discoveries. Nor is it cynical to speak of the culture of science, its ways of thinking about careers and what is admirable about scientists and many other things that are not in themselves "science." In the last couple of decades, we have learned a great deal about the culture and social organization of science, and it continues to be an active and growing area of research in anthropology.

MEDICINE AND SCIENCE

Even in the hard sciences, ideas are expressed in metaphor. When astronomers discovered a feature of the cosmos with properties so bizarre as to be unimaginable, they nevertheless needed a label that was comprehensible to the layperson. The title "black hole" made sense because even light is drawn into it and disappears. Needless to say, everyone thinks of Alice's endless fall into Wonderland, and that is more or less how black holes are portrayed in space dramas. There are no areas of science that operate without the use of metaphor.

This phenomenon is even more inescapable in medicine where the focus is the human body itself. Obviously, people all over the world encounter disease, and need some cultural account of it. In some places it involves witchcraft, as we saw in Chapter Seven, and the sufferer needs the assistance of a diviner. Elsewhere, the cause is described in terms of soul loss, and only a shaman can help. What is less obvious is that doctors in the West also have to translate their diagnoses into language understandable in their patients' folk understanding of illness. Moreover, the technical language of the doctors themselves is shot through with analogy. So, for instance, recent research in medical anthropology reveals a shift in the metaphors used by doctors and the lay public in talking about the international crisis caused by the AIDS pandemic. Previously, the dominant concept was one of hygiene. The body had to be kept free of unclean and dangerous things that might penetrate the skin. In case of failure, drugs needed to be mobilized to expel the alien organisms. Interestingly, this model parallels that of the nation-state, preserving itself by guarding its borders. But AIDS operates in a different and even more frightening way. Instead of being a disease in itself, it is instead a "deficiency" – a vulnerability to whatever diseases comes along, resulting in the endless torments of the AIDS sufferer. It is as if the individual has lost control of his or her borders, and all manner of alien things are now circulating within it. This shift in language comes at an historical moment when economic globalization is indeed making the boundaries of nation-states more porous, because international agreements about "open markets" limit the powers of governments to control what goes in and out.

Let us be clear about what is being argued here. Medical anthropologists are not suggesting that globalization caused the AIDS epidemic, nor vice-versa. What they see happening is a change in peoples' thinking because, in worrying first about one, then the other, *they* have connected the two. Moreover, this has its consequences. At an early stage of the epidemic no one really understood what was going on, including medical specialists. An early government report listed sources of infection within the country including homosexuals, intravenous drug users – and Haitians. However, over the next few years it became clear, first, that AIDS was introduced to Haiti from the USA and not the reverse, and second, that AIDS was no more common among Haitians than other populations. In the hysteria of the moment, AIDS had been over-reported by doctors dealing with a new disease whose symptoms were still imperfectly understood. If we ask why that occurred, it is not a far stretch of the imagination to see that Haitians were formidably alien, with their history of rule by a tyrant, the infamous Papa Doc, who cultivated the reputation of a sorcerer and a raiser of the dead. Haitians provided an instance of the alien within. The fact that they were *legal* immigrants only made it clear to panicky Americans that the borders lay undefended.

CRITICIZING NATIONALISM

To harp on the failures of modern medicine may seem to be mere obstruction, so we must say again that this is not so. No medical anthropologist is interested in impeding the best health care possible for everyone. The critical role is to pay attention to cultural factors that scientists and medical researchers may not notice because their attention is focused elsewhere. With regard to nationalism, however, critical anthropology has been more outspoken. The reason for this is simple: modern history is littered with occasions when a proper love of country has spilled over into outright chauvinism and useless warfare.

The crucial premise of the anthropology of nationalism is that there is nothing "natural" about a nation. This skepticism towards whatever it is that is being called a nation follows directly from the problems that ethnographers have had in bounding particular "cultures" and "societies," as described in Chapter Eight. We have learned to look sideways at such categories. Each time one is invoked, we want to know how it is "socially constructed," how a particular proper name came into being, and how it is used.

But nationalism achieves political force only insofar as it is not questioned. Militant nationalists are convinced that the origins of their race and language are lost in the mists of time, and have been imbued in generation after generation of their ancestors. Usually it takes only a little historical research to show how unrealistic these claims are. This is true even for long-established nations. It would, for instance, be absurd to imagine that the English constitute a "race," or ever did. On the contrary, early medieval history reveals a bewildering sequence of conquests and migrations, in which Britons, Gaels, Romans, Saxons, Vikings, and Normans mixed promiscuously. The English language has equally diverse roots, with a simplified Germanic grammar and a large part of its vocabulary borrowed from Latin via French. Moreover, no uniformity existed in the language until modern times. Mutually unintelligible dialects persist in England to this day. Had an English king succeeded in making himself also king of France, as several tried to do, England would now be a province of France. Certainly, it would have its own folk traditions and language, but the same is true of regions that *are* provinces of France, such as Brittany, the Basque country and the Occitan-speaking south.

The point is that politics creates nationalisms, rather than the reverse. Examples are not hard to find in recent times. The state of Yugoslavia was created by fiat in 1918, after the collapse of the

Austrian and Ottoman empires. It was designed by the "Great Powers" at the international peace conference in Versailles for the purpose of bringing together all the displaced Slavic peoples under their own government, hence the name "Southern Slavs." After World War Two, Yugoslavia came under Soviet domination, but its fiercely independent leader, Marshal Tito, insisted on shaping his own destiny. After Tito died in 1980, however, there was no one of his stature to follow him. Instead, local leaders set about carving out niches for themselves, and in the ensuing violence the nation fell apart. The response of political pundits across the world was that ancient feuds had re-emerged in an area famous for its violent history. The implication was that there was nothing to be done. Meanwhile, neighbors who had lived side by side for generation began to murder each other, and the phrase "ethnic cleansing" entered our vocabulary. The most infamous of the petty dictators who set out to whip up nationalist fervor for his own ends was the Serbian leader Slobodan Milosevic, currently on trial in The Hague for war crimes. There is nothing "natural" or "inevitable" about the appalling violence that such men provoke.

It would of course be absurd to imagine that anthropologists are going to stop such wars. But the critical function remains. Whenever nationalist rhetoric is cranked up the question to ask is: whose agenda is being served here? When people begin to say "my country, right or wrong," chauvinism is out of control. A better response to nationalist rhetoric is summarized in Bertrand Russell's maxim: the first duty of a citizen is to distrust his leaders.

FAR FROM HOME, CLOSE TO HOME

In the twentieth century, anthropologists set out to explore other peoples' worlds, where lives unfolded according to different understandings of the natural order of things. Even when they began this project, there were already few places around the world that had not felt the impact of imperialism and the rapidly emerging global economy. Their task required considerable adaptability. In Tikopia, for instance, Firth was able to engage in participant observation with people who still practiced their indigenous religion and maintained their "house" structure. As we saw in Chapter Three, even in the 1920's this did not imply that Tikopia was untouched by the outside world. But on the other side of the Pacific, in Hawai'i, change had gone much further. Land had been annexed wholesale, and immigrants brought in to work the plantations. As for the Hawai'ian religion, it was barely even a memory. It could only be studied from documents left behind by missionaries and their converts. Between these extremes, ethnographers adjusted their methods as appropriate. In much of sub-Saharan Africa, they could largely replicate Firth's experience, because many pre-colonial states had lost their independence within living memory, and still existed within a system of "indirect rule." In North America, harried remnants of many of the "first nations" allowed only "salvage anthropology" of cultural resources such as myth and folklore. In South America, some ethnic groups were extinct while others maintained a wary distance from settlers. Across the whole of Eurasia, from Europe to China, indigenous minorities had existed for centuries within ancient civilizations, or on the edges of them, and often proved remarkably successful in coping with change.

Under the circumstances, what was achieved was remarkable. There is hardly a corner of the globe that lacks an ethnographic literature, whose value will only increase in decades to come. But anthropology is not dependent on some dwindling resource. Even by the middle of the twentieth century, ethnographers were already turning their attention to new cultural forms emerging in the face of globalization. The first task that Godfrey Wilson, director of the newly founded Rhodes Livingstone Institute, set himself was to study migrant workers in the rapidly expanding cities. Before long African migrants were arriving in Paris and New York as well, while East and West Indians were migrating to London. Politicians spoke ironically of "the Empire coming home." Some welcomed it, some not, but it became increasingly clear that the movement of people around the globe was unstoppable. In the 1950's Margaret Mead remarked, half-jokingly, that the rate of technical and social change was so great that in future the job of anthropologists would be to explain the generations to each other. It is plain that there is more work than ever for anthropologists to do, and they will need to be even more enterprising in finding cultural niches, and adapting their intimate methods of research.

There are innumerable journeys of exploration yet to be made. You are ready to set out on your own. *Bon voyage.*

Summary

There is no inherent reason why anthropologists should take the part of those they study. With a couple of exceptions, the first generation of anthropologists in the nineteenth century certainly did not. Instead, their evolutionary paradigm constantly skirted the edge of racism. The easiest answer to the question that motivated them was a kind of implicit genetic determinism. To Herbert Spencer it seemed self-evident that those peoples who had advanced to civilization were inherently superior to those stuck in savagery or barbarism, and his views dominated the thinking of Europeans during the age of High Imperialism. It lingers on to this day. It has become the logic of people who consider themselves "realists," people who have never heard of Spencer but have absorbed the doctrines and policies of "Social Darwinism." Meanwhile, Spencer's logic can now be seen to be wrong. We now understand the mechanisms of genetics, and know that human beings share the potential to acquire any culture whatsoever. We also know that most of the characteristics that Spencer considered inherent or inborn were in fact cultural features subject to change, even within a single generation. This finding is no mere curiosity; it has immediate political consequences.

As first-hand fieldwork became standard in anthropology, the whole tenor of the discipline changed. Having made it their task to try to see the world from other peoples' point of view, it became inevitable that they would become critical of policies that oppressed or denigrated their hosts. This continues to be the case as ethnographers document the effects of "globalization" on people outside the "First World." While economists hail it as the salvation of mankind, its effects for disempowered people in the "Third World" have often been disastrous.

Critique, however, goes beyond negative judgment. Anthropology provides a vantage point from which we may look back at our own cultures, seeing anew their values and assumptions. For example, anthropology has played an important role in modern feminism. That role has not been simply to confirm the claims of feminist activists, but rather to assess their claims in worldwide perspective. This has presented a conundrum for feminist ethnographers, caught between respecting the values of those they study and representing their own deeply held convictions. But this turns out to be only an example – if a particularly agonizing one – of a general problem in fieldwork.

Ethnographers are not required to approve of everything their hosts do. The only way to preserve a reasonable balance is to be ready to turn the critical view onto the pieties of our own culture, such as the infallibility of medicine and the unfailing worthiness of patriotism.

FURTHER READING

In Chapter Four, I cited Marvin Harris (1968) as the best brief summary of nineteenth-century social evolutionism. Since Harris' goal was to rid evolutionism of its legacy of racism, he also presents an excellent summary and rebuttal of the doctrines of "Social Darwinism." The effects of globalization are discussed in *Modernity at Large: Cultural Dimensions of Globalization* (1996) by Arjun Appadurai. For an overview of the development of feminist anthropology, see *Gender at the Crossroads of Knowledge* (1991). The introductory essay by the editor, Micaela di Leonardo, is particularly useful.

An influential study of the construction of nationality is Richard Handler's *Nationalism and the Politics of Culture in Quebec* (1988). Other cases are described in *The Politics of Difference: Ethnic Premises in a World of Power* (1996), edited by Edwin Wilmsen and Patrick McAllister.

BIBLIOGRAPHY

Ahmed, Akbar (1976) *Millennium and Charisma among Pathans*, London: Routledge and Kegan Paul.

Appadurai, Arjun (1996) *Modernity at Large: Cultural Dimensions of Globalization*, Minneapolis: University of Minnesota Press.

Asad, Talal (ed.) (1973) *Anthropology and the Colonial Encounter*, Atlantic Highlands, NJ: Humanities Press.

Bailey, Frederick (1969) *Stratagems and Spoils: A Social Anthropology of Politics*, New York: Schocken.

Barley, Nigel (1987) *A Plague of Caterpillars: A Return to the African Bush*, London: Penguin.

Barth, Fredrik (1959) *Political Leadership Among Swat Pathans*, London: Athlone.

Bellwood, Peter (1979) *Man's Conquest of the Pacific: The Prehistory of Southeast Asia and Oceania*, New York: Oxford University Press.

Benedict, Ruth (1934) *Patterns of Culture*, Boston: Houghton Mifflin.

Boas, Franz (1938, original 1911) *The Mind of Primitive Man*, New York: Macmillan.

Bodley, John (1990) *Victims of Progress,* Mountain View, CA: Mayfield.

Campbell, Bernard (2001) *Humankind Emerging,* 8th concise edition, NY: Allyn and Bacon.

Clifford, James (1988) *The Predicament of Culture: Twentieth-Century Ethnography, Literature and Art,* Cambridge: Harvard University Press.

Darwin, Charles (1958, original 1859) *On the Origin of Species by Means of Natural Selection,* NY: Mentor.

Descola, Philippe and Gisli Palsson (eds.) (1996) *Nature and Society: Anthropological Perspectives,* London: Routledge.

Dumont, Jean-Paul (1978) *The Headman and I: Ambiguity and Ambivalence in the Fieldworking Experience,* Prospect Heights, Illinois: Waveland.

Durkheim, Emile (1965, original 1912) *The Elementary Forms of the Religious Life,* New York: Free Press.

—— (1982, original 1893) *The Rules of the Sociological Method,* New York: Free Press.

Engels, Frederick (1954, original 1884) *Origins of the Family, Private Property, and the State,* Moscow: Foreign Languages Publishing House.

—— (1958, original 1844) *The Condition of the Working Class in England,* Oxford: Oxford University Press.

Evans-Pritchard, Edward (1956) *Nuer Religion, Oxford: Clarendon.*

—— (1969, original 1940) *The Nuer: A Description of the Modes of Livelihood and Political Institutions of a Nilotic People,* Oxford: Oxford University Press.

—— (1970, original 1940). African Political Systems. London: Oxford University Press.

Fallers, Lloyd (1956) *Nuer Religion,* Oxford: Oxford University Press.

—— (1965, original 1956) *Bantu Bureaucracy: A Century of Political Evolution among the Basoga of Uganda,* Chicago: Chicago University Press.

Firth, Raymond (1967) *The Work of the Gods in Tikopia*, London: Athlone.

—— (1983, original 1936) *We, the Tikopia: A Sociological Study of Kinship in Primitive Polynesia*, Stanford: Stanford University Press.

Fortune, Reo (1932) *Sorcerers of Dobu*, London: E.P. Dutton.

Frazer, James (1922) *The Golden Bough: A Study in Magic and Religion*, New York: Macmillan.

Freeman, Derek (1970) *Report on the Iban*, London: Athlone Press.

—— (1983) *Margaret Mead and Samoa: The Making and Unmaking of an Anthropological Myth*, Cambridge: Harvard University Press.

Good, Byron (1994) *Medicine, Rationality, and Experience: An Anthropological Perspective*, Cambridge: Cambridge University Press.

Goody, Jack (ed.) (1962) *The Development Cycle in Domestic Groups*, Cambridge: Cambridge University Press.

Gould, Stephen (1981) *The Mismeasure of Man*, New York: Norton.

Gregory, Chris (1982) *Gifts and Commodities*, London: Academic.

Handler, Richard (1988) *Nationalism and the Politics of Culture in Quebec*, Madison: University of Wisconsin Press.

Harris, Marvin (1968) *The Rise of Anthropological Theory*, New York: Thomas Crowell.

Hays, Terence (ed.) (1992) *Ethnographic Presents: Pioneering Anthropologists in the Papua New Guinea Highlands*, Berkeley: University of California Press.

Holmes, Lowell (1987) *Quest for the Real Samoa: The Mead/Freeman Controversy*, Boston: Bergin and Garvey.

James, Lawrence (1994) *The Rise and Fall of the British Empire*, New York: St. Martin's.

Johnson, Thomas and Carolyn Sargent (eds.) (1990) *Medical Anthropology: A Handbook of Theory and Method*, New York: Greenwood.

di Leonardo, Micaela (ed.) (1991) *Gender at the Crossroads of Knowledge: Feminist Anthropology in the Postmodern Era*, Berkeley: University of California Press.

Lévi-Strauss, Claude (1969, original 1949) *The Elementary Structures of Kinship*, Boston: Beacon.

—— (1995, original 1978) *Myth and Meaning: Cracking the Code of Culture*, New York: Schocken.

Lutz, Catherine (1988) *Unnatural Emotions: Everyday Sentiments on a Micronesian Atoll and their Challenge to Western Theory*, Chicago: University of Chicago Press.

MacCormack, Carol and Marilyn Strathern (eds.) (1980) *Nature, Culture, and Gender*, Cambridge: Cambridge University Press.

Mair, Lucy (1977) *African Kingdoms*, Oxford: Clarendon.

Malefijt, Anne de Waal (1968) "Homo monstrosus", *Scientific American*, 219:4, p. 113.

Malinowski, Bronislaw (1961, original 1922) *Argonauts of the Western Pacific: An Account of Native Enterprise and Adventure in the Archipelagoes of Melanesian New Guinea*, New York: Dutton.

Mauss, Marcel (1967, original 1924) *The Gift: Forms and Functions of Exchange in Archaic Societies*, New York: Norton.

Mead, Margaret (1928) *Coming of Age in Samoa*, New York: William Morrow.

Metcalf, Peter (2002) *They Lie, We Lie: Getting On With Anthropology*, London: Routledge.

—— (2003) "Hulk Hogan in the Rainforest", in Timothy Craig and Richard King (eds.) *Global Goes Local*, Vancouver: University of British Columbia Press, pp. 15–25.

Metcalf, Peter and Richard Huntington (1991) *Celebrations of Death: The Anthropology of Mortuary Ritual*, Cambridge: Cambridge University Press.

Middleton, John (1960) *Lugbara Religion: Ritual and Authority among an East African People*, Oxford: Oxford University Press.

Middleton, John and David Tait (eds.) (1958) *Tribes Without Rulers: Studies in African Segmentary Systems*, London: Routledge and Kegan Paul.

Montagu, Ashley (1945) *Man's Most Dangerous Myth: The Fallacy of Race*, New York: Columbia University Press.

Montagu, Lady Mary Wortley (1994, original 1763) *Turkish Embassy Letters*, London: Virago.

Morgan, Lewis Henry (1851) *League of the Ho-de-no-sau-nee, or Iroquois*, Rochester, NY: Sage and Broa.

Moskowitz, Breyne (1978) "The Acquisition of Language", *Scientific American*, 239: 5, pp. 92–109.

Needham, Rodney (ed.) (1973) *Right and Left: Essays in Dual Symbolic Classification*, Chicago: University of Chicago Press.

Patterson, Francine (1979) "Life with Koko", *National Geographic*, 161: 1, October.

Polo, Marco (1997) *The Travels*, Ware, Hertfordshire: Wordsworth.

Radcliffe-Brown, Alfred (1952) *Structure and Function in Primitive Society*, Oxford: Oxford University Press.

Said, Edward (1979) *Orientalism*, New York: Vintage.

Salmond, Anne (1975) *Hui: A Study of Maori Ceremonial Gatherings*, Wellington, NZ: Reed.

Sapir, Edward (1921) *Language*, New York: Harcourt, Brace.

Schneider, David (1968) *American Kinship: A Cultural Account*, Chicago: University of Chicago Press.

Strathern, Marilyn (ed.) (1987) *Dealing with Inequality: Analysing Gender Relations in Melanesia and Beyond*, Cambridge: Cambridge University Press.

Taylor, Stephen (ed.) (1969) *Cognitive Anthropology*, New York: Holt, Rinehart, & Winston.

Trask, Robert (1995) *Language: The Basics*, London: Routledge.

Turner, Victor (1967) *The Forest of Symbols*, Ithaca, NY: Cornell University Press.

——(1968) *The Drums of Affliction*, Oxford: Clarendon.

Wallerstein, Immanuel (1983) *Historical Capitalism*, London: Verso.

Whiting, John and Irvin Child (1953) *Child Training and Personality: A Cross-Cultural Study*, New Haven: Yale University Press.

Williams, Patrick and Laura Chrisman (eds.) (1994) *Colonial Discourse and Post-colonial Theory: A Reader*, New York: Columbia University Press.

Wilmsen, Edwin and Patrick McAllister (eds.) (1996) *The Politics of Difference: Ethnic Premises in a World of Power*, Chicago: University of Chicago Press.

Wolf, Eric (1982) *Europe and the People Without History*, Berkeley: University of California Press.

INDEX

American Sign Language 97
analogy 85–6, 11–2, 175–6, 178, 180, *see also* metaphor
ancestors 42–3, 112, 128–9
Asian world economy 149–50
Atoni 119–24, 138
Australian aborigines 142, 144, 166, 175
Austronesian 93, 98
Azande 9, 129

barbarians 139–41
Barth, Frederik 177–8, 181
Bateson, Gregory 174
Bemba 60–3, 74, 178, 185
Benedict, Ruth 168–70, 179, 181, 192
Boaz, Franz 100–1, 112, 143, 167–8, 172, 180
Borneo 15, 24, 117, 124, 148–51, 153–4, 159–61, 165, 176

capitalism 108, 147, 155, 190, 193
chauvinism 6, 38, 89, 101, 169, 186, 198, 202–3
cognatic 71
collective representations 40–3, 45, 52, 77, 109, 11, 136, 179

Comparative Method 80–1, 99, 118, 140, 161
Condorcet, Maquis de 187
Cook, James 7, 140
corporate group, *see* group
counter culture 185, 192
Cunningham, Clarke 119
culture 19, 84, 100, 139, 146, 159, 164, 166, 168, 179, 184, 190; culture defined 2, critique of the concept of culture 154–6; a narrower definition 135–6
culture and personality school 174, 180
culture shock 2–3, 5, 8, 11, 52, 198
Cushing, Frank Hamilton 8, 90

Darwin, Charles 29, 80, 83, 87, 103, 186–91, 193
death 127–9, 138, 175–6
Dobu 169–71
dreams 164
Durkheim, Emile 40–1, 44, 52–3, 76, 108, 113, 115, 175

Economic Man 178
Engels, Frederick 193

ethnocentrism 6, 21, 87, 92
ethnography, definition of 17
ethnoscience 103–5, 199
Evans-Pritchard, E.E. 9, 64, 74, 76, 129, 173
evolutionism, social 80–2, 87, 91, 98, 112, 126, 140, 142 –3, 147, 170, 186, 187–8, 191

Fallers, Lloyd 88
feminist anthropology 111, 115, 117, 192–7, 205
feud 65–8, 177
fieldwork 8–11, 15–7, 53, 86, 172–3, 195, 198, 205
Firth, Raymond 42–3, 153, 203–4
Fortune, Reo 168–9
four fields approach 91–2
Frazer, James 118
Freeman, Derek 71, 173, 181
Freud, Sigmund 82, 106, 148, 164, 167, 174
functionalism 76–8, 82–7, 154, 176, 181

Geertz, Clifford 154
gender 123–7, 137, 170, 196
global economy 18, 139, 151–6, 161, 196
201–4
Gluckman, Max 60
group, definition of 51

Haddon, Alfred Cort 8
Harris, Marvin 88
Herodotus 6
Hertz, Robert 115–17, 121–2, 136, 138, 157
High Imperialism 78–9, 81, 205
hominids 25, 164

India 79, 90, 92, 155
Indo-European 183
indirect rule 75
informants 13–14
institution see collective representation
intelligence quotient 31–2
individualism 41, 44, 179

Jakobson, Roman 105

Kenyatta, Jomo 77
kinship 45, 49, 59, 71, 109–10, 123, 135, 153
Kipling, Rudyard 81
Koko 97
Kwakiutl 101, 168–9

language 3, 9–10, 11, 24, 93–114, 136, 153
di Leonardo, Micaela 195, 198
Lévi-Strauss, Claude 105–13, 146, 162
lies 4, 39, 97, 173
linguistics 10, 93, 180, 182, see also language
Linnaeus 23–6, 27, 30, 105
Lugbara 22–3

Malinowski, Bronislaw 8–9, 11, 13–4, 16–8, 20, 77, 82–3, 103, 126, 152
Malthus, Thomas 187–8
Maori 103, 117, 119, 144–5
Marx, Karl 86, 147–8, 155, 157, 162, 179, 193
Mauritius 155–6
Mauss, Marcel 108, 181
marriage 109–10, 123, 135, 153, 171
matrilineage 60–1, 194
Mead, Margaret 172–4, 181, 192, 204
mediation 124
medical anthropology 131, 133–4, 138, 200–2
Mendel, Gregor 191
metaphor 117, 154, 178, 200, see also analogy
Middleton, John 22, 36
Montaigne, Michel de 7, 90–1
Morgan, Lewis Henry 8, 90, 152, 193
myth 103–5, 199

New Guinea 7, 77, 87, 99, 102, 143, 149, 152, 194
Nuer 9, 64–70, 74, 76, 185
Ndembu 118, 130
norm see collective representation

Ojibwa 104–5

participant observation 11, 18, 86, 203
patrilineage 59, 69, 194
person 49–52, 168, 180
personality 168–9, 174, 179–80
physical anthropology 18, 30, 34–5, 91–2
politics, definition of 54–6
post-colonial studies 86, 88
post-modernism 155–6
"primitive" 7, 80–83, 87, 98, 122, 126, 141, 183, 195
Psychic Unity 170. 175–6
psychology 12, 21, 39, 55, 107, 161, 167, 170, 175, 180

race 27–37, 91, 206
racism 27, 36, 81, 91, 101, 147, 171, 205
Rivers, W.H.R. 8
Royal Anthropological Institute 75
reductionism 40, 98, 173, 175, 180
reflexive 133, 184, 195, 199
relativism, 55, 72, 77, 83, 90–1, 137, 170–3, 180, 193–5, 198–9
religion 12, 118, 122, 130, 157, 178, 185, 203, see also ritual
Richards, Audrey 60, 192
ritual 15, 84, 118, 124, 130, 142, 153, 180, see also religion
role see status

Said, Edward 88
Samoa 172–3
Sapir, Edward 101–2
savages 90, 139–41
Schneider, David 135–6, 138, 146

semiotics 102
sex, see gender
shaman 132, 168, 200
slavery 115, 197
Social Darwinism 186–92, 195, 205, 206
socialization 4, 38, 39, 84
social psychology 12
society, definition of 49
sociology 12, 21, 55
sorcery 117, 169, 201 see also witchraft, magic
Spencer, Herbert 187–91, 205
status 45, 86, 174–5
stereotypes 171–2, 174, 180, 198
structure 51, 60, 85, 106–11, 126, 154
structural–functionalism 77
symbolism 118–9, 136–7

television 18, 159–61
Tikopia 42–3, 45–51, 111, 152–3, 203
tool use 25
transformation 102, 107, 110
transactionalism 178, 181
Trobriand islands 9, 11, 13, 18, 82, 84, 126
Turner, Victor 118, 130, 138

unconscious 82, 103, 106, 110, 164

Wallerstein, Immanuel 148, 162
Whiting, John and Beatrice 174, 181
Whorf, Bejamin 96
Wilson, Godfrey 204
witchcraft 22, 129–30, 200
Wolf, Eric 78

Zulu 56–60, 74